THE GREAT IRISH FAMINE

THE **BROADVIEW**
SOURCES SERIES

The Great Irish Famine

A HISTORY IN DOCUMENTS

edited by KAREN SONNELITTER

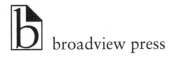

broadview press

BROADVIEW PRESS – www.broadviewpress.com
Peterborough, Ontario, Canada

Founded in 1985, Broadview Press remains a wholly independent publishing house. Broadview's focus is on academic publishing; our titles are accessible to university and college students as well as scholars and general readers. With over 600 titles in print, Broadview has become a leading international publisher in the humanities, with world-wide distribution. Broadview is committed to environmentally responsible publishing and fair business practices.

The interior of this book is printed on 100% recycled paper.

Library and Archives Canada Cataloguing in Publication

Great Irish famine (Peterborough, Ont.)
    The great Irish famine : a history in documents / edited by Karen Sonnelitter.

(The Broadview sources series)
Includes bibliographical references.
ISBN 978-1-55481-377-3 (softcover)

    1. Ireland—History—Famine, 1845-1852—Sources. I. Sonnelitter, Karen, editor II. Title. III. Series: Broadview sources series

DA950.7.G74 2018   941.5081   C2018-905369-0

Broadview Press handles its own distribution in North America:
PO Box 1243, Peterborough, Ontario K9J 7H5, Canada
555 Riverwalk Parkway, Tonawanda, NY 14150, USA
Tel: (705) 743-8990; Fax: (705) 743-8353
email: customerservice@broadviewpress.com

Distribution is handled by Eurospan Group in the UK, Europe, Central Asia, Middle East, Africa, India, Southeast Asia, Central America, South America, and the Caribbean. Distribution is handled by Footprint Books in Australia and New Zealand.

Canada Broadview Press acknowledges the financial support of the Government of Canada for our publishing activities.

Copy-edited by Juliet Sutcliffe
Book design by Em Dash Design

PRINTED IN CANADA

CONTENTS

ACKNOWLEDGEMENTS

I would like to thank the anonymous reviewers of the proposal for this volume and of the completed volume. Their insightful comments were greatly appreciated. I would also like to thank Brett McLenithan and Stephen Latta from Broadview who helped develop the idea for this volume and to pull it all together. Thanks to John Raymond and Sean Conley at the Siena College Library for their help in acquiring many of the sources used here. Special thanks to my research assistant Gordon MacCammon, who sorted through years' worth of newspaper coverage and made many important contributions to this volume. Thanks to the Siena College Center for Undergraduate Research and Creative Activity, which helped to fund the research that went into this book. Finally, thanks to my family for their support of this project and my dog Maddie, who sat patiently at my side during much of the writing process waiting for her walk.

INTRODUCTION

It was in October of 1845 that the prime minister of the United Kingdom of Great Britain and Ireland, Sir Robert Peel, received the first of several "very alarming" reports that warned of a mysterious blight which threatened to destroy that year's potato crop.[1] In a letter to the **Lord-Lieutenant**, Lord Heytesbury, Peel worried over the "great evil with which we are threatened."[2] He was right to be concerned: by 1851, one million people would be dead of famine or related diseases and at least one million more had left the island either by choice or coercion. It is estimated that Ireland lost 25 percent of its population in only six years.

Lord-Lieutenant: Often called the viceroy, this was the crown's chief representative in Ireland and the official head of the Irish executive.

The documents presented here come from a variety of sources both inside and outside of Ireland and are intended to guide us to a greater understanding of the causes, the course, and significance of the Great Irish Famine. As with all primary sources, they must be read critically with attention paid to the medium, the audience, the author, and the intent of the document. With that in mind, these documents provide insight into both what happened during the famine and the response to the famine within Ireland, within the United Kingdom, and around the world. To aid in this analysis this volume begins with a brief introduction to contextualize the famine itself and the historical interpretations of it, a chronology of events, a glossary, and a list of questions to consider.

BACKGROUND TO THE FAMINE

Even before the Great Famine, Ireland was a problem for England. In many ways Ireland had been a problem for hundreds of years. Conquered by King Henry II of England in the twelfth century, Ireland was an uneasy possession of the English crown, frequently rebellious and never as profitable as it was supposed to be. Ireland's legal status with respect to England shifted over the centuries. It was first a **lordship** of the King of England, with its own independent, but legally subordinate, parliament established in 1297. In 1542 it became a separate kingdom, and King Henry VIII of England was given the separate title of King of Ireland. The Irish Parliament continued to legislate for the country, and continued to be subordinate to the English Parliament. For a brief period under the protectorate of Oliver

lordship: Refers to the period of English feudal rule in Ireland, generally 1177–1542, when the King of England's title in Ireland was Lord of Ireland.

---

1   Robert Peel, *The Memoirs of the Right Honourable Sir Robert Peel*, 2 vols. (John Murray: London, 1857), 2:121.

2   Ibid., 121.

Reformation: The Protestant Reformation was a period of religious schism in the sixteenth and seventeenth centuries, beginning with Martin Luther's 95 Theses in 1517.

Henry Grattan: Grattan (1746–1820) was an Irish politician and prominent member of the Irish House of Commons, best known for this campaign for legislative independence for Ireland in the late eighteenth century.

Acts of Union: Parallel acts of the parliaments of Great Britain and Ireland which dissolved the independent Irish Parliament and created the United Kingdom of Great Britain and Ireland.

Irish question: Phrase used by British elites in the nineteenth and early twentieth centuries to describe the problem of Irish nationalism and Irish independence.

Cromwell Ireland did send members to England's Parliament. The passage of the Crown of Ireland Act in 1542, which cemented Henry VIII's title, was part of a plan to better secure the Tudors' position in Ireland following their break with the Catholic Church. To go along with this new political status the Tudors began an extensive campaign of reconquest and settlement to better establish their authority and their religion over the island. The official Tudor policy was known as surrender and regrant, Irish lords were encouraged to surrender their holdings to the crown and then have them regranted under a royal charter if they swore an oath of loyalty to the crown. Irish nobles responded to this campaign and to the **Reformation**, also imposed on the orders of the Tudor dynasty, with a series of rebellions and wars. It was not until King William III's victories at the Battle of the Boyne (1690) and the Battle of Aughrim (1691) that the rebellious elements in Irish society were brought to heel. The eighteenth century in Ireland was generally peaceful, and allowed the descendants of English soldiers and Scottish settlers, groups known as the Anglo-Irish and the Ulster Scots, to consolidate their political power. These so called "new Irish" came to resent Ireland's political treatment and developed a sense of Irish patriotism and an Irish identity. Irish Protestant politicians, such as **Henry Grattan**, campaigned for a stronger Irish Parliament and greater legislative autonomy for the country, while writers like Jonathan Swift (Document 1) used satire to mock British policy towards Ireland. Other members of this class, inspired by the ideologies of the American and the French Revolutions, organized an Enlightenment-inspired liberation movement in Ireland as well. The rebellion of 1798 sought to unify all the religious groups of Ireland behind the common cause of Irish independence from British rule. While it gained widespread support, it failed to overthrow British rule. In the aftermath, political leaders in both Great Britain and Ireland agreed to a political union between the two countries. In 1801 Ireland's legal status changed yet again as the **Acts of Union** made it a part of the new United Kingdom. Ireland ceased to be a legally separate country and its independent parliament was dissolved. From 1801 on Ireland sent representatives to England to sit in Parliament at Westminster. By 1845, of the 658 members of Parliament in Westminster only 105 represented Ireland, despite the fact that Ireland made up 40 percent of the population of the United Kingdom.[3]

The Acts of Union established Ireland's political status but it did not settle the **Irish question** despite hopes to the contrary. Ireland remained a problem for its English rulers. Politically Ireland was still prone to unrest and rebellion as an elite minority continued to rule over a disenfranchised majority.

---

3   Christine Kinealy, *This Great Calamity: The Irish Famine 1845–1852*, (Dublin: Gill & Macmillan, 1994), chap. 1.

The last violent uprising before the famine was led by **Robert Emmet** in 1803. Still English authorities tended to fear that all Irish political action might lead to violent insurrection. Prior to the famine **Daniel O'Connell's** movements for **Catholic Emancipation**, achieved in 1829, and later to Repeal the Acts of Union attracted large crowds. Despite the fact that O'Connell explicitly rejected violence as a political tool, the size of the crowds he attracted worried English political leaders. O'Connell's movements led to a wave of Irish nationalism, and in the 1840s several younger members of O'Connell's Repeal Association, associated with the new nationalist newspaper *The Nation*, would split to form the Young Ireland movement. Young Irelanders wanted Irish independence and were eventually willing to endorse the use of force to achieve it.

Aside from its politics, Ireland was considered by many in Great Britain as an economic burden on the United Kingdom. In the eighteenth century Ireland's poverty was a regular source of concern. At that time Ireland was thought to be underpopulated, a result of the wars and famines that had devastated the country in the seventeenth century. **Mercantilism**, the prevailing economic theory of the era, held that the strength of a nation resided in its population. Mercantilism instilled in countries what Eli Heckscher has called "an almost frantic desire to increase population."[4] According to mercantilism, Ireland in the eighteenth century was poor in part because it was too thinly peopled. Anglo-Irish patriots complained bitterly about Ireland's political subservience to England, about the wealth that Ireland lost through absentee landlords, and about economic policy that favored England. One such Anglo-Irishman was Thomas Prior, who gained notoriety in 1729 for publishing *A List of the Absentees of Ireland* (Document 2). Prior devoted most of his career to encouraging economic development in Ireland.

Ireland was also distressingly prone to famine. In the sixteenth and seventeenth century Ireland was devastated by man-made famines. English armies destroyed crops in rebellious regions as a military tactic. The **Confederate Wars** from 1641 to 1653 were particularly devastating: when **Oliver Cromwell** and his **New Model Army** arrived in 1649, they began a campaign to remove all resistance to English rule. One strategy was the destruction of foodstuffs and crops. It is impossible to know how many died in the wars and famines of this period, but **William Petty**, who served under Cromwell, surveyed the island in 1672 for his *A Political Anatomy of Ireland* and estimated that over 600,000 had been killed, or about 40 percent of the population.[5]

Robert Emmet (1778–1803): Irish nationalist who led an abortive rebellion against British rule in 1803.

Daniel O'Connell (1775–1847): Irish politician who led a successful campaign for Catholic Emancipation; often referred to as 'the Liberator' as a result.

Catholic Emancipation: The Roman Catholic Relief Act of 1829 repealed earlier legislation which had disenfranchised Catholics, allowing qualified Catholic landowners to vote and sit in Parliament.

Mercantilism: Economic theory popular from the sixteenth through the eighteenth century focused on trade and the accumulation of wealth.

Confederate Wars: The Irish theater of the Wars of the Three Kingdoms, which began as a conflict between Irish Catholics and English and Scottish settlers.

Oliver Cromwell (1599–1658): An English military leader for parliamentary forces during the English Civil War. Later led a devastating campaign to subdue Ireland before becoming Lord Protector of England until his death in 1658.

New Model Army: The parliamentary army during the English Civil War. Formed in 1645, it was considered a new model for an army since it consisted of full-time paid soldiers who could be sent anywhere.

William Petty (1623–87): English scientist who conducted a land survey of Irish land that was to be confiscated and given as payment to Cromwell's soldiers, including himself.

---

4 Eli Heckscher, *Mercantilism*, 2 vols. (London: Allen and Unwin, 1935), 2:158.

5 Charles Carleton, "Civilians," in *The Civil Wars: A Military History of England, Scotland, and Ireland, 1638–1660*, ed. John Kenyon and Jane Ohlmeyer (Oxford: Oxford UP, 1998), 272–306.

At the beginning of the eighteenth century it is estimated that Ireland had about two million people. Periodic famine remained a problem.[6] The famines of the eighteenth and early nineteenth century were not human-made. They were subsistence crises caused usually by crop failures and weather conditions. There were harvest failures and isolated reports of famine in 1708–09, 1721–22, 1728–29.[7] The most severe of these was between 1739 and 1741; a freak early frost destroyed crops, and unusual weather conditions and unseasonable cold continued for months afterwards. The historian David Dickson has estimated that this famine killed between 310,000 and 480,000 people at a time when the Irish population was about 2.4 million. If these estimates are accurate then the famine of 1741 actually killed a higher percentage of the population than the Great Potato Famine a century later. When the potato crop failed in 1845 the population was about 8 million, three times larger than it had been in 1741.[8] A number of less severe famines occurred between 1741 and 1845. Famine was reported in parts of the country in 1756, 1766, 1782, and 1798–1800, the potato crop failed in 1801 causing much concern, and there was famine again in 1817, 1821–22, 1825, 1831, 1835, and 1839. Most of these were comparatively minor and short term. The almost routine nature of these shortages points to larger issues within Ireland than those associated with the Great Famine of the mid-nineteenth century. Many predate the overpopulation of Ireland noted in the 1841 census and while potato failures are a factor in several, they have a variety of causes. In many instances potatoes kept the Irish alive while other crops failed.

By the nineteenth century Ireland was still a cause for concern and still had a tendency towards famine, but it was no longer underpopulated. In 1776 Adam Smith published *An Inquiry into the Nature and Causes of the Wealth of Nations* (Document 4). Smith's work helped to change the economic consensus on mercantilism. Meanwhile in 1798, Thomas Malthus published his *An Essay on the Principles of Population*, which challenged accepted ideas on population growth. As a result of Malthus' work English commentators now worried that Ireland was over-populated and that the large mass of poor, overwhelmingly Catholic, Irish peasants were overly dependent on a single crop—the potato. Thomas Malthus would directly comment on Ireland's population in the *Edinburgh Review* (Document 5).

When and who introduced the potato to Ireland is not precisely known. The plant itself is native to South America, and most credit Sir Walter

---

6   Sean Connolly, *Religion, Law and Power: The Making of Protestant Ireland 1660–1760* (Oxford: Oxford UP, 1992), 144–45.

7   "William Wilde's Table of Irish Famines, 900–1850," in *Famine: The Irish Experience, 900–1900*, ed. E. Margaret Crawford (Edinburgh: Donald, 1989), 11–13.

8   David Dickson, *Arctic Ireland: The Extraordinary Story of the Great Frost and Forgotten Famine of 1740–41* (Belfast: White Row Press, 1997), 69, 72.

Raleigh with bringing the potato to Ireland; this is unverifiable but it was widely believed in the Victorian period.[9] Traditionally the Irish had lived off animal husbandry, milk and its derivatives, grain, and oats. Following the wars of the sixteenth and seventeenth centuries, land was confiscated and redistributed to loyal Protestant settlers from England or Scotland. Potatoes caught on with the Irish peasantry—they did not require as much land as livestock, nor did they require the granaries, mills, or ovens that oats and grain needed and which Ireland did not have. Potatoes were not as easily burned, stolen, or trampled by armies. In sum, a family could live off the potatoes they grew on a small plot of poor land.[10] After the wars and land redistribution this was often the only type of land available to Irish Catholics, and even then it was only available for them to lease.

In the nineteenth century mercantilism fell out of favor, and the English tended to view Ireland through the lens of political economy.[11] By that calculation Ireland was overpopulated and overly dependent on the potato. The potato was too easy to grow; it allowed the Irish peasantry to have too many children, which contributed to overpopulation; and it made them idle and rebellious. Potatoes were criticized as a "lazy" crop; the Irish reliance on them was thought to reflect a weakness of character.[12] This interpretation nicely fit into pre-existing stereotypes about Ireland and the Irish, but it was also inaccurate. Ireland did not consist entirely of desperately poor Catholic peasants in ramshackle stone houses living only off potatoes. Ireland in the years before, and even during the famine, exported corn and grain to Great Britain. In the 1840s two million people in Britain were fed by food imported from Ireland.[13] But the potato was a staple food for many across Ireland: potatoes, which were not easily shipped, were grown for subsistence not for sale. In fact the consumption of potatoes is what allowed for the export of so much grain. Potatoes had many advantages: they were easy to grow and easy to cook, required minimal processing, they were nutritious, and when combined with buttermilk supplied ample protein and nutrients for a healthy diet. The Irish peasantry were considered by many, including Adam Smith, to be remarkably healthy and hardy and this was generally attributed to the potato. Mr and Mrs Samuel Carter Hall (Document 8) wrote of the Irish, "It is universally admitted that a finer or hardier race of

9 William H. McNeill, "The Introduction of the Potato into Ireland," *Journal of Modern History* 21, no. 3 (1949): 218.

10 K.H. Connell, "The Potato in Ireland," *Past & Present* 23 (1962): 57–58.

11 Kinealy, *This Great Calamity*, 1.

12 Michael De Nie, "Curing 'The Irish Moral Plague,'" *Eire-Ireland* 32 (1997): 70–72.

13 Kinealy, *This Great Calamity*, 4.

peasantry cannot be found in the world."[14] Potatoes come in many varieties, but in Ireland in the 1840s the most popular was a white potato known as the "Irish Lumper," which grew well in the poor soil that many Irish peasants, particularly in the west, farmed for their subsistence.[15] Gradually over the course of the eighteenth and early nineteenth century, the potato went from a food that supplemented the Irish diet to a staple of the Irish diet. By 1840, potatoes were the primary food for over three million people in Ireland.[16]

To the Irish, potato dependency was only a problem in hindsight. In the years leading up to the famine the larger problem was not potatoes, but the land system which necessitated so many in Ireland to live off potatoes. One of the many benefits of the potato was that it could be grown in even poor quality land. Potato cultivation was "the linch-pin of the whole system of tillage."[17] It was possible to grow enough potatoes on a small plot of land to feed a family, which allowed more land to be devoted to the cultivation of corn and wheat for export. The potato was praised by many for its reliability. The Irish political economist Mountifort Longfield (Document 11) defended the potato and those who relied upon it by noting that, "those little husbandmen, too, are necessarily bad farmers. They have no selection of land in which to plant their potatoes; they are obliged to put up with any land they can get." The potato, he noted, was generally a regular crop not liable to failures. It is hearty enough to provide good yields in ordinary years and is less prone to weather conditions than corn.[18] Prior to 1845 the potato generally served the Irish peasantry well. Most previous crop failures were corn or wheat destroyed by inclement weather, while the hardy potato survived. As Longfield noted, the Irish peasantry had little choice but to rely on the potato since they had little choice in land and potatoes would grow anywhere.

Irish farmers had little choice in their land because by the early nineteenth century there were few substantial Irish Catholic landowners in Ireland; instead, most land was owned by Anglo-Irish families, a group popularly called the Anglo-Irish Ascendancy. They were primarily the descendants of Protestant soldiers and settlers to whom English authorities had given the land that they had confiscated from Catholic Irish inhabitants in the sixteenth and seventeenth centuries. A number of major Anglo-Irish

---

14 Samuel Carter Hall and Anna Hall, *Ireland: Its Scenery, Character, etc.*, 3 vols. (London: How & Parsons, 1841), 1: 83.

15 Ireland, Department of Agriculture, Fisheries and Food, *Potato Varieties of Historical Interest in Ireland* (James Choiseul, Gerry Doherty, and Gabriel Roe, Ireland: 2008).

16 Kinealy, *This Great Calamity*, 12.

17 Cormac Ó Gráda, "Poverty, Population, and Agriculture, 1801–1845," *A New History of Ireland* vol. 5 (Oxford: Clarendon P, 1989), 112.

18 Mountifort Longfield, *Lectures on Political Economy* (Dublin: Richard Milliken and Son, 1834), 254–56.

landowners were absentees: they lived abroad, usually in England, and so most of the income generated by their land was spent abroad. Large landowners generally regarded their Irish estates only as a source of income and felt little sense of responsibility towards their tenants.[19] They also felt little responsibility to improve or invest in their land so long as they continued to profit from it. Since the eighteenth century, absentees had been condemned by Irish patriots, both Catholic and Protestant, as drains on Ireland's wealth, but the problem persisted.

Absentee landlords generally entrusted the management of their estates to middlemen or to a land agent. Landlords would sublet large tracts of land to middlemen who would sublet the property in smaller plots to Irish peasants at a higher rate. Some landlords rented land directly to Irish tenants, but if they lived abroad they entrusted a land agent to collect the rent for them. Irish peasants leased small plots of land through this system. By 1841 45 percent of landholds in Ireland were smaller than five acres.[20] The smallest of these holdings were held by people termed cottiers, who essentially held a cottage and a small patch of land and paid their rent through working for their landlord. To feed themselves and their families these smallholders relied on the potatoes they grew on their own land. Irish peasants could also obtain land through a system called conacre, but only particularly desperate tenants would rent land in this way. Under conacre peasants sublet a small portion of land for a single season. The land had generally already been prepared for planting, the rates were often high, and if anything damaged the crop the tenant was ruined since they had contracted to pay a high rent. Because of its speculative nature, conacre tenants were particularly vulnerable to eviction, although no Irish tenant was free of that concern.[21]

For English commentators the largest cause for concern in Ireland was the ubiquity of poverty. Official sources in England suggested that two million or more in Ireland were impoverished. The census of 1841 showed that two-fifths of all families lived in what was classified as fourth-class accommodation, a single room with little to no furniture.[22] In the 1830s a commission was appointed to investigate the condition of the poor in Ireland (Document 9) and it described the living conditions of the poor in cities and included reports on rural areas as well. For most of its history Ireland was not governed by a statutory poor law, as compared to England, which passed its first poor law in 1601. In 1838 this changed with the passage of the Irish Poor Law. The law itself took several years to develop. In

---

19 Cecil Woodham-Smith, *The Great Hunger* (New York: Penguin, 1991), 21.

20 Ibid., 34.

21 Gerard McCann, *Ireland's Economic History: Crisis and Development in the North and South* (London: Pluto Press, 2011), 18.

22 Ó Gráda, "Poverty, Population, and Agriculture," 110.

George Nicholls (1781–1865): British Poor Law Commissioner upon the creation of a new system of poor relief in Great Britain in 1834.

outdoor relief: Assistance to the poor that did not require them to enter the workhouse.

workhouses: Institutions in Great Britain and Ireland that provided accommodation and paid work to the destitute poor; conditions were intentionally harsh to discourage people from applying for poor relief.

Law of Settlement: Law under the English Poor Law that allowed people to obtain relief in a parish they were not born into. This did not exist in Ireland.

1833 a royal commission was appointed to survey Irish poverty. Later an English Poor Law Commissioner, **George Nicholls**, was sent to Ireland to determine if the English system of workhouse relief could be extended to Ireland. Nicholls determined that it could and so the Irish Poor Law Bill of 1838 was modeled on the English Poor Law of 1834. The aim of both systems was to relieve destitution while discouraging dependency on the government. There were, however, several important differences: in Ireland relief could only be administered through the workhouse. According to the 1838 law there was to be no **outdoor relief**; there was no right to relief, so when **workhouses** became full there was no obligation to provide aid in other forms; and finally there was no **Law of Settlement**—Irish people could not acquire a right to relief in a different district. Overall the law was harsher than its English counterpart, and it reflected an intense aversion to outdoor relief in Ireland.[23]

The new poor law divided Ireland into 130 Poor Law Unions each with its own elected board of guardians and its own workhouse, financed by local rates. To qualify for relief applicants had to be destitute and they and their family had to reside in their union's workhouse. The purpose of a workhouse, and requiring the poor to reside in them, was to discourage people from applying for relief. These strict qualifications for relief were deemed necessary in Ireland, which it was thought would be unable to financially support a more liberal system. The workhouses were constructed quickly and the new poor law system was in place by 1845.[24]

THE COURSE OF THE FAMINE

In 1844 a mysterious disease began to affect potatoes in America, and by 1845 that same disease had begun to appear in Europe. It appeared in England, Scotland, Belgium, and Holland, and by that fall it had appeared in Ireland as well. A horticultural magazine, the *Gardener's Chronicle,* referred to it as "a blight of unusual character."[25] The Home Secretary, Sir James Graham, wrote to Prime Minister Sir Robert Peel in September 1845 that the disease had appeared in Ireland. At first the reports were not excessively alarming: the potatoes were destroyed in some regions but fine in others, and the oat and barley harvest was not damaged. By October reports began to change. Edward Buller, the Secretary of the Royal Agricultural Improvement Society of Ireland, wrote to Peel that conditions were worse than expected. When

---

23   Christine Kinealy, "The Poor Law During the Great Famine: An Administration in Crisis," in *Famine: The Irish Experience,* ed. E. Margaret Crawford (Edinburgh: J. Donald, 1989), 158.

24   Ibid., 159.

25   Qtd. in Kinealy, *This Great Calamity,* 31.

farmers dug out their potatoes they found them rotten from the blight. Buller wrote that "a panic has seized all parties" and that he was writing privately to Peel regarding the severity of this issue so that "no time should be lost in adopting the necessary measures of precaution and relief for this country."[26]

At the time what exactly was happening was unknown. Peel would put together a scientific commission to study the blight and Ireland to determine if there was a cure, but none could be found. Investigators were not able to identify the disease and instead theorized that the wet conditions might be to blame; the commission was ultimately unable to offer any useful suggestions. The actual cause of the blight would only be identified in 1890.[27] Ireland and the rest of Northern Europe had fallen victim to the oomycete *Phytophtora infestans*, as a result of which infected potatoes decayed and turned into a rotten mush. The extent of infestation was often unclear until harvest; before that it appeared only as dark blotches on the leaves of the plants. Completely unaware of this, scientists and Irish famers focused on ways to dry the crops, believing that wet conditions were causing them to rot.[28]

The potato crop of 1845 was 33 percent smaller than usual. In 1846 it was 75 percent smaller than normal. By 1847 only 284,000 acres were under potato cultivation, down from two million.[29] Starvations began in 1846, but most of the dead fell victim to diseases such as typhus fever, dysentery, scurvy, and cholera. The harvest of 1847 was actually a success, but so little land was under cultivation and there were so few seed potatoes that there were still food shortages.[30] In 1848 and 1849 the blight struck again, further damaging the harvest, and the quantity of potatoes produced remained far lower than pre-1845 levels. These conditions did not abate until 1852. In the intervening years mortality more than tripled as people died of starvation and an array of diseases.[31]

Meanwhile in London, the seat of government for the United Kingdom, the response to the famine became a political issue. In 1846 Peel chose to respond to the crisis by ordering the importation of food from America. Here he ran into problems within his Conservative (Tory) Party. At the time a series of protectionist trade laws called the Corn Laws was in place, which sought to protect domestic farmers by banning the importation of food, fixing grain prices to favor British farmers. The Corn Laws set a price

---

26 *Memoirs of Sir Robert Peel*, 2:110–28.

27 Ian Miller, *Reforming Food in Post-Famine Ireland: Medicine, Science, and Improvement, 1845–1922* (Manchester: Manchester UP, 2014), 25.

28 T.P. O'Neill, "The Scientific Investigation of the Failure of the Potato Crop in Ireland, 1845–6," *Irish Historical Studies* 5, no. 18 (1946): 124–38.

29 L.A. Clarkson and Margaret Crawford, *Feast and Famine: A History of Food and Nutrition in Ireland, 1500–1920* (Oxford: Oxford UP, 2002), 88.

30 Miller, *Reforming Food*, 25.

31 Kinealy, *This Great Calamity*, 168.

threshold for British grain; when it was met the importation of cheaper foreign grain was allowed. Essentially the laws made it impossible for the poor to buy cheap food. Peel had inherited the legislation, but the policy was very popular with his fellow Tories. After much deliberation, he sought to repeal the Corn Laws—a decision which was intensely controversial in England and within his own party. Some in Parliament accused Peel of exaggerating the Irish situation in order to repeal the Corn Laws. In the end Peel did manage to repeal the legislation, but it cost him his position.[32] In 1846 Peel's Tory Party lost the election and he was replaced as prime minister by Lord John Russell and the **Whig Party**.

Whig Party: British political party that first emerged in the late seventeenth century. Generally associated with liberal politics at the time: it sought to reduce the power of the crown, supported bankers and merchants, and supported limited voting reform.

The importation of corn, which was sold cheaply, was intended to help ease the situation in Ireland in the early months of the crisis. The potato crop failures had led to food shortages, and what food was available was prohibitively expensive. However, importing corn caused its own problems. Most Irish peasants were unfamiliar with cornmeal and had no idea how to prepare it; they also could not afford the flour or oatmeal that was supposed to be mixed with cornmeal to make it more digestible.[33] Many suffered stomach problems from the sudden switch to a new food source. Peel organized a Relief Commission to sell the imported food at cost, and set up public work schemes, the wages of which were generally sufficient to buy the imported corn. The other issue was that despite the potato shortage Irish landowners were still exporting grain. The grain crop had not been damaged, and landowners who cultivated grain continued selling it in English markets. This simply drove up food prices in Ireland even more. Both Peel and later Russell chose not to interfere with this trade, and despite many calls to ban exports of food from Ireland during the famine, Irish grain continued to be sold abroad.[34] Most in Ireland regarded Peel's measures as relatively effective. The Irish newspaper the *Freeman's Journal* praised that "no man died of famine during his administration."[35] The effectiveness of Peel's measures is difficult to measure given that his administration ended in 1846.

The new Whig government believed that government should interfere in trade as little as possible and so it stopped the policy of food imports, leaving that up to local merchants. Instead it concentrated on the public works schemes, dictating that the cost of such schemes be paid for through local taxes. Pay on the public works was low and generally not enough to support a family. In addition, the public works had the unintended consequence of keeping Irish farmers away from their fields, so the amount of land under

---

32 Iain McLearn and Camilla Bustani, "Irish Potatoes and British Politics: Interests, Ideology, Heresthetic and the Repeal of the Corn Laws," *Political Studies* XLVII (1999): 817–36.

33 Miller, *Reforming Food*, 27.

34 Kinealy, *This Great Calamity*, 89.

35 Qtd. in Kinealy, *This Great Calamity*, 37.

cultivation dropped precipitously.[36] The Whig response to the crisis was to focus on local relief, which in some ways made sense, since the impact of the famine was uneven across Ireland. The problem, though, was the insistence that local poor relief should be financed locally, which placed an impossible burden on regions whose economy had been devastated by the blight.[37]

It is clear that there were problems in the system of famine relief; what many historians have disagreed on is whether the causes were ideological or institutional. The political and economic philosophies of the era certainly made the British government reluctant to engage in large-scale relief. But given the scale of the crisis, was it possible to provide effective relief? The insistence on making relief a local responsibility almost certainly hampered effectiveness and led to an increase in mortality, evictions, and emigration.[38] The regions that were most affected were already the poorest even before the famine.[39] Traditionally, British policy is attributed to a strict adherence to laissez-faire economics by the Russell administration. Others have suggested that the scale of the crisis was simply too vast to allow an effective response by the government. L.M. Cullen and T.C. Smout have said that "the Irish [famine] problem was too huge for the British state to overcome."[40] Racial ideology also certainly played a part in how the Irish were viewed and therefore in how Britain responded to the famine. Thomas Campbell Foster reflects some of this ideology in his *Letters on the Condition of the People of Ireland* (Document 10).

Charles Trevelyan, the assistant secretary of the Treasury, who oversaw famine relief efforts for the Liberal government, was certainly devoted to laissez-faire economics. In private correspondence he noted that "it forms no part of the functions of government to provide supplies of food ... it falls to the share of government to protect the merchant and agriculturists in the free exercise of their respective employments."[41] Trevelyan blamed Irish landlords for the condition of the Irish peasantry and thought that famine relief ought to be their responsibility. Numerous popular articles and histories have quoted Trevelyan as saying, "the judgement of God sent the calamity to teach the Irish a lesson, that calamity must not be too much

36 Ibid., 90–91.

37 Kinealy, "The Poor Law During the Great Famine," 157.

38 Ibid., 141.

39 William J. Smyth, "'Variations in Vulnerability': Understanding Where and Why the People Died," in *Atlas of the Great Irish Famine*, eds. John Crowley, William J. Smyth, and Mike Murphy (New York: New York UP, 2012), 180.

40 L.M. Cullen and T.C. Smout, "Economic Growth in Scotland and Ireland," in *Comparative Aspects of Scottish and Irish Economic and Social History 1600–1900*, eds. L.M. Cullen and T.C. Smout (Edinburgh: John Donald, 1978), 11.

41 "Letter from Trevelyan to Lord Monteagle," in *The Irish Famine: A Documentary*, eds. Colm Tóibín and Diarmaid Ferriter (New York: St Martin's P, 2001), 71.

mitigated."[42] According to Robin Haines, this phrase, which Trevelyan never actually wrote, is the result of a misinterpretation by historian Jennifer Hart in her 1960 article, "Sir Charles Trevelyan at the Treasury."[43] Haines argues that Trevelyan's most contemptuous words were for Irish landlords, and he was known at the time for his empathy towards Irish Catholics.[44] Historians disagree considerably on Trevelyan's exact role in and responsibility for famine relief policy. Excerpts from his 1848 book *The Irish Crisis* (Document 25) are included in this volume and readers can judge his views for themselves.

Joel Mokyr has argued that the root of Britain's lack of action during the worst years of the famine was that "Ireland was considered by Britain an alien and even hostile country."[45] Mokyr contends that this attitude explains the lack of British investment before the famine, the comparatively harsher views of Irish poverty, and the lack of resources put towards famine relief. He argues that if a similar crisis had occurred in England or Wales, the British government would have provided aid on a much larger scale. Instead, during the years of the famine the treasury spent only £9.5 million on famine relief, compared to the £69.3 million that would be spent on fighting the Crimean War between 1853 and 1856.[46] Whatever the motivation, the relatively small amount of money expended on aid to Ireland during the famine had major repercussions for people in Ireland.

For Irish smallholders unable to support themselves through the public works, the only other option was the workhouse. Under the Poor Law of 1838 Ireland was divided into Poor Law Unions, and the administration of each union was the responsibility of a local board, funded by local rates. By 1847 workhouses, never popular because of their many restrictions, had filled to capacity. To receive relief Irish families had to consent to confinement in the workhouse. Many came to be filled to overcapacity, allowing disease to spread easily amongst the people kept there.[47] The Poor Law did not allow for outdoor relief during the early years of the famine. Eventually, following pressure from the population, the law was amended in 1847 to

---

42 This exact phrasing is used in Tim Pat Coogan, *The Famine Plot: England's Role in Ireland's Greatest Tragedy* (New York: Palgrave Macmillan, 2012), 63–64. It also appears in numerous other books and contemporary news articles discussing the famine.

43 Robin Haines, *Charles Trevelyan and the Great Irish Famine* (Dublin: Four Courts Press, 2004), 2–4. Jennifer Hart, "Sir Charles Trevelyan at the Treasury," *English Historical Review*, 75, no. 294, (1960), 99.

44 Haines, 7.

45 Joel Mokyr, *Why Ireland Starved: A Quantitative and Analytical History of the Irish Economy, 1800–1850* (London: George Allen & Unwin, 1983), 291.

46 Ibid., 292.

47 Kinealy, *This Great Calamity*, 113.

allow workhouses to offer outdoor relief to the sick and disabled; the able-bodied could only receive outdoor relief if the workhouse was at capacity (Document 26).

As the crisis worsened, the government passed the Destitute Poor Act in 1847, the public works schemes were disbanded and outdoor relief or soup kitchens were set up in most of Ireland's Poor Law Unions. Food imports into Ireland reached their peak in 1847 at the same time that exports were at their lowest levels, but 1847 was still the worst year of the famine. The rations at soup kitchens were small, and disease ravaged the country affecting both the poor and relief workers. By the time of the harvest of 1847 the government believed the crisis to be ending, which was incorrect, but based on this assumption they scaled back relief efforts. The Irish Poor Law Extension Act of 1847 stated that Poor Law Unions were to take control of the relief efforts and that they should derive all of their money from local funds. This act did allow for outdoor relief, although again only under certain conditions, such as if the workhouse was full, or if the applicant was old or infirm. It allowed the commissioners to alter the size of unions and increased the number of workhouses. The act also contained two provisions—one called the Gregory Clause, named for a Dublin MP William Gregory who suggested it, and another called the £4 clause. The Gregory Clause stated that anyone who owned more than a quarter of an acre of land was not eligible for relief. Meanwhile, the £4 clause made landlords responsible for all taxes on holdings valued under £4. Between this and the Gregory Clause, many landowners were financially motivated to rid themselves of smallholders.[48]

Since landlords were liable to pay the poor rates on smallholdings under the £4 clause, clearing estates of these tenants was a way to avoid paying poor rates. Estimates are that around 500,000 people were evicted during the famine, and that small farms, those under five acres, virtually disappeared. In turn evictions placed additional burdens on the poor rates, as evicted families either had to secure new lodgings so they could receive outdoor relief or face going into the workhouse. However, it was generally agreed upon by the government and the Poor Law Commissioners at the time that these evictions, which allowed for the consolidation of property, were in the long-term interests of Ireland. The hope was that the removal of smallholders and the consolidation of estates would allow for agricultural improvements.[49]

Irish smallholders, cottiers, and laborers had reason to fear eviction for years. While large-scale farmers had long, fixed-term leases of at least twenty-one years, many smallholders were either **at-will tenants** or rented

at-will tenants: Tenants without a lease or other written agreement with their landlord.

---

48 Kinealy, "The Poor Law During the Great Famine," 161–62.

49 Ibid., 164.

on a yearly basis. The situation changed drastically during the famine as smallholders were rendered unable to pay their rents. Landlords meanwhile faced the financial burdens of the loss of rental income and the requirement to pay the Poor Law rates, which they were largely liable for. The government preferred to have poor relief financed through the Poor Law system and paid for entirely by local rates. Policymakers tended to scapegoat landlords, who were portrayed as shirking their responsibilities, while ignoring the financial impact the famine had on them.[50] Some Irish landlords felt forced to resort to large-scale evictions of at-will tenants and smallholders with expired leases by the financial burdens of the poor law. Meanwhile, eviction allowed landlords to consolidate their holdings into larger, more economically viable farms. Both the British government and economists generally considered consolidation to be best in the long term. The complication was that the large-scale eviction led to mass destitution. Dispossessed tenants were directed to the overcrowded and overburdened workhouses, or in some cases they were directed to emigrate.[51]

Another consequence of evictions was the increased rate of emigration. Emigration was already an established trend, but during the famine the rates increased markedly as desperation drove more and more people to leave Ireland. Recently evicted families did not themselves have the resources to fund their own emigration. Many destitute Irish families took advantage of, or were forced to take advantage of, landlord-funded emigration schemes. Landlords often paid the passage of the tenants that they evicted in order to clear their estates. In other cases Poor Law Unions or charities would pay the fares to Britain, Canada, or the United States. Most emigrants were young, unskilled, and Catholic; many spoke only Irish.[52]

Emigration was responsible for more population loss during the famine and in the succeeding years than death. Between 1845 and 1851 it is thought that one million people left Ireland,[53] and high emigration rates continued for years afterwards. Many emigrants were sick from disease and starvation, and illnesses spread quickly in the cramped cargo holds of nineteenth-century sailing vessels (Document 39). Ships taking Irish emigrants to Canada or the United States came to be labeled as coffin ships because of the high death rates among emigrants on board. Quarantine centers were established in both Canada and the United States to stop the spread of the diseases that many migrants brought with them (Documents 40 and 41). In many cases, while initial passage was paid for by the landlord, little to no arrangement was

---

50 Kinealy, *This Great Calamity*, 39.

51 Ibid., 190.

52 Kinealy, *This Great Calamity*, 314–16.

53 William J. Smyth, "Exodus from Ireland—Patterns of Emigration," in *Atlas of the Great Irish Famine*, 494.

made for the migrants upon their arrival. Those who did survive the journey found themselves in unfamiliar environments with little means of support.[54]

In Ireland and around the world private charity stepped in as best it could; the Society of Friends, or the Quakers, raised money in America and Britain and distributed it in local areas. The British Relief Association managed to raise money from some of the most prominent individuals in the world, including Queen Victoria and the Sultan of the Ottoman Empire.[55] The political considerations that affected state poor relief did not apply to private philanthropy, and private organizations at times acted at the request of the British government.[56] Numerous smaller organizations emerged, and communities large and small around the world raised money "for the relief of the suffering Irish."[57] The Irish Famine led to an unprecedented wave of international philanthropy, with assistance coming even from the Chocataw and Cherokee nations, both of whom had been forcibly relocated to reservations only a decade before.[58]

The actual number of deaths that can be attributed to the famine is unknown; the best historical estimate is at least 1.1 million deaths in excess of the average mortality rate, and then at least 400,000 averted births due to the famine's effects on fertility.[59] Most "excess mortality" during this period was the result of contagious diseases, which swept through the population weakened by lack of food. Famine fever, usually either typhus fever or relapsing fever, and chronic dysentery were the most common, but tuberculosis, smallpox, and measles were all rampant. In 1848 Ireland was even hit by a cholera epidemic. While Ireland had a network of medical charities that predated the famine, they were inadequate to the scale of the crisis that hit during the famine. Emergency fever hospitals were built, and the Central Board of Health attempted as best they could to regulate the conditions. Space frequently proved to be a problem, and overcrowding in hospitals and workhouses further contributed to the spread of disease.[60]

---

54 Kerby A. Miller, "Emigration to North America in the Era of the Great Famine, 1845–55," in *Atlas of the Great Irish Famine*, 214–15.

55 Christine Kinealy, *Charity and the Great Hunger in Ireland: The Kindness of Strangers* (London: Bloomsbury, 2013), 196.

56 Ibid., 3.

57 Anelise Hanson Shrout, "'Distressing News from Ireland': The Famine, the News and International Philanthropy" (PhD Dissertation: New York University, 2013), 11.

58 Anelise Hanson Shrout, "A 'Voice of Benevolence from the Western Wilderness': The Politics of Native Philanthropy in the Trans-Mississippi West," *Journal of the Early Republic* 35 no. 4, (2015): 553–54.

59 Joel Mokyr, *Why Ireland Starved: A Quantitative and Analytical History of the Irish Economy, 1800–1850*, 2nd ed. (London: Taylor & Francis, 1985), 263–68.

60 Laurence Geary, "Medical Relief and the Great Famine," in *Atlas of the Great Irish Famine*, 199–204.

Within Ireland there was large-scale suffering—and widespread social unrest (Document 18). The famine led to increased incidences of crimes such as theft and vagrancy but also seems to have contributed to rioting and murder. British officials feared that Irish discontent might manifest as revolutionary outrage. The Lord-Lieutenant in 1848, George Villiers, Lord Clarendon, advised Prime Minister Russell that the government needed to focus on "relieving distress which causes much of the bad feeling now, and if we can pay off a revolution in that way, it will be an economy."[61] There was a small uprising in the summer of 1848, led by members of the Young Ireland movement, which was quickly put down and the captured leaders were transported to either Bermuda or Australia. The government suspended habeas corpus in the hopes of preventing further rebellions.[62] They also took pains to ensure that there was sufficient military and police presence in the event of another uprising. By the summer of 1848 there were 100,000 troops and 13,000 police in Ireland.[63] Aside from the 1848 uprising, most crime did not seem to aim at revolution but was in response to the desperation and dislocation brought on by hunger and evictions. Writing years later of the failure of the 1848 rebellion, the Irish nationalist Maud Gonne noted that it was no surprise the uprising failed: "It is a fallacy to think that the poorer and more miserable a people are the better they will fight; there is a degree of misery and poverty which saps all energy, moral and physical."[64]

Aftermath

Conditions slowly improved in 1851, and by 1852 the famine is generally considered to have ended. However, its impact lingered on in ways both great and small. Ireland's population had dropped by about one quarter and would never recover to pre-famine levels. As of the 2016 census the population of the Republic stood at 4.77 million people, while Northern Ireland had 1.8 million as of the 2011 census. It is estimated that about one million died as a direct result of the famine, approximately one-eighth of the pre-famine population of 8.5 million. At least one million more emigrated during the years of the famine, and emigration remained a feature of Irish life for decades to follow.[65] The emptiness and desolation of post-famine Ireland was noted by many contemporaries. **John O'Donovan** wrote to a friend that a "solemn and awful stillness reigns which seems to forebode some

John O'Donovan (1806–61): Irish language scholar and topographer who worked for the Irish Ordnance Survey and was later professor of Celtic Languages at Queen's University, Belfast.

61 Kinealy, *This Great Calamity,* 203.

62 Ibid., 203. There was a wave of revolutions and rebellions across Europe in 1848 and the uprising in Ireland was a small part of that broader trend.

63 Christine Kinealy, *Repeal and Revolution: 1848 in Ireland* (Manchester: Manchester UP, 2009), 280.

64 Qtd. in Kinealy, *Repeal and Revolution,* 281.

65 Cormac Ó Gráda and Phelim P. Boyle, "Fertility Trends, Excess Mortality, and the Great Irish Famine," *Demography* 23, no. 4 (November 1986).

dreadful reaction and frightful commotion."[66] In the immediate aftermath of the famine British census commissioners noted that depopulation had addressed many of the issues afflicting pre-famine Ireland. (The eighteenth-century idea that Ireland's problems were caused by underpopulation was no longer prevalent.) The reduction in population and the accompanying reduction in small landholders meant an increasing number of large farms and promised improved economic conditions.[67]

The Irish language had been in decline for some time, but the since the famine and emigration had disproportionately affected Irish speakers in the west, the language declined even more. While levels of emigration went down once the famine ended, they never returned to pre-famine levels. Up to half of each generation continued to leave Ireland for the remainder of the nineteenth century.[68] This trend of emigration created the Irish diaspora; the number of people claiming Irish descent today exceeds the population of Ireland by a factor of ten. The experience of the famine had enormous resonance for the first-generation of famine emigrants. Their attitude was shaped by Irish nationalists, who aimed to mobilize hostility towards the British into active financial support of Irish revolutionary activity.[69] In a more immediate sense the community of famine exiles continued to play an important role in Ireland. By 1852 emigrants were sending £7,404,000 back to their home country annually.[70] In her novel *Bessy Conway* (Document 43) Mary Ann Sadlier illustrated this trend by having the virtuous Irishwoman Bessy return home to Ireland after a series of trials in America just in time to save the family farm.

Economically in Ireland it took decades for conditions to truly improve. Evictions remained widespread in the 1850s, and many people still lived at the subsistence level. However, in the long term people became less dependent on potatoes, and subsequent failures of the crop never again had such severe consequences. The famine also inspired new political movements. Pre-famine political movements like the Repeal Association and Young Ireland lost momentum or were silenced in the wake of the famine. However, new issues soon emerged, particularly the land question. Tenants' groups began to be established as early as 1849 with the objective of obtaining lower rents, fixed tenure, and legal protections for tenants. The Tenant Right League was founded in 1850, although it shut down by 1859. The goals of these earlier organizations was picked up by the Land League, which was officially established in 1879, following years of agitation. The land question was the

---

66 Qtd. in Willie Nolan, "Land Reform in post-Famine Ireland," in *Atlas of the Great Irish Famine*, 570.
67 Ibid., 570.
68 Piaras Mac Éinri, "Famine and the Irish Diaspora," in *Atlas of the Great Irish Famine*, 589–95.
69 Ibid., 589–95.
70 Nolan, "Land Reform," 570.

central political issue in Ireland in the late nineteenth century.[71] Meanwhile the Irish Republican Brotherhood, founded in 1858, was the descendant of the Young Ireland movement. The Brotherhood focused on achieving political independence from the United Kingdom and advocated the use of violence towards that end.[72]

Nationalist movements of the late nineteenth and early twentieth century were heavily influenced by popular memory of the famine. That memory was transferred to new generations through songs and folklore, as the memory of the famine became a part of the Irish oral tradition.[73] The association between the famine and Irish nationalism began before the famine even ended. In his famous 1847 "Lecture on the Antecedent Causes of the Famine" (Document 36), given to raise money for famine relief efforts, the Bishop of New York John Hughes laid the cause of the famine on the long history of English occupation and oppression. Once the famine had ended, one of the most powerful and influential early interpretations of the events was written in 1861 by the exiled Irish nationalist John Mitchel (Document 45). Mitchel portrayed the famine as *The Last Conquest of Ireland (Perhaps)* and blamed English policy for both creating the conditions that led to the famine and for a failure to provide sufficient relief. Like Hughes, Mitchel connected the famine to a long history of British misrule in Ireland, but, unlike Hughes, Mitchel was an open advocate for the use of physical force to change this. Mitchel was a member of the Young Ireland movement and a former writer for the *Nation*. In 1848 he was convicted under the Treason Felony Act of 1848, a new piece of legislation recently passed in response to British fears that the famine would lead to political revolt. Mitchel was transported first to Bermuda, from where he escaped in 1853 and fled to the United States, where he established a radical Irish newspaper called the *Citizen*. He continued to advocate vocally for Irish nationalism and he also became a vocal pro-slavery advocate in the years leading up to the American Civil War. *The Last Conquest of Ireland (Perhaps)* is polemical, intended to promote a particular view of the famine and to encourage the kind of radical and violent Irish nationalism that John Mitchel had been advocating for years.[74]

The writings of John Mitchel and other members of the Young Ireland movement helped to inspire the tenants' rights movement and its leaders

---

71 Ibid., 570–71.

72 Ibid., 571–72.

73 Roger McHugh, "The Famine in Irish Oral Tradition," *The Great Famine: Studies in Irish History 1845–52*, ed. R. Dudley Edwards and T. Desmond Williams (New York: New York UP, 1957), chap. 7.

74 Graham Davis, "Making History: John Mitchel and the Great Famine," in *Irish Writing: Exile and Subversion*, ed. Paul Hyland and Neil Sammells (London: Palgrave Macmillan, 1991), 98.

such as **Michael Davitt**. They directly inspired movements like the **Fenian Brotherhood**. Furthermore, by successfully crafting a particular narrative of the famine in *The Last Conquest of Ireland (Perhaps)*, Mitchel inspired generations of Irish-Americans to provide support from abroad. Mitchel rejected peaceful agitation, the kinds of tactics practiced by Daniel O'Connell during his pre-famine Repeal Movement. A non-violent nationalist movement continued to advocate for Home Rule in late-nineteenth and early-twentieth century Ireland. However, increasingly, inspired by John Mitchel, nationalist movements advocated for the use of physical force to achieve their ends. These "advanced nationalists" would found movements such as the Irish Republican Brotherhood and would organize uprisings like the 1916 Easter Rising.[75]

Michael Davitt (1846–1906): Irish republican and agrarian campaigner who founded the Land League.

Fenian Brotherhood: An Irish republican organization founded in the United States in 1858, and a sister organization to the Irish Republican Brotherhood.

Historiography of the Famine

Both the scale of the famine and its long-term effects have made it perhaps the most well-known period in Irish history. Oddly, despite this, it has been relatively understudied by Irish historians. There are a variety of explanations for this, but essentially for years it has been impossible to separate interpretations of the famine from attitudes toward Irish nationalism and Irish politics. Different groups of historians have approached and interpreted the famine in different ways. John Mitchel's *The Last Conquest of Ireland (Perhaps)* articulated a powerful and in many ways compelling interpretation of the famine, but it did so in the service of a clear political agenda. His analysis was highly influential, but with its overt political agenda it came to be rejected by a new wave of twentieth-century historians who appeared in Ireland following independence. These "revisionist" historians sought to free the study of Irish history from the service of politics and to apply a "value-free" approach to the study of history; revisionist historians sought to distance themselves from anti-British polemics such as John Mitchel's.

Nationalist historians tend to take their cue from Mitchel's most famous line, "the Almighty, indeed, sent the potato blight, but the English created the famine."[76] In the twentieth century, Cecil Woodham-Smith's *The Great Hunger* (1962) introduced a similar interpretation of the famine to a new generation of readers. The famine and the conditions which led to its severity are blamed on British government policy, the evils of the land system, and the negligence of the landlord class. Charles Trevelyan is singled out for his role in shaping famine relief policy. Revisionists, meanwhile, in seeking to distance themselves from the anti-British interpretations of nationalists, have portrayed the famine as unfortunate but inevitable, the result of

---

75 Kinealy, *Repeal and Revolution*, 285–86.
76 John Mitchel, *The Last Conquest of Ireland (Perhaps)*, (Dublin: Irishman Office, 1861), 323.

overpopulation and Ireland's economic backwardness at the time. They have argued that the Famine is not a watershed moment in Irish history and that it was not as demographically devastating as had been supposed.[77]

In recent decades, both of these interpretive frameworks have been overshadowed by the post-revisionist school of thought. This school is best exemplified by the work of Christine Kinealy (*This Great Calamity: The Irish Famine 1845–1852*) and Cormac Ó Gráda (*The Great Irish Famine*). The post-revisionist framework which now dominates is an attempt to move beyond the political divisions of the earlier schools. Post-revisionist historians integrated new developments in economic, social, and cultural history into the study of the famine, and have challenged the revisionist view and reintegrated serious discussion on issues of blame and the scale of the catastrophe. They have not, however, gone so far as to endorse claims that the famine constituted a genocide, as was claimed under more extreme versions of the nationalist/traditionalist view. As Ó Gráda put it, "Food availability was a problem; nobody wanted the extirpation of the Irish race."[78]

When reading the documents included here, keep in mind that they can be interpreted in many ways. Every author has their own particular motives for writing, but most write within the established conventions of the time. In particular this work contains several travel accounts from British visitors to Ireland written both before and during the famine. British travel accounts of pre-famine Ireland and famine Ireland were distinct from later travel writing which emphasized tourist travel. Instead these accounts, such as Mr and Mrs Samuel Carter Hall's *Ireland: Its Scenery, Character, etc.* (Document 8), doubled as commentaries and analyses that sought to diagnose the political, economic, and social ills that were thought to affect Ireland.

In addition this work contains a number of newspaper sources. Mid-nineteenth-century newspapers differ significantly from most contemporary American newspapers. Most notable for the sources used here is that objectivity was not considered essential to journalism, and several papers took a clear political stance. The *Freeman's Journal* and the *Nation* were both open proponents of Irish nationalism. The *Times* of London was a traditionally conservative paper, opposed to Irish nationalism. The coverage of these papers shaped the opinions of contemporary readers on issues like blame and how to respond.[79] Most nineteenth-century newspapers did not have foreign correspondents, so English newspapers routinely reprinted from Irish newspapers, and Irish newspapers routinely reprinted from each other.

---

77 Roy Foster, *Modern Ireland* (London: Penguin, 1988), 318.

78 Cormac Ó Gráda, *Ireland Before and After the Famine: Exploration in Economic History, 1800–1925* (Manchester: Manchester UP, 1988).

79 Anelise Shrout, "'Distressing News from Ireland': The Famine, the News and International Philanthropy," 10.

Most Irish and British newspapers got their information from local correspondents or letter writers. American newspapers generally reprinted clips from British or Irish newspapers.[80]

The documents that follow fall into six sections: first, those that reveal conditions in Ireland before the famine from the early eighteenth-century until 1846. Next, a broad range of accounts of the famine in Ireland and reactions abroad. Finally, literary and political documents from the years following the famine. The famine was widely reported on around the world, and many English travelers who visited Ireland in those years in either a personal or a professional capacity wrote accounts of their experiences. This collection attempts to balance such narratives with newspaper coverage and government documents in order to demonstrate how contemporaries both within and outside Ireland understood and reacted to the famine. Editorial interventions have been kept to a minimum, but all documents have been edited for length. This is a classroom edition and the intention has been to keep the texts accessible and to include as broad a range of sources as possible.

---

80 Ibid., 27–28.

CHRONOLOGY

1740–41 ● Severe famine, called *Bliain an Áir* (the year of the slaughter), strikes Ireland. It is estimated to have killed 38 percent of the Irish population, which was then an estimated 2.4 million.

1798 ● A republican group known as the United Irishmen inspired by the French Revolution seeks to overthrow British rule in Ireland.

1801 ● January 1: The Acts of Union go into effect, formally uniting Ireland with Great Britain and abolishing the Irish Parliament. Ireland loses legislative independence.

The potato crop fails, threatening to cause famine among the peasantry.

1817 ● Weather conditions lead to general crop failures, but the potato crop was "abundant."

1821 ● First national census of Ireland takes place. It recorded Ireland's population as 6,801,827.

1829 ● Thanks to Daniel O'Connell, Catholic Emancipation is granted, giving Catholics in the United Kingdom the right to sit in the Westminster Parliament and to vote if they meet property qualifications.

1831 ● Census shows Irish population to be 7,767,401; a growth of 14.3 percent since the previous census.

1833 ● A Royal Commission is appointed to enquire into the condition of the poorer classes in Ireland, and a three-year survey is carried out. The Commission estimates that 2,385,000 people are out of work in Ireland and need assistance for thirty weeks of the year. It recommends encouraging emigration and economic development. Parliamentary leaders oppose the idea of government intervention.

1835 ● Failures of the potato crop in some districts lead to severe distress. Areas that suffered crop failures were relieved by shipments of potatoes from places like Galway and Wexford, which were unaffected.

1837 ● Victoria comes to the throne of the United Kingdom of Great Britain and Ireland.

1838 ● A Poor Law modeled on the English Poor Law is introduced in Ireland. The country is divided into 130 Poor Law Unions each with a workhouse.

1841 ● Census shows the Irish population stands at 8,175,124. It has grown 5.5 percent since 1831 and an estimated 50 percent since 1800. The census shows that the rural workforce has increased by 50 percent, while the industrial workforce has declined by 15 percent.

1842 ● A group referred to as Young Ireland establishes the newspaper the *Nation* which promotes Irish cultural nationalism.

1845 ● August: First report of the blight in Ireland.

October: One-third of potato crop lost to blight.

November: Sir Robert Peel orders purchase of Indian corn in United States. Relief Commission established.

114,000 relieved in Workhouses.

1846 ● March: Public Works Act to provide employment begins. Sale of Indian corn begins.

June: Peel virtually eliminates duties on corn. Lord John Russell replaces Peel as prime minister.

July: Blight reappears, three-quarters of crop lost. Emigration escalates.

August: Poor Employment Act passes—new round of public works.

November: Unusually harsh winter, mortality soars thanks to epidemics of fever and dysentery. Society of Friends forms a relief committee.

December: 390,000 people reported on public works. 244,000 relieved in workhouses.

1847 ● January: British Relief Association formed.

March: 714,000 on relief works. Soup kitchens begin replacing relief works.

April: Fever Act passes to cope with epidemics.

May: Daniel O'Connell dies while on pilgrimage to Rome.

June: Poor Relief Act providing for outdoor relief for vulnerable populations.

July: Blight is not as serious but potato harvest is 25 percent of normal. Separate Poor Law Commission established for Ireland. Soup distributed to three million people daily.

October: Soup kitchens close with relief to be provided by Poor Law Unions and workhouses.

Estimated 220,000 people emigrate.

417,000 relieved in workhouses.

1848 July: General failure of potato crop, only one-third of usual crop saved. Young Ireland rising in County Tipperary.

September: Parliaments stops extraordinary government relief measures. Poor Law rules are to be strictly enforced and rates raised. First Encumbered Estates Act passed.

November: Cholera epidemic begins. Rural evictions increase from 1847 level.

Estimated 182,000 people emigrate.

610,000 relieved in workhouses.

1849 May: Blight confined to west and south. Rate-in-Aid Act distributes Poor Law rates equally over all Poor Law Unions.

June: 800,000 on outdoor relief. Society of Friends (Quakers) gives up relief work.

August: Visit of Queen Victoria and Prince Albert.

December: Workhouse accommodation available for 250,000; most of it is occupied.

Estimated 220,000 people emigrate.

932,000 relieved in workhouses.

16,686 families evicted.

1850 August: Potato harvest is largely healthy; isolated instances of the blight occur.

Tenant Right League is established by Charles Gavan Duffy and Frederick Lucas. They advocate for the Three Fs: fair rent, fixity of tenure, and free sale. Political opposition and emigration causes the League to peter out by 1859.

Right to vote is extended to farmers who hold twelve acres or more.

Estimated 214,000 people emigrate.

805,000 relieved in workhouses. A further 363,000 receive outdoor relief.

1851 August: Poor Relief Act provides for the establishment of dispensaries.

Census shows that the Irish population has fallen from 8,175,124 in 1841 to 6,552,385 in 1851.

Estimated 255,000 people emigrate.

707,000 relieved in workhouses.

1852 Outdoor relief is virtually phased out.

Estimated 369,000 people emigrate.

504,000 relieved in workhouses.

1853	Estimated 193,000 emigrate.
	396,000 relieved in workhouses.
1854	Estimated 150,000 people emigrate.
1855	Estimated 79,000 people emigrate.
1858	James Stephens founds the Irish Republican Brotherhood.
1860	The Partry Evictions take place: 68 families are turned out of their homes by Thomas Plunket, the Church of Ireland Bishop of Tuam.
1867	March: The Irish Republican Brotherhood, aka the Fenians, organize a failed rebellion against British rule.
	Thomas J. Kelly and Timothy Deasy, leaders of the IRB, are arrested in Manchester; during a successful rescue attempt a policeman is killed. Subsequently 62 members of the IRB are transported to Australia. William Philip Allen, Michael Larkin, and Michael O'Brien are executed in Manchester for the murder of the police officer; they are eulogized in Irish Republican circles as the Manchester Martyrs.
1870	The Home Government Association is established by Isaac Butt to advocate for the repeal of the Acts of Union.
1879	Famine strikes again. *An Gorta Beag* (the mini-famine) caused hunger and severe distress but not many deaths thanks to aid sent from Irish-Americans and the swift response of the British government.
	Irish National Land League is founded in County Mayo by Michael Davitt, the son of an evicted tenant farmer. Charles Stewart Parnell is elected president. Andrew Kettle, Michael Davitt, and Thomas Brennan are honorary secretaries. The League will advocate for the Three Fs.

QUESTIONS TO CONSIDER

1. Prior to 1845, what did people feel were the positives and negatives of potato cultivation?

2. Prior to 1845, the potato provided cheap, easy food for millions of Irish citizens, so why did some commentators condemn the reliance on it?

3. What forces were at play in Ireland prior to 1845 that contributed to the famine? Would a crisis of some sort have occurred even without the appearance of the blight?

4. John Mitchel (Document 45) famously stated, "The Almighty, indeed, sent the potato blight, but the English created the famine." What evidence from the documents supports this statement? What evidence from the documents does not support it?

5. Many in both England and Ireland blamed landlords, in particular absentee landlords, for the conditions in Ireland before and during the famine. What role did absentee landlords play in creating the conditions in Ireland that contributed to the famine?

6. How did news sources in the United States and England perceive the famine? In what ways do their interpretations differ from Irish news sources? In what ways are they similar?

7. In what ways did pre-existing attitudes towards Ireland and the Irish shape British state policy towards the famine? In what ways were those policies shaped by the political philosophies of the time?

8. What were the biggest challenges towards providing effective relief for famine victims?

9. Based on the documents, what impulses motivated the international philanthropic response towards the famine? What is significant about that response?

10. What sense do these documents give of how nineteenth-century people defined the role of the "state"? What responsibilities do they feel a state has towards its citizens?

11. How did British visitors to Ireland before and after the famine view the country?

12. How did Sir Robert Peel's and Lord John Russell's attitudes and approaches towards famine relief differ? What were the positives and negatives of each approach?

13. In *The Irish Crisis* (Document 25), how does Charles Trevelyan justify his response to the famine?

14. Compare and contrast the politics expressed in the *Dublin University Magazine* (Document 32) with those expressed in the *Nation* (Documents 12, 17, 38). Does their interpretation of the famine differ?

15. Many in Ireland condemned the removal of Sir Robert Peel from office in 1846. Why did they prefer his government's response to the famine? What were the flaws in that response?

16. During the famine, did being part of the United Kingdom benefit or hurt Ireland? What views on this do the documents express?

17. Why was there such resistance to the concept of providing outdoor relief in Ireland during the famine?

18. After 1846, British policymakers preferred to rely on local taxes to fund famine relief. Why? What were the consequences of this policy? Why was it problematic?

19. In an area like Grosse-Île in Canada, was there anything that could have been done to reduce the mortality of famine migrants?

20. Why were the death tolls on Irish "coffin ships" so high?

21. Based on the documents, what caused the high rates of emigration during the famine?

22. Did social norms and the bonds of society hold during the famine or did they bend or break?

PART 1

Conditions in Ireland before the Famine

DOCUMENT I:

Extracts from Jonathan Swift, *A Modest Proposal* (Dublin, 1729)

Jonathan Swift's (1667–1745) most famous satirical essay, *A Modest Proposal for preventing the Children of poor people from being a burden to their parents or country, and for making them beneficial to the Public*, argues that the poor in Ireland could improve their lot by selling their children to the rich. Mercantilist economic policy of the eighteenth century viewed population as central to a nation's wealth, and many English commentators wanted to grow Ireland's population. Swift intended to mock the heartlessness of such schemes, which in his view built the wealth of a nation on the poverty of its citizens.[1]

ᛞ

I t is a melancholy object to those, who walk through this great Town, or travel in the Country, when they see the Streets, the Roads, and Cabin-Doors, crowded with Beggars of the female Sex, followed by three, four, or six Children, all in Rags, and importuning every Passenger for an Alms. These Mothers instead of being able to work for their honest livelihood, are forced to employ all their time in strolling, to beg sustenance for their helpless infants, who, as they grow up either turn Thieves for want of work, or leave their dear native Country to fight for the **Pretender in Spain**, or sell themselves to the **Barbadoes**.

I think it is agreed by all parties, that this prodigious number of children, in the arms, or on the backs, or at the heels of their mothers, and frequently of their fathers, is in the present deplorable state of the Kingdom, a very great additional grievance; and therefore whoever could find out a fair, cheap and easy method of making these Children sound and useful Members of the

Pretender in Spain: Refers to the Catholic descendants of the deposed King James II. In 1729 this refers to James II's son James Francis Edward Stuart then living in exile following the failed rebellion of 1715.

Barbadoes: A thriving Caribbean sugar colony at this time, where many Irish were sent as indentured laborers.

---

1   Louis Landa, "'A Modest Proposal' and Populousness," *Modern Philology*, 40, no. 2 (1942): 161–70.

common-wealth would deserve so well of the public, as to have his Statue set up for a preserver of the Nation.

But my intention is very far from being confined to provide only for the Children of professed beggars, it is of a much greater extent, and shall take in the whole number of Infants at a certain age, who are born of parents in effect as little able to support them, as those who demand our charity in the streets....

The number of Souls in this Kingdom being usually reckoned one Million and a half, Of these I calculate there may be about two hundred thousand Couple whose Wives are breeders, from which number I Substract thirty Thousand Couples, who are able to maintain their own Children, although I apprehend there cannot be so many, under the present distresses of the Kingdom, but this being granted, there will remain an hundred and seventy thousand Breeders. I again Subtract fifty Thousand for those Women who miscarry, or whose Children dye by accident, or disease within the Year. There only remain an hundred and twenty thousand Children of poor Parents annually born: The question therefore is, How this number shall be reared, and provided for, which, as I have already said, under the present Situation of Affairs, is utterly impossible by all the methods hitherto proposed, for we can neither employ them in Handicraft, or Agriculture; we neither build Houses, (I mean in the Country) nor cultivate Land: they can very seldom pick up a Livelyhood by Stealing until they arrive at six years Old, except where they are of towardly parts, although, I confess they learn the Rudiments much earlier; during which time they can however be properly looked upon only as Probationers, as I have been informed by a principal Gentleman in the County of Cavan, who protested to me, that he never knew above one or two Instances under the Age of six, even in a part of the Kingdom so renowned for the quickest proficiency in that Art.

I am assured by our merchants, that a boy or girl, before twelve years old, is no saleable commodity, and even when they come to this age, they will not yield above three pounds, or three pounds and half a crown at most on the Exchange, which cannot turn to account either to the parents or the Kingdom, the charge of nutriments and rags having been at least four times that value.

I shall now therefore humbly propose my own thoughts, which I hope will not be liable to the least objection.

I have been assured by a very knowing American of my acquaintance in London, that a young healthy child well nursed is at a year old, a most delicious, nourishing, and wholesome food, whether stewed, roasted, baked, or boiled, and I make no doubt that it will equally serve in a fricasie, or ragout.

I do therefore humbly offer it to public consideration, that of the hundred and twenty thousand Children, already computed, twenty thousand may be reserved for breed, whereof only one fourth part to be males, which is more than we allow to sheep, black cattle, or swine, and my reason is, that these children are seldom the fruits of marriage, a circumstance not much regarded by our savages, therefore, one male will be sufficient to serve four females. That the remaining hundred thousand may at a year old be offered in sale to the persons of quality, and fortune, through the Kingdom, always advising the mother to let them suck plentifully in the last month, so as to render them plump, and fat for a good table. A child will make two dishes at an entertainment for friends, and when the family dines alone, the fore or hind quarter will make a reasonable dish, and seasoned with a little pepper or salt will be very good boiled on the fourth day, especially in winter.

I have reckoned upon a medium, that a child just born will weigh 12 pounds, and in a solar year if tolerably nursed encreaseth to 28 pounds.

I grant this food will be somewhat dear, and therefore very proper for Landlords, who, as they have already devoured most of the parents, seem to have the best title to the children....

After all I am not so violently bent upon my own opinion, as to reject any offer, proposed by wise men, which shall be found equally innocent, cheap, easy and effectual. But before something of that kind shall be advanced in contradiction to my scheme, and offering a better, I desire the author, or authors will be pleased maturely to consider two points. First, as things now stand, how they will be able to find food and **raiment** for a hundred thousand useless mouths and backs. And secondly, there being a round million of creatures in humane figure, throughout this Kingdom, whose whole subsistence put into a common stock, would leave them in debt two millions of Pounds Sterling adding those, who are beggars by profession, to the bulk of farmers, cottagers and labourers with their wives and children, who are beggars in effect; I desire those politicians, who dislike my overture, and may perhaps be so bold to attempt an answer, that they will first ask the parents of these mortals, whether they would not at this day think it a great happiness to have been sold for food at a year old, in the manner I prescribe, and thereby have avoided such a perpetual scene of misfortunes, as they have since gone through, by the oppression of landlords, the impossibility of paying rent without money or trade, the want of common sustenance, with neither house nor clothes to cover them from inclemencies of weather, and the most inevitable prospect of intailing the like, or greater miseries upon their breed forever.

I Profess in the sincerity of my heart that I have not the least personal interest in endeavouring to promote this necessary work having no other motive than the public good of my country, by advancing our trade, providing for infants, relieving the poor, and giving some pleasure to the rich. I have **no children**, by which I can propose to get a single penny; the youngest being nine years old, and my wife past child-bearing.

raiment: Clothing.

no children: Swift himself never married and had no children.

Extracts from Thomas Prior, *A List of the Absentees of Ireland* (Dublin, 1729): 19–20, 20–21, 22–23, 32–33

> Thomas Prior (1680–1750) is best known as the founder of the Royal Dublin Society, a philanthropic society established in 1731 to help Ireland develop economically. Like Jonathan Swift, Prior was an Anglo-Irish patriot concerned with British policy towards Ireland. He first published his *A List of the Absentees of Ireland, and the yearly value of their estates and incomes spent abroad* anonymously to criticize Anglo-Irish landowners who in his view contributed nothing to the country which was the source of their wealth.

Thus we continued for some time in a tolerable condition; but of late, that treasure, which was the fruit and acquisition of many years, hath gradually flowed from us; which makes us daily more sensible of the scarcity of money, which could formerly be easily had at 6 per cent interest, but now cannot, without some difficulty, be had at 7. This want of money in the kingdom, throws a damp upon all business; manufacturers can't be set to work, materials purchased, or credit subsist; and people, who are willing to support themselves by their industry, are left to struggle with poverty, for want of employment.

We are not now at a loss to point out the principal source of all our misfortunes, and the chief cause of all this distress; it appears plainly, from the list of absentees, and the estimate of the quantity of species, they may be reasonably supposed to draw yearly out of the kingdom, that no other country labours under so wasteful a drain of its treasure, as Ireland does at present, by an annual remittance of above 600000 **l.** to our Gentlemen abroad, without the least consideration or value returned for the same: this is so great a burden upon us, that, I believe, there is not in history, an instance of any one country, paying so large a yearly tribute to another....

It is believed by many, who understand our money affairs, that there is less **species** now in the kingdom, than was at any one time since the **Revolution**, if not since the **Restoration:** The most sanguine do not reckon, that we have 400000 l. now remaining; if so, 'tis impossible to subsist much longer under such a drain; for if the quantity of money exported vastly over balances any income or gain we have by trade (as plainly appears by examining the said list, the balance of our trade herein set forth, and a constant course of exchange against us) it evidently follows, that all our remaining species, will, in a little time, be carry'd off: the consequence therefor will be, that we shall

l: Pounds sterling, also symbolized using £.

species: Coined money.

Revolution: The Glorious Revolution of 1688, when William III and Mary II displaced the Catholic King James II as King of England, Scotland, and Ireland.

Restoration: The Restoration of Charles II to the monarchy in 1660 following the Civil War and the Protectorate of Oliver Cromwell.

be utterly disabled from carrying on our foreign and domestic commerce, paying rents, or discharging the public establishment....

'Tis melancholy to observe, that, now we are labouring under great disadvantages in trade, and struggling with penury and want: the humour of living, and spending abroad still increases among our men of quality and station, and has even infected our ladies, who may sooner be found out at London, Paris, Rome, or any foreign place of expense, than at home.

If those gentlemen, who draw of out of the kingdom yearly 600000 l. could be prevailed upon, to spend the same at home, the advantages and good effects thereof, would be soon visible in the improvement of lands and houses; in the increase of people, arts, and manufactures, in a greater produce in the excise and customs, and in a better support of the government: whereas now by the means of our nobility and gentry deserting their own country, and spending all abroad, our people are left without employment, and are forced to shift to foreign countries, even to America, to get a livelihood; and the public funds fall very short of the necessary establishment, and must grow worse every day; so that, in time of peace, we shall be driven to the necessity, either of lessening the establishment, or increasing our taxes, without any ability to pay them.

'Tis too much in reason for these Gentlemen to expect, that we shall patiently bear with the loss of our trade, loss of our money, and additional taxes; for no other reason, but to gratify the vanity of those, who have thus wantonly abandoned their country, and riot abroad in its ruin: there is no way left to save us, but by obliging them to live at home, or making them pay for living abroad....

It cannot be supposed, that our Irish Landlords, who live abroad, and consume no part of the produce or manufacture of their country, pay the least share of the duties or taxes thereof; or relieve any of its poor, whose miseries they never see; or make any improvements, who never mean to live among us. Nay, their living abroad seems to have so far alienated their affections from their country, and hardened their tempers towards it, that they, above all others, are remarkable for setting their estates as at **Rack Rent**, so as hardly to allow a livelihood to their poor tenants, by whom they are supported.

Rack Rent: A highly excessive rent.

There is no country in Europe, which produces, and exports so great a quantity of beef, butter, tallow, hides, and wool, as Ireland does; and yet our common people are very poorly cloath'd, go barelegged half the year, and very rarely taste of that flesh meat, with which we so much abound; we pinch ourselves in every article of life, and export more, that we can well spare, with no other effect or advantage, than to enable our Gentlemen and Ladies to live more luxuriously abroad.

And they are not content to treat us thus, but add insult to ill usage; they reproach us with our poverty, at the same time, that they take away our money; and can tell us, we have no diversions or entertainments in Ireland for them, when they themselves disable us from having better, by withdrawing from us.

But 'tis to be hoped, that our **Legislature** will take care, that those Gentlemen, who spend their fortunes abroad, and are thereby the greatest, and almost only cause of its poverty and distress, shall not be the only persons favoured, and exempted from paying the taxes thereof.

A tax of four shillings in the pound on the estates of absentees, would in all likelihood, remove the evils complain'd of, by stopping in a great measure those wasteful drains of our money; and would in all respects, answer the occasions of the government; for if these Gentlemen, will notwithstanding, still live abroad, then a considerable fund will arise out of their estates to defray the public charges; and if they should return home, then the public revenue will increase by a greater produce in the excise and customs, in proportion as the home consumption would be enlarged by the spending of so much more money among us; either way the public occasions would be supply'd; and the people relieved.

Legislature: In the eighteenth century Ireland had an independent Parliament; this was dissolved following the Acts of Union in 1801.

DOCUMENT 3:

Extracts from *The Groans of Ireland: In a Letter to a Member of Parliament* (Dublin, 1741), 3–5

This anonymous pamphlet was written as a commentary on the famine of 1740–41, until that point the worst subsistence crisis in Irish history. This famine was caused by severe weather conditions which destroyed both the potato and the grain harvest. It is thought to have killed 38 percent of the Irish population, which was a higher percentage than the potato famine a century later.[2] The author of the pamphlet attributes the severity of this famine and the regular appearance of famine in Ireland to agricultural policy.

e

I have been absent from this Country for some years, and on my return to it last summer found it the most miserable scene of universal distress, that I have ever read of in history: want and misery in every face; the rich unable almost, as they were willing, to relieve the poor; the roads spread with dead and dying bodies; mankind the colour of the **docks** and nettles which they fed on; two or three, sometimes more, on a car going to the grace for want of bearers to carry them, and many buried only in the fields and ditches where they perished.

> **docks:** A type of herb with edible, green leaves.

This universal scarcity was ensued by **fluxes** and **malignant fevers**; which swept off multitudes of all sorts: whole villages were laid waste by want and sickness, and death in various shapes; and scarce a house in the whole island escaped from tears and mourning....

> **fluxes:** Dysentery, a common ailment during times of famine.
>
> **malignant fevers:** Probably typhoid fever, another common famine ailment.

Sir, when a stranger travels through this country, and beholds its wide extended and fertile plains, its great flocks of sheep and black cattle, and all its natural wealth, and conveniences for tillage, manufactures and trade, he must be astonished, that such misery and want could possibly be felt by its inhabitant; but you, who know the **Constitution**, and are acquainted with its weaknesses, can easily see the reason....

> **Constitution:** Ireland in the eighteenth century had no formal written constitution, but many in Ireland complained about the prevailing idea that Ireland was bound by acts of the English Parliament.

That this country, one of the most fertile in the world, is subject to such frequent wants and famines as it feels; this is the third I have seen in the compass of twenty years: 'tis indeed the severest, and attended with the most dismal consequences: but about twelve or thirteen years ago, there was one very near as bad; and from whence can this proceed, Sir?—From the want of proper tillage laws to guide, and to protect the husbandman

---

2   David Dickson, *Arctic Ireland: The Extraordinary Story of the Great Frost and Forgotten Famine of 1740–41* (Belfast: White Row Press), 1997.

in the pursuit of his business; one scarce year sets all hands to the low, this begets a great plenty; there are neither granaries to receive, nor bounties to encourage the exportation of this plenty; the husbandman cannot get for his grain, what the labour cost him, he sinks under its weight, deserts the plow, stock with sheep, and in a few years there is another scarcity, another famine: this is the known course of tillage in this country; and it must ever be so, whilst laws are wanting.

DOCUMENT 4:

Extract from Adam Smith, *An Inquiry into the Nature and Causes of the Wealth of Nations*, vol. 1 (London, 1776), 249–51

Scottish economist Adam Smith was already well-known when he published his most famous work, *The Wealth of Nations*, in 1776. In it he lays the foundation for classical free market economic theory, which was the prevalent economic theory among British political leaders during the Irish Famine. In this section he reflects on the utility of potatoes for supporting populations, particularly the Irish population.

ев

The food produced by a field of potatoes is not inferior in quantity to that produced by a field of rice, and much superior to what is produced by a field of wheat. Twelve thousand weight of potatoes from an acre of land is not a greater produce than two thousand weight of wheat. The food or solid nourishment, indeed, which can be drawn from each of those two plants, is not altogether in proportion to their weight, on account of the watery nature of potatoes. Allowing, however, half the weight of this root to go to water, a very large allowance, such an acre of potatoes will still produce six thousand weight of solid nourishment, three times the quantity produced by the acre of wheat. An acre of potatoes is cultivated with less expense that an acre of wheat; the fallow, which generally precedes the sowing of wheat, more than compensating the hoeing and other extraordinary culture which is always given to potatoes. Should this root ever become in any part of Europe, like rice in some countries, the common and favourite vegetable food of the people, so as to occupy the same proportion of the lands in tillage which wheat and other sorts of grain for human food do at present, the same quantity of cultivated land would maintain a much greater number of people, and the labourers being generally fed with potatoes, a greater surplus would remain after replacing all the stock and maintaining all the labour employed in cultivation. A greater share of this surplus too would belong to the landlord. Population would increase, and rents would rise much beyond what they are at present.

The land which is fit for potatoes, is fit for almost every useful vegetable. If they occupied the same proportion of cultivated land which corn does at present, they would regulate, in the same manner, the rent of the greater part of other cultivated land....

The chairmen, porters, and coal heavers in London, and those unfortunate women who live by prostitution, the strongest men and the most beautiful women perhaps in the British dominions, are said to be the greater part of them, from the lowest rank of people in Ireland, who are generally fed with this root. No food can afford a more decisive proof of its nourishing quality, or of its being peculiarly suitable to the health of the human condition.

DOCUMENT 5:

Extracts from Thomas Malthus, "Newenham and Others on the State of Ireland," *Edinburgh Review*, vol. 24 (1808) 337, 339–40, 341–44

Thomas Malthus (1766–1834) was an English clergymen and scholar already well known for his *Essays on the Principle of Population* published in 1798. Malthus's earlier work had not specifically addressed Ireland, although many regarded his ideas on the dangers of population increase as relevant to that nation. He was asked to write an article reflecting on the population of Ireland in the *Edinburgh Review*. In this article, published anonymously, he comments on the implications of Irish population growth as had been noted by writers such as Thomas Newenham.

e

Among the subjects peculiar to the state of Ireland, which have hitherto been comparatively but little noticed, is the extraordinary phenomenon of the very rapid increase of its population. While many of the countries of Europe have been slumbering on with a population nearly stationary, or, at most, increasing very slowly; while even the most prosperous (except the newly civilized country of Russia) have not approached towards doubling their numbers during the course of the last century, Ireland, in the same period, has more than quadrupled them....

The introduction of the potato into Ireland, and its becoming the general food of the common people, seems to have fermented this particular case; and to be the single cause which has produced the effects that excite our astonishment. At what period potatoes became the staple support of the Irish poor, it is difficult precisely to ascertain; but, whenever this event took place, it would necessarily occasion a most prodigious facility in the payment and production of labour. The way in which the means of subsistence practically regulates the increase of population in civilized societies, is, by limiting and determining the real wages of the labourer, of the number of persons which the labour of one man will support upon the staple food of the country. In England, at present, reckoning labour at ten shillings a week, the quarter loaf at a shilling, and allowing a half peck loaf a week to each individual, the earnings of a single man will support, on bread alone, five persons. With his weekly wages he will be able to purchase 43 pounds 7 ounces of bread, his usual nourishment.

In Ireland, at the time that **Mr. Young** made his tour, the average price of labour was 6 ½ **d.**, and the prime cost of potatoes to the cultivator 1 ½ d. the stone of 14 pounds. At these rates, the labourer would be able to

Mr. Young: Arthur Young was an English agricultural writer who toured Ireland in 1776–77 and wrote about his experiences in a well-known travelogue, *Arthur Young's Tour in Ireland* (1780).

d: Pence, the smallest unit of British/Irish currency at the time. There were 12 pence in a shilling, and 20 shillings in a pound.

procure, with his weekly earnings, 364 pounds of potatoes, and, allowing four pounds of potatoes to one of bread, 91 pounds of solid nourishment, —above double the quantity earned by the higher wages of the English labourer, and adequate to the weekly support of above double the number of persons....

The **indolence** of the Irish peasantry, which has been so frequently the subject of remark, has naturally been occasioned by this redundancy of labour, combined with the habit of working for the farmers, on whose lands they are settled at a fixed and under-price [rent]. But, paradoxical as it may at first appear, it is probably that this indolence, and the number of holidays that it prompts them to keep, has rather rendered to improve than to lower their condition, and has been one, among other causes, which has prevented the price of labour from falling, in proportion to the cheapness of the food on which it is supported.

But though it is certainly true that the Irish peasant has hitherto been able to command a greater quantity of the food to which he is accustomed, than the English labourer can of bread, yet it by no means follows that his general condition should be proportionally better. Something else besides food is required to make life comfortable; and the surplus potatoes of the Irishman, when converted into money, will have but a small power in purchasing other articles. Owing to the deficiency of manufacturing capital in Ireland, and the indolent habits of workmen in general, the conveniences of clothing, furniture, etc. are as dear as in England; while the pecuniary wages of the Irish labourer are not equal to half the earnings of the Englishman. Hence arises the unsparing meal of potatoes noticed by Mr. Young, at which the beggar, the pig, the dog, the cat, and the poultry, seem all equally welcome; while the cabin that affords shelter to all these various inhabitants, is hardly superior to an English pigsty;—its furniture confined almost exclusively to the pot in which the potatoes are boiled; and the clothing of its human inmates as deficient in quantity as it is wretched in quality....

This kind of support, though it might be sufficient to give play to the strong principle of increase among a people long oppressed and degraded, could never present very flattering prospects of happiness; and when joined to the occasional difficulty of getting sufficient employment to enable them to pay the rent of their potato grounds, would naturally prompt them to emigration. Ireland has in consequence, long been considered as the great *officina militum*, not only for England, but for other countries....

The consequences of such a rapid rate of increase deserve our most serious attention. Either the increase will continue at its present rate, or it will not. If the rate continue, Ireland will contain **twenty millions of people** in the course of the present century; and we need not insist upon the result. With such a physical force, it is quite impossible that it should

indolence: The supposed laziness of the Irish was a common stereotype of the period.

officina militum: Latin for "workshop of soldiers," a reference to the thousands of Irish soldiers who joined the British army, and in some cases the French army.

twenty millions of people: Thomas Newenham estimated that Ireland had 5,400,000 people in 1804.

remain united to Great Britain, without sharing, in every respect, the full benefits of its constitution.

If the rate do not continue to the end of the century, which is certainly the more probable supposition, it will be interesting to ask ourselves, what will be the principal causes of its retardation, and in what manner they will practically operate? The cause first generally felt, will be the dearness of land; and the advance of rent will continue, till the usual quantity of land considered as necessary to support a large family, cannot be obtained for the amount of the average earnings of a year's labour. Smaller portions will then be taken; but even these, in time becoming scarce, and difficult to be procured, the cotter system will be gradually destroyed, and give place to a set of labourers earning their pecuniary wages like the peasantry of England, but still living upon potatoes as their principal food. These potatoes will then be raised by the farmers, and will become a principal object of cultivation for the market, as the great staple food of the country.

The other, and ultimate cause of retardation, will be such a rise in the price of potatoes, compared with the price of labour, as will give the labourer no greater command over subsistence in the shape of potatoes, than he has at present over corn, in some of the stationary, or slowly-increasing countries of Europe. When the Irish peasant can only earn the maintenance of five, instead of ten persons, the habit of early marriages will necessarily be checked; the rearing of families will be impeded; and the cabins will cease to swarm, as they do at present, with overflowing broods of healthy children.

But before this last cause has produced an approach to a stationary population, Ireland will contain, in proportion to its size, a prodigious mass of people. It is the first and only country that has yet fully taken to a species of food, which, at the most, requires only one third of the land necessary to yield the same nourishment in wheat. Its effects, hitherto, have been truly astonishing; and, in its future progress, it may be expected to produce proportionate results.

Extract from J. Bellingham, *Hints to Farmers on the Culture of Potatoes* (Newry, 1813), 12–14

This brief pamphlet directed farmers in the United Kingdom on the best methods to cultivate potatoes and expounded upon the utility of the crop.

From the numerous kinds, and their affinity, each sort bearing twenty different names, and every district having its favourite, it would be idle in my to attempt classing them, or point out the kind, or season, in which it is most proper for each to be planted. The potato that requires most time to come to perfection, ought certainly to be first planted, and may be depended upon to keep the longest and produce the best dish, when the early, I may say, all the white kinds, are unfit for use. The apple potato, well known in Ireland, will keep good until late in the month of July, and requires six months to bring it to perfection; it may be had at every sea-port town in the island.

It would be idle in me to expatiate on the vast benefit that would result to society, by cultivating this most valuable of all roots in the spirited manner it deserves: no crop will produce to man and beast so much good, wholesome food, from the square of the surface it occupies, or leave the ground in finer order. In 1812, a fair crop would have sold for more than would pay the fee-simple of the land.

DOCUMENT 7:

Extracts from William Cobbett, *Cobbett's Weekly Political Register*, vol. 86, no. 4 (25 October 1834) 194, 195–98

William Cobbett (1763–1835) was an English farmer and member of Parliament, who ran a weekly newspaper the *Political Register*. Cobbett saw himself as a champion of traditional rural life, and he favored parliamentary reform and opposed the corn laws. In 1834 he traveled to Ireland on the invitation of Daniel O'Connell. The letter below details some of his experiences; it is made out to Charles Marshall, a laborer on Cobbett's English farm, who could neither read nor write, but to whom Cobbett addressed ten letters on Ireland that were subsequently printed in his newspaper.

e

To Charles Marshall, Labourer, **Normandy Tithing, Parish of Ash**, Farnham, Surrey

Cork, 17. Oct. 1834

Marshall,

Since the date of my last letter I have been in the City of Kilkenny, and have, in a long speech, urged the justice and necessity of poor-laws, such as we have always had in England. In another letter, when I get more time, I will tell you how our poor-laws came to be, and I will prove to you, that, in case of need, you have as clear a right to relief out of my farm, as I have to my cows or my corn, or as **Mr. Woodruffe** has to the land or the timber. Our rights are very clear; but not more clear than yours are. At present I must speak to you of some little part of what I have recently seen and heard. When I get back to Normandy, I shall make a book, relating to everything about this country.

From Kilkenny I came to Clonmell, the capital of the county of Tipperary, which is deemed one of the finest in Ireland. The land, in this distance of about 35 English miles, is very fine, except in a few places. But, only four turnip fields all the way. The harvest was here all got in. But, the grass! The fine grass fields covered with herds of fine cattle; fine oxen; fine cows; fine sheep; all seemed fat; and to every miserable thing called a house, a fine hog, so white, clean, and fat, so unlike the poor souls who had reared it up

Normandy Tithing, Parish of Ash: This is the name of Cobbett's farm and the parish in which it resided. Parishes were the basic unit of local government in both England and Ireland.

Mr. Woodruffe: Colonel Woodruffe was the landowner from whom Cobbett rented his own farm.

offal: The internal organs of an animal used for food.

eight score to twenty score: As a unit of measurement a score is a weight of approximately 20 pounds. A hog weighing eight score weighs about 160 pounds.

firkins: A cask for storing liquids or butter, approximately a quarter of a barrel.

Scotch vagabonds: Cobbett could be quite prejudiced against Scotland and many Scottish people. He tended to blame Scottish political economists and merchants specifically for the condition of the country.

haulm: The stem or stalk of a plant.

and fatted it, and who were destined never to taste one morsel of it; no, not so much as the **offal**.

At the town of Clonmell, I went to see one of the places where they kill and salt hogs to send to England. In this one town, they kill every year, for this purpose, about sixty thousand hogs, weighing from **eight score to twenty score**. Every ounce of this meat is sent out of Ireland, while the poor half-naked creatures, who raise it with such care, are compelled to live on the lumpers, which are such bad potatoes, that the hogs will not thrive on them, and will not touch them, if they can get other potatoes. The rooks, which eat the good potatoes, will not eat these though they be starving. And, yet, this is the stuff that the working people are fed on. There are about eighty thousand **firkins** of butter, and, perhaps, a hundred thousand quarters of wheat, and more of oats, sent away out of this one town; while those who raise it all by their labour, live upon lumpers! [...]

But, now, Marshall, I am coming nearer home; and I beg you all to pay great attention to what I am going to say. You will think it strange, that all this food should be sent out of the country, and that the people should get nothing back for it. You will think, that we must send them clothes and household goods and tea and sugar, and soap in return for the hogs and other things. To the rich we do; and to the barracks; but, the millions of working people have only rags for parts of their bodies, and they have neither goods nor tea nor sugar nor plate nor knife nor fork nor tea-kettle nor cup nor saucer.

The case is this: the owners of all the great estates live in England or in France or in Italy. The rents are sent to them; and, as there are no poor-rates, they get all the produce of the land from the miserable farmer, except just enough to keep him alive. They spend those rents out of Ireland; so that the working people here, who might eat meat three times a day are compelled to live upon lumpers! And, you be assured, that this would be the lot of the English working people, if the **Scotch vagabonds** could succeed in their projects for sweeping away our poor laws....

I went to a sort of Hamlet near to the town of Middleton. It contained about 40 or 50 hovels. I went into several of them, and took down the names of the occupiers. They all consisted of mud-walls, with a covering of rafters and straw. None of them so good as the place where you keep your little horse. I took a particular account of the first that I went into. It was 21 feet long and 9 feet wide. The floor, the bare ground. No fire-place, no chimney, the fire (made of potato-**haulm**) made on one side against the wall, and the smoke going out of a hole in the roof. No table, no chair; I sat to write upon a block of wood. Some stones for seats. No goods but a pot, and a shallow tub, for the pig and the family both to eat out of. There was one window, 9 inches by 5, and the glass broken half out. There was a mud-wall about

4 feet high to separate off the end of the shed for the family to sleep, lest the hog should kill and eat the little children when the father and mother were both out, and when the hog was shut in; and it happened some time ago that a poor mother, being ill on her straw, unable to move, and having her baby dead beside her, had its head eaten off by a hog before her own eyes! No bed: no mattress; some large flat stones, to keep the bodies from the damp ground; some dirty straw and bundle of rags were all the bedding. The man's name was Owen Gumbleton. Five small children; the mother, about thirty, naturally handsome, but worn into half-ugliness by hunger and filth; she had no shoes or stockings, no shift, a mere rag over her body and down to her knees. The man BUILT THIS PLACE HIMSELF, and yet he has to pay a pound a year for it with perhaps a **rod** of ground! Others, 25 s. a year. All built their own hovels, and yet have to pay this rent. All the hogs were in the hovels to-day, it being coldish and squally; and then, you know, hogs like cover. Gumbleton's hog was lying in the room; and in another hovel there was a fine large hog that had taken his bed close by the fire. There is a nasty dunghill (no privy) to each hovel. The dung that the hog makes in the hovel is carefully put into a heap by itself, as being the most precious. This dung and the pig are the main things to raise the rent and to get fuel with. The poor creatures sometimes keep the dung in the hovel, when their hard-hearted tyrants will not suffer them to let it be at the door! So there they are, in a far worse state, Marshall, than any hog that you ever had in your life.

rod: A unit of land area measuring about 30.25 square yards.

Lord Middleton may say, that HE is not the landlord of these wretched people. Ah! But this tenant, his middleman, is their landlord, and Lord Middleton gets the more rent from him by enabling him to let these holes in this manner. If I were to give Mr. Dean a shilling a week to squeeze you down to twelve shillings a week, who would you think was most to blame, me or Mr. Dean?

Now, Marshall, pray remember, that this horrible state of things never could take place if the Irish people had those poor-laws, which the Scotch vagabonds would advise the Parliament to take from us. For then THE LAW would compel those who have the estates to pay sufficiently those without whose labour the land is worth nothing at all.

And even without poor-rates, the people never could have been brought to this pass without the ever-damned potatoes! People CAN keep life in them by the means of this nasty, filthy, hog-feed; and the tyrants make them do it, and have thus reduced them to the state of hogs.

I repeat to you, therefore, that if any person bring a potato into my house, for any purpose whatever, Mr. Dean is hereby authorized and directed to discharge that person. And, Marshall, while I will give you, or any man, and all the men, in the tithing, the finest cabbage, carrot, parsnip, beet, and any other seed, and my corn to plant, I will never again give constant employment to any man in whose garden I shall see potatoes planted. I have no right to dictate to you what you shall plant, but I have a right to employ my money as I please, and it both my pleasure and my duty to discourage in every way that I can the cultivation of this damned root, being convinced that it has done more harm to mankind than the sword and the pestilence united.

DOCUMENT 8:

Extracts from Mr and Mrs Samuel Carter Hall, *Ireland: Its Scenery, Character, etc.*, 2 vols. (London: 1841–43), 1:82–83, 123–24

Samuel Carter Hall (1800–89) was an Irish born journalist of the Victorian era. Along with his Irish wife Anna Maria Fielding (1800–81), who wrote as Mrs. S.C. Hall, they were well-known for their portrayals of Ireland and Irish life. This account was based on years of touring Ireland in the early nineteenth-century.

ح

It is unnecessary to state, that for above a century and a half, the potato has been almost the only food of the peasantry of Ireland. They raise corn, indeed—wheat, barley, and oats, in abundance—but it is for export; and although the assertion may startle many, we have no hesitation in saying there are hundreds in the less civilized districts of the country who have never tasted bread. Whether the Irish have to bless or ban the name of **Sir Walter Raleigh** is a matter still in dispute—some siding with **Cobbett** in execrating "the lazy root," "the accursed root" as, if not the originator, the sustainer of Irish poverty and wretchedness; others contending that the introduction of the potato is an ample set-off against the wars and confiscations of Elizabeth, her counsellors, and her armies. It is universally admitted that a finer or hardier race of peasantry cannot be found in the world; and although it is considered that their strength fails them at a comparatively early age, it is impossible to deny the nutritive qualities of a food upon which so many millions have thriven and increased. But there can be as little doubt that the ease with which the means of existence are procured has been the cause of evil. A very limited portion of land, a few days of labour, and a small amount of manure, will create a stock upon which a family may exist for twelve months....

In considering this melancholy and embarrassing subject, it should never be lost sight of, that although in England a tenant who cannot or will not pay his rent, and is therefore removed from his holding, may either become a day-labourer or obtain land elsewhere, in Ireland the case is different. The peasant has his "bit of land," out of which to procure the means by which he and his family are to exist; during a large portion of the year he can obtain no employment, and the potatoes he digs keeps them alive until work comes round. If deprived of it, he cannot, or rather dare not, seek for ground elsewhere: for if he eject another holder, his doom is sealed. "Land is to the Irish peasant (we quote from the evidence of Mr. Blackburne, the

Sir Walter Raleigh: Raleigh (1552–1618), an English explorer sometimes popularly credited with introducing the potato to Ireland, although there is no evidence to support this.

Cobbett: William Cobbett (1763–1835), an English pamphleteer who condemned potato cultivation and wrote of his desire to contain it.

present Attorney-General for Ireland) a necessary of life, the alternative being starvation." He reasons, that, "You do take his life, if you do take the means by which he lives[.]" ...

We do not hesitate to affirm—and our conviction is formed after visiting nearly every county of Ireland—that the landlords who must be characterized as bad landlords are now very limited in number. Public opinion and improved habits have equally wrought to produce an altered state of things; and the "middle-men"—the evil productions of a long-continued evil system—have nearly, if not altogether, vanished from the country....

A middle-man was usually, in his origin, "one of the people" who having made money, took a farm, or an estate—rented a hundred, or, as was often the case, a thousand acres; the landlord in chief, generally an absentee, looked to him alone for the payment of his half-yearly rent, and knew nothing whatever of the condition of the cottiers who dwelt upon his estate; if we add that he cared nothing, as well as knew nothing, we shall not be far from the truth: for, while pursuing a course of pleasure in the metropolis—in Dublin sometimes, but in London more frequently—he was far away from the sight of their sufferings—"And wherefore should the clamorous voice of woe intrude upon his ear?" The peasantry, badly housed, badly clothed, badly fed, were in no way necessary either to his luxuries or his necessities; the middle-man was always a punctual paymaster, and he was the only person upon his estate with whom the landlord was brought into contact, or called upon to correspond. This middle-man had to transmit to his employer, perhaps three or four thousand pounds, often more, every year. And how was he to procure it? First, his system was to parcel out the estate into small bits seldom more than two or three acres to each, but generally averaging an acre. These "bits" were invariably let annually, and never on lease; the occupier, therefore, had no temptation to cultivate the land. His slip of ground seldom bore any other produce than potatoes; these were designed solely for the consumption of his own household and the support of a pig, which, if it lived, and no unusual misfortune attended the family, was "to pay the rent"; Of course, the land was let at the highest possible rate, and to the highest or most thoughtless bidder; the middle-man had to pay the landlord, and to grow rich himself; as the tenant was invariably in arrear, he was at all times in the power of the middle-man; and the putting on a new coat, the addition of a trifling article of furniture, or the appearance of anything like comfort in or around his dwelling, was a sure and certain notice that the bailiff would be "down upon him", ere the sun had set. This infamous system is, as we have said, almost at an end; out of it arose the wretchedness of the Irish peasantry, and, unhappily, it originated a war between landlord and tenant, the effects of which have not disappeared with the cause.

DOCUMENT 9:

Extracts from Commissioners for Inquiring into the State of the Poorer Classes in Ireland, *Poor Inquiry (Ireland)* (London, 1836)

Established in 1833, the Royal Commission on the Poorer Classes in Ireland conducted an extensive survey over three years intended to find out the cause of widespread destitution in Ireland at the time. The commissioners took evidence from a wide range of sources and, following the completion of their investigation, published a series of reports on their findings.

ев

Report on the City of Cork (Appendix C, Part I, 25–26)

The common wages of a labourer are 1s. per diem, which is much lower than formerly, but since the labouring population live almost entirely on potatoes, their way of estimating their wages is by the price of that article of food; by this rule their condition will appear to be much bettered, the same quantity being now purchased for 5d. which at the end of the war cost 1s.

Most families keep a pig, and collect manure; this latter is either sold or applied to a patch of land generally from one quarter to half an acre. The south-west of the town is entirely laid out in these gardens at a rental from £7 to £10 an acre; they appear highly cultivated. Mr. Henley represented the labourers in his employ as greatly benefited by having these gardens; he sometimes, however, found it necessary to allow them a day or two to work at them; still he considers that they are of more advantage than the wages would be which they lose in consequence....

The improved condition of the labouring class may be attributed to their being generally in constant employ, from the demand for labour occasioned by the improvements which have been made and are still in progress in the city and its vicinity....

When we come, however, to the portion which are enumerated as "destitute" the case is different. As an example we shall describe a house in Three Hatchet-lane, a populous part of the city.... The whole of these persons slept upon straw, very dirty and old, which was stowed in a corner during the day, or put into a box used as a seat; the only covering besides their day clothes were three rags of blankets amongst them all; pots to boil potatoes, and stools for seats, constituted the rest of their furniture. There was a little fire in two of the rooms only; it was a cold day in February. The men, excepting one who was sick, were out at work. Nearly the whole of the children were out, and stated to have gone begging: they go chiefly into the country and return with potatoes given by farmers. It may be observed, that of the women and children the greater number were healthy; some, however, on the contrary, appeared half-starved and sickly.

Answers to Queries for Parishes in Large Towns (Appendix C, Part I, 2, 5, 14)

12. On what kind of food do the labourers and working tradesmen of your Parish usually subsist?

Loughrea—Labourers on potatoes and salt, or sometimes buttermilk, or salt herring; tradesmen generally have butter and eggs and sometimes meat....

Galway-Parish of St. Nicholas—Labourers live on potatoes, and, when they can procure them, either milk or fish of the worst description....

Carlow—Potatoes twice or three times a day, with milk or a salt herring perhaps one-half of the year constitute the food of the labourer....

Report upon Vagrancy and Mendicity in the City of Dublin (Appendix C, Part II, 40)

Commentary from T. Abbott, Esq, of the Association for the Suppression of Mendicity

I think I can, in some degree, explain the causes of what would certainly, at first, seem to impeach the efficacy of our institution. From the accompanying table, which comprises the price of potatoes with the numbers on our books, it appears that an increase in the price of potatoes, almost uniformly produces an increase in our numbers, and a fall in their price, an immediate and opposite effect. I would therefore assign the variations in the cost of the chief food of the poor as the principal cause of the variations alluded to....

Year.	Daily Average of Poor in the Institution.	Average Price of Potatoes per Ton.		Year.	Daily Average of Poor in the Institution.	Average Price of Potatoes per Ton.	
		s.	d.			s.	d.
1818	2,624	.	.	1826	1,238	67	0
1819	1,584	64	7	1827	1,838	51	6
1820	1,050	46	1	1828	1,728	29	0
1821	836	34	10	1829	2,004	42	1
1822	691	40	7	1830	2,517	55	6
1823	784	37	6	1831	2,810	37	9
1824	1,184	60	8	1832	1,917	27	10
1825	1,335	62	5	1833	1,776	33	10

Actual Condition of the Poor (Appendix C, Part II, 101)

The Rev. Thomas R. Shore, curate of St. Michan's parish, and honorary secretary of the **Society for the Relief of Sick and Indigent Roomkeepers**, states… "that the condition of the poor has for the last seven years been decidedly growing worse. St. Michan's parish contains 25,000 inhabitants, one-eighth of the whole population of Dublin, and two-elevenths of the poor reside therein; 10,000 totally destitute in Michan's parish, who know not in the morning how they will obtain support in the day; 40,000 or 50,000 so destitute in Dublin; there are 15,000 persons in Michan's parish who would be considered objects of the society; not about 6,000 or 7,000 who are above receive relief. The poor may be divided into three classes, viz., persons quite destitute, near 25,000 or 26,000, in the city of Dublin; next those who have but occasional employment, 25,000 or 26,000; the third class, who are in occasional distress, these are principally poor tradesmen, who would not get an employment in a shop and are below the rank of a journeyman (they might be about 16,000 or 18,000 in Dublin, and such would be applicants to the Roomkeeper's Society); a fourth class, who might be reduced to distress by sickness. Of the classes above mentioned, I think the second and third are more rapidly increasing in number. Vast numbers of persons—women—have been reduced from the third class to the second. I think the moral condition of the poor sinks with their necessities; they acquire a degree of indifference from which it is impossible to arouse them. I think that the usual condition of the very lowest is deteriorated in the last seven years. I have heard of several instances of persons dying of starvation. A great many are worn out and die nominally of some other disease, 200 or 300 a year."

Society for the Relief of Sick and Indigent Roomkeepers: A charitable organization founded in 1790 to provide assistance to all the poor in Dublin regardless of their religion.

DOCUMENT 10:

Extracts from Thomas Campbell Foster, *Letters on the Condition of the People of Ireland* (London: 1846), x–xi, 43–44, 286–88

A lawyer and legal writer, Thomas Campbell Foster traveled extensively in Ireland in 1845 on behalf of the *Times*. This book is based on a series of articles he wrote for that paper. In the excerpt below he explains what he sees as the racial differences between the English (Saxon) and Irish (Celtic) peasantry.

ev

In other words, it is the industry and persevering energy of England which has accomplished her greatness; it is the want of these qualities which keeps Ireland poor and steeped in misery. To hide this true reason of Irish poverty, however amiable the motive, is simply to aid in perpetuating Irish poverty. Make apparent the true cause of Irish distress, and the Government will then have some chance of being able to propound measures calculated to lessen that cause, and to drag forward and urge on the people. [...]

If there be one characteristic which more than another distinguishes the lower class of the Celtic population, it is that they are content to live hardly and upon little: and if there is any one quality which distinguishes the lower class of the Saxon race more than another, it is this, that, however hard they may be content to work, they will live comfortably and well. It is because the poor Celt is content to put up with bad fare, and worse clothing and shelter, that he is made to put up with them. It is because the man of Saxon descent will live comfortably and well, or, if his exertions cannot accomplish this, make his grumblings heard and felt, that he does live comfortably and well. Let any man of observation travel through the Celtic population of the county of Leitrim into the adjoining mixed population of the county of Fermanagh, and I think he must be convinced that race has more to do with the distinguishing characteristics of Ulster than either politics or religion. At any rate, until it is proved that **Orangeism** and Protestantism will add six inches to the average height and proportionate bulk to the men, and tall figures and good looks to the women, as well as better dress, I shall continue of opinion that these great differences in the appearance of the people themselves, as well as the differences which may be observed in their dress, and in their houses and mode of living, must chiefly be attributed to the characteristics of the race. [...]

There still remained another point to inquire into, and that was, how far is this wretchedness the fault of the people themselves, or, in other words, have they made the most of those advantages which they possess? If they

Orangeism: Another term for Irish Protestants, referring to their support of the Protestant William of Orange during the Glorious Revolution.

have not, then, however blameable may be that oppression and want of encouragement, on the one hand, which retards and freezes every attempt at improvement, and which I have never hesitated to condemn, still, on the other hand, the people themselves are not blameless; and it would neither be impartial nor just to attribute their wretchedness, which in a great measure is the fault of their own apathy and indifference, entirely to the fault of the landlords.

I came not here as a party man—to make out a case, but to state the facts as I found them. I have therefore not hesitated to describe that undeniable apathy which exists among the people of the west of Ireland, under the influence of which they neglect and lose advantages unequalled by any other part of the empire, and which, if profited by—if used by them, would certainly have produced wealth and prosperity, in spite of either bad landlords or bad laws, as their almost universal neglect of these advantages has resulted in general poverty and wretchedness, in the accomplishment of which as good or bad landlord is not the most material consideration. [...]

Their [the Celtic people's] capacity of long endurance, their easy tractability of disposition, and their contentment with almost any lot, are virtues which the English people have not. The Englishman is patient, forbearing; but he will not endure—he is tractable only so long as he is well used, and I never yet met with a contented Englishman. But it is these very qualities of the people, not virtues, which make England what she is. Her people will endure no oppression, no injustice; treat them ill and they are turbulent, and every man is always striving up the ladder for the step above him, urging on for something he does not possess. And it is the very virtues of the poor Celtic peasant which tend to this deterioration and wretchedness. He endures oppression, and he has therefore been oppressed and hardly used; his easy tractability of disposition has been taken advantage of; he has been put upon, screwed down without compunction, because it was found he would bear it. His contentment has made him rest satisfied with shelter and a turf fire, and potatoes and water to live upon. He rests content and satisfied with the very worst house, and clothes, and food, is happy so long as he can get them, and he strives for nothing better. Yet it is his worst misfortune to have that contented disposition, which one almost envies, that can make him feel "as happy as a prince if he can get potatoes and buttermilk." It is impossible for a man so constituted to rise unless he is forced and urged upwards.

Extracts from Mountifort Longfield, *Lectures on Political Economy* (Dublin: 1834), 249–56

Mountifort Longfield was an Irish lawyer and academic. In 1832 he was appointed the first Professor of Political Economy at Trinity College Dublin. In 1867 he would become a member of the Irish privy council and helped to draft bills proposed by the administration of Prime Minister William Gladstone. His thoughts on potatoes appear in his most important work, *Lectures on Political Economy*, primarily as an appendix to his second lecture where he presents the major criticisms then current of potatoes and his own defense of them.

ej

Potatoes appear to be in very bad repute among political economists. Some even hint that the poverty of Ireland is in a great measure to be attributed to the use of this food. The reader may form some idea of the horror with which they have been viewed, by looking to the Index to Mr. McCulloch's edition of Smith's *Wealth of Nations*, where, under the title "Potatoes," he will find a reference for the "rapid and alarming progress of potatoes in France." Such language would be more applicable, if they eat men instead of feeding them. Something however may be said to vindicate them from the charge of creating or aggravating the poverty that prevails in Ireland. The strongest objection which is urged against the potato arises from the impossibility of storing them from one year to another. "The whole crop must necessarily be exhausted in a single year; so that when the inhabitants have the misfortune to be overtaken by a scarcity, its pressure cannot be alleviated, as is almost uniformly the case in corn-feeding countries, by bringing the reserves of former years into the market. Every year is thus left to shift for itself." This is undoubtedly a disadvantage, which, however, I think is compensated by the utility of potatoes as food for cattle....

In the three years terminating the 5th January, 1826, the annual average number of swine exported from Ireland to Great Britain was 74,000. Besides that large number of swine, there were exported 340,000 **cwts.** of bacon and pork. The immense quantity of potatoes which was consumed in fattening those animals, formed a resource out of which the wants of the human population could have been supplied had a scarcity occurred. Although potatoes cannot easily be hoarded or exported, yet pigs can; and potatoes may be considered as the raw materials of which pigs are manufactured. But whatever be the staple food of the people, if the nation is poor, a death

cwts: A hundredweight, unit of measurement mostly used for livestock and agricultural commodities. In the United Kingdom a hundredweight is equivalent to 112 lb.

will occasionally occur; and if we look to the history of England, or of any country at a time when it was as poor as Ireland is now, we shall find that dearths and famines were more frequent there, and more tremendous in their effects than they have been in Ireland during the last thirty years.

A second objection, is that on account of the bulk and weight of potatoes, a scarcity can never be materially relieved by importation. Now, in the case of a poor country with a perfect freedom of trade existing between it and a rich one, which has a similar soil and climate, as in the case of England and Ireland, this immobility of potatoes is rather an advantage to the poorer country. If a scarcity here cannot be relieved by importation, neither can it be aggravated by exportation. If potatoes could easily be transported from place to place, the latter event would most frequently take place. Their price would necessarily rise to the same height in both countries. But prices rise faster in proportion to the scarcity, in a rich than in a poor country, and therefore whenever there was a scarcity common to both countries, exportation would take place from Ireland to England....

What gives an appearance of plausibility to the common declamations against the use of potatoes is, that they confound the custom of living chiefly upon potatoes with the poverty which introduces that custom. And then it is argued that people who live upon bread and beef, can more easily purchase articles of furniture and clothing, and will form a richer and more comfortable population than those who have the means of procuring nothing more expensive than potatoes. This is true. But the question is, whether the use of the potato produces poverty, or aggravates its evils, or the contrary. On this head the principal complaint is that it is a cheap, and wholesome, and palatable food, and consequently produces an inconvenient increase of population, and that this increase of population lowers the wages and depresses the condition of the labourer. Also it is said to be favourable to the comfort of the population, that the price of subsistence should bear a high proportion to the price of comforts and decencies, for that then the number of those who enjoy such comforts and decencies will bear a high proportion to the number of those who possess but the means of a bare subsistence. And it is said that the introduction of such a cheap food as potatoes, prevents the existence of that high proportion. I shall consider separately those arguments, which indeed are not very consistent with each other.

It is certain that in any given state of the population, the cheapness of food, arising from a facility of production, cannot be injurious to the inhabitants. It will not lower their habits, nor depress their condition, but it will have the directly contrary effect. The real wages of their labour do not depend upon the price of provisions, but upon the value of the articles which their labour produces. Of that sum, the less is required to purchase food, the more will remain to purchase other things.... An increase of population produced by cheapness of food cannot therefore be deemed an evil, unless a man is prepared to maintain, that cheap food, which would otherwise be a good, is an evil, merely because of its tendency to increase the population, and that an increase of population, which would otherwise be a good, is an evil, merely because of its tendency to raise the price of food....

Another charge I brought against the potatoes, which, if it were well founded, would indeed be a most serious one. It is alleged that the potato crop is irregular, uncertain, and extremely liable to failures.... But the variations which take place from year to year are not entirely to be laid to the blame of the potato. Our customs and husbandry are the principal cause. First, in many parts of Ireland, potatoes are not a regular marketable article. It is the custom for every labourer to take from a **rood** to an acre of land, on which he plants potatoes for his own family.... Those little husbandmen, too, are necessarily bad farmers. They have no selection of land in which to plant their potatoes; they are obliged to put up with any land they can get, and from want of capital they are unable to lay out a sufficient quantity of manure upon the land. So hardy is the potato, that in ordinary years it yields a tolerable crop, and it ought not hastily to be reputed a variable crop if it fails in bad seasons, when badly cultivated upon land in which it ought never have been planted....

I have merely alluded concisely to the arguments that may be urged in defence of potatoes, because I think that the presumption is entirely in their favor. He who argues against them should make out a very strong case. Providence has bestowed upon the world a prolific, wholesome, and palatable vegetable. These qualities must insure its general cultivation in all countries adapted to its growth. And it is a hard matter to believe that the introduction of this plant should naturally and almost inevitably introduce general distress. It would be a singular instance of permanent national unhappiness, being introduced by anything except a course of irreligion, vice, or folly.

rood: An area equal to one-quarter of an acre.

PART 2

Effects of the Blight

DOCUMENT 12:

Newspaper Accounts of the Blight

The potato blight was caused by *Phytophthora infestans*, an oomycete. It first emerged in the United States and first appeared in Ireland in 1845. It infected the insides of potatoes, making them look healthy from the outside but causing them to rot and blacken on the inside. During the 1840s the blight was little understood, and the cause was not positively identified until 1890. Between 1846 and 1852 newspaper coverage of the potato blight regularly highlighted the extent of the distress that it caused.

ᴇ

Freeman's Journal, 22 July 1846

PROGRESS OF THE POTATO DISEASE

We (says the *Tyrone Constitution*) cannot longer conceal the fact—we have again been visited by the potato blight of last year. Round by Strabane, Clogher, and even in our own neighbourhood, great quantities of the reds, blacks, burrowees, and kidney sorts are found to be diseased. This is sad news, so early in the season.

The Following is from the *Ballyshannon Herald:*—"We regret to state that in many places throughout this country (Donegal), a disease of an alarming nature has made its appearance in the growing crops—the stalks in many cases appear healthy and strong at top, but at the bottom they are decayed and the potatoes in a putrid state.

London Illustrated Times, 15 August 1846

FAILURE OF THE POTATO CROP

A letter from Dublin, dated August 11, says, "In various letters, received this morning, there is melancholy confirmation of the previous accounts of the spread of the destructive blight in the potato crop. Along the western coast, in Mayo, the ravages of the disease have been terrible, and all classes have been struck with dismay. Already, oatmeal is advancing in price. Potato fields, that had been green and healthy in appearance on Saturday, presented a mass of rottenness on Sunday. There will be great distress and suffering; and, during the winter and spring, unless more extensive measures of relief even than those of the late Government shall be adopted, we shall have the country in a frightful condition, and a large proportion of the population in a state of starvation."

London Illustrated Times, 22 August 1846

IRELAND

There is no political news of consequence this week from Ireland; but we regret to state that the Irish papers contain the most melancholy descriptions of the disease in the potatoes. The disease appears to be general.

The Tralee Chronicle gives a lamentable sketch of the state of the barony of Iveragh. It is furnished on the authority of the Rev. J. B. Tyrwhitt, a benevolent and highly intelligent Englishman, and a clergyman of the Established Church:—"His account of the prospects of the people of this very poor barony, and all along from the river Kenmare, Sneem, Darrynane, to Cahirciveen, and thence towards Killorglin, is harrowing and startling. The whole potato-crop is literally destroyed; while, over a very wide surface, the oat crop presents an unnatural lilac tinge to the eye; at the same time, in too many instances, the head is found flaccid to the touch, and possessing no substance. The barley crop, too, in many places, exhibits the effect of a powerful blight. In some places, also, where turnips have been grown, they present—as, indeed, has been the case in other parts of the county—a healthy exterior in top and skin; but, on being opened, are found deeply impregnated with a taint similar to that which has smitten the potatoe, to such an extent, that one cannot stand in the blackened fields without being overpowered by the offensive effluvia."

Nation, 22 **August 1846**

THE POTATO CROP

From Every district of Ireland the cry of apprehended famine swells to the certainty of that terrible visitation.—The *total* failure of the potato crop of this season is confirmed from every quarter of the land. In some parts of the country apprehensions are entertained that the corn crops have been visited by the mysterious blight which has converted the potato fields into a mass of rottenness.

London Illustrated News, 5 **September 1846**

THE TOTAL FAILURE OF THE POTATO CROP IN IRELAND

The Times says:—"The accounts we continue daily to receive from all parts of Ireland leave no room to doubt the failure of the potato crop. From the Giant's Causeway to Cape Clear, from Limerick to Dublin, not a green field is to be seen. The disease having attacked the plant at a much earlier period this year than it did in 1845, the root has been arrested in its growth, and prevented from arriving at maturity. Thus, what was last year but a partial destruction is now a total annihilation; and it is become a very general belief that the month of December will not find a single potato in the country. Ireland is, therefore, doomed to suffer a recurrence (if it should not rather be called a continuance) of that distress which has well nigh pauperized the whole population."

London Illustrated News, 5 **September 1846**

DISTRESS AND IMPENDING FAMINE

There have been meetings in various parts of Ireland, at which lamentable accounts have been given of the scarcity of food and the prevalence of distress. The Dublin Correspondent of the Morning Chronicle says:—"The entire country is in motion. In all directions the gentry are assembling, in the hope of devising measures to avert the impending famine, and to save the country from the terrible evils by which we are threatened. It is no longer necessary to enter into details of distress. Universally is it admitted that, within a few weeks, millions of our population will be totally destitute of food; and the question everywhere for consideration is, how is employment to be provided with the least degree of positive loss to the owners of the soil."

London Illustrated News, 2 **November 1846**

DEATHS FROM STARVATION

(From the Cork Examiner, Nov 2—We are again—and it is a revolting duty—compelled in justice to charge the Board of Works with the deaths of two more victims; and we do so on the unquestionable authority of the Rev. Mr. Mulcahy, parish priest of Castlehaven, Myross. These men died of starvation, although at work under the Board, and on the public road. Their pay was kept from them for a fortnight and three weeks; and, although these wretched victims were partly relieved by the charity of wretches as poor and forlorn as themselves, they could not hold out against the destroyer, and fell victims to hunger and the Board of Works.)

London Illustrated News, 19 **December 1846**

ANOTHER DEATH FROM STARVATION

A Dublin paper states that from some of the remote districts the most horrifying details have been received of the sufferings of the poorer classes; and also various particulars of deaths from starvation. On the 6th instant an inquest was held by A. Hosty, Esq, coroner, at Lisheenager, on view of the body of Michael Walsh. Mary Walsh having been sworn and examined, said—The deceased was my husband. We had neither potatoes nor corn for the last twelve weeks, nor did deceased get but six days' work during that time. There were no public works in the neighbourhood but one road, and he was unable to get employment. The only support ourselves and three children had were a few turnips, and, occasionally, a little meal we used to get from a neighbour. We lived upon one meal a-day, and often suffered from hunger for the last three weeks. Deceased took ill on the 1st instant, and died on the Thursday following. During that time myself and my children lived on a few boiled turnips, without meal or any other mixture, and we are all suffering from hunger.

London Illustrated News, 1 January 1847

PROGRESS OF THE FAMINE

There were nearly 20 deaths by starvation reported from the southern and western counties on Monday morning. In a list of seven specified in the Galway Mercury, there is an account of the death of a man named Walker, who a few years ago was the proprietor of a veterinary establishment in Marlborough-street, Dublin. It appears that on Thursday (last week) he fell down suddenly in the town of Loughrea, and after a few minutes expired. An inquest was held on the body, and the jury returned a verdict of "Died of starvation." Several additional inquests on persons who died of starvation, were reported on Tuesday from the counties of Cork, Clare, Limerick, and Waterford.

Nation, 13 February 1847

PROGRESS OF FAMINE—KERRY

The correspondent of the *Kerry Examiner* writes from Dingle, under date, February 8th:—The state of the people of this locality is horrifying. Fever, famine, and dysentery are daily increasing, deaths from hunger daily occurring, averaging weekly twenty—men, women, and children thrown into the graves without a coffin—dead bodies found in all parts of the country, being several days dead before discovered—no inquests to inquire how they came by their death, as the hunger has hardened the hearts of the people.

BOY AND GIRL AT CAHERA.

London *Times*, 2 May 1847

The Cork Examiner of yesterday contains the following shocking statement;—

"We this day witnessed a most horrifying and appalling spectacle at the Shandon guard house, at the foot of Mallow Lane. Under the sheds attached to the building lay some 38 human beings—old and young men, women, children, and infants of the tenderest age all huddled together, like so many pigs or dogs, on the ground, without any other covering but the rags on their persons, and these in the last stage of filth and hideousness."

Nation, 22 May 1847

STATE OF THE COUNTRY—MAYO

To the Editor of the Nation
Dear Sir—The people of this parish are, I regret to say, suffering dreadfully from the want of food; and, if something be not immediately done to relieve them, I fear life and property will not be safe. On yesterday several hundreds of them came into this town loudly demanding work or food, and were prevented with great difficulty from breaking into the bread shops to get something to eat. Words cannot describe their sad state. All the public works in this extensive parish were suspended on the 1st of May; and, though the roads are all in the most unfinished state, and large sums of money in hands—over 10,000l.—the poor are left idle to starve, or to die, if they wish, to carry out, I suppose, the political economy of our Whig rulers.[1]

Nation, 18 March 1848

MISERABLE STATE OF THE COUNTRY

Reports from all parts of Ireland contain accounts of the suffering condition of the people. Inadequate relief and eviction—the operations of the infamous Gregory clause[2] are producing their fatal results everywhere. Among those places most afflicted, Galway seems to hold a lamentable pre-eminence. The county jail of Galway is more of a pestilent hospital than a prison. From the 20th February to the 7th instant, one hundred and fifteen human beings had perished in it. A letter of the Rev. G. Commins, **P.P.**, chaplain of the prison, which appears in the Galway papers, gives us the most shocking details of its condition. We perceive from it that the jail, independently of the hospital, was intended to accommodate 110 persons, while on last Saturday it contained no less than 903 prisoners and 34 children! [...]

P.P.: parish priest.

"The hospital is crowded to excess; there are two in each bed; and in many instances three. I saw one woman and six children, varying in age from 8 to 14 years, lying on the same bed. I see living persons lying on the same bed with a corpse, whose fetid condition renders it dangerous to approach. I frequently see persons lying on the cold flags, or on the boards in hospital, whose deaths may be announced before the next morning, waiting for other

---

1 A commentary on the laissez-faire approach of then prime minister John Russell and his Whig Party, who halted the food imports and relief works adopted by the previous administration led by Sir Robert Peel.
2 See Glossary.

creatures to die, that they may seize on the portions of the beds occupied by them."

London Illustrated News, 18 May 1848

POTATO DISEASE

The King's County Chronicle says—"We regret to state that the potato disease is again manifesting its symptoms in this locality. During this week the Earl of Rosse's gardener presented some specimens of new potatoes at our office, which were entirely infected—by a disease having all the appearance of the late epidemic. The specimens, however, were cultivated under glass, and not in open exposure."

London Illustrated News, 27 July 1850

THE POTATO BLIGHT

—The Limerick Reporter states that the old potato blight had shown itself in a virulent form in some localities in the rich soils of the counties of Limerick and Tipperary, the odour from the fields already infected being most offensive, and the leaves of the plant being throughout blackened. That Journal remarks—"The disease did not appear to any extent before the night of Monday; but on Tuesday morning, in several parts of the country, the blight alarmed several who had hoped for the best previously. Meantime, we trust the disease is but partial." It must be recollected, however, that the present is one of the most extensive potato crops grown for many years in Ireland and that even if a fourth part were blighted there would still be an immense supply for food, and a stoppage of the drain for foreign corn, which for four years past has so greatly exhausted the resources of the country. Accounts from Tralee, Ardfert, Castleisland, and other parts of Kerry, also announce the rapid spread of the potato disease. One of the letters says:— "The potatoes are all gone in this part of the country, and the greatest alarm and despondency prevail. The people are flying from all parts of this country."

Freeman's Journal, 12 **September 1850**

DISEASE OF THE POTATO CROP IN CONNAUGHT

(From a western correspondent)
For some weeks past I have been watching, with great anxiety, the progressive steps of the fatal potato blight, and, not wishing to be alarmist, I forbore giving publicity to the result of my observations. Whilst exaggerated statements regarding the extent of the calamity can serve no purpose, neither can any useful object be obtained by attempting to conceal what now is too notorious in this locality. Landlords do not wish to have it appear another year of famine, Connaught are again entering upon another year of famine, lest common humanity might interpose a check to their demands for exorbitant rents, which will be made now at the ripening of the harvest crop.

DOCUMENT 13:

James Mahony, "Condition of Ireland: Illustrations of the New Poor-Law," *Illustrated London News*, 22 December 1849

> James Mahony (1810–79) was an artist and engraver living in Cork when he was asked by the *Illustrated London News* to produce a series of illustrations and reports on the distress. Mahony's images of the distress have been iconic representations of the famine. This story from 1849 is an example of his reporting.

ev

Kilrush: A town in County Clare in the west of Ireland. This refers to the much larger Poor Law Union with a workhouse which encompassed 13 electoral districts.

Having last week introduced this important subject to our readers, and given them some of the statistics of **Kilrush**, we shall henceforward allow our Correspondent to speak for himself:—

I assure you (he says) that the objects of which I send you Sketches are not sought after—I do not go out of my way to find them; and other travellers who have gone in the same direction, such as Lord Adair, the Earl of Surrey, and Mr. Horsman, will vouch, I am sure, for the accuracy of my delineations. The Sketch of Moveen, to which I now call your attention, is that of another ruined village in the Union of Kilrush. It is a specimen of the dilapidation I behold all around. There is nothing but devastation, while the soil is of the finest description, capable of yielding as much as any land in the empire. Here, at Tullig, and other places, the ruthless destroyer, as if he delighted in seeing the monuments of his skill, has left the walls of the houses standing, while he has unroofed them and taken away all shelter from the people. They look like the tombs of a departed race, rather than the recent abodes of a yet living people, and I felt actually relieved at seeing one or two half-clad spectres gliding about, as an evidence that I was not in the land of the dead. You may inquire, perhaps, and I am sure your readers will wish to know, why it is that the people have of late been turned out of their houses in such great numbers, and their houses just at this time pulled down, and I will give you my explanation of this fact.

The public records, my own eye, a piercing wall of woe throughout the land—all testify to the vast extent of the evictions at the present time. Sixteen thousand and odd persons unhoused in the Union of Kilrush before the month of June in the present year; seventy-one thousand one hundred and thirty holdings done away in Ireland, and nearly as many houses destroyed, in 1848; two hundred and fifty-four thousand holdings of more than one acre and less than five acres, put an end to between 1841 and 1848: six-tenths, in fact, of the lowest class of tenantry driven from their now roofless or annihilated cabins and houses, makes up the general description of that desolation of which Tullig and Moveen are examples. The ruin is great and complete. The blow that effected it was irresistible. It came in the guise of charity and benevolence; it assumed the character of the last and best friend of the peasantry, and it has struck them to the heart. They are prostrate and helpless. The once frolicsome people—even the saucy beggars—have disappeared, and given place to wan and haggard objects, who are so resigned to their doom, that they no longer expect relief. One beholds only shrunken frames scarcely covered with flesh—crawling skeletons, who appear to have risen from their graves, and are ready to be returned frightened to that abode. They have little other covering than that nature has bestowed on the human body—a poor protection against inclement weather; and, now that the only hand from which they expected help is turned against them, even hope is departed, and they are filled with despair. Than the present Earl of Carlisle there is not a more humane nor a kinder-hearted nobleman in the kingdom; he is of high honour and unsullied reputation; yet the Poor-law he was mainly the means of establishing for Ireland, with the best intentions, has been one of the chief causes of the people being at this time turned out of their homes, and forced to burrow in holes, and share, till they are discovered, the ditches and the bogs with otters and snipes.

The instant the Poor-law was passed, and property was made responsible for poverty,[3] the whole of the landowners, who had before been careless about the people, and often allowed them to plant themselves on untenanted spots, or divide their tenancies—delighted to get the promise of a little additional rent—immediately became deeply interested in preventing that, and in keeping down the number of the people. Before they had rates to pay, they cared nothing for them; but the law and their self-interest made them care, and made them extirpators. Nothing less than some general desire like that of cupidity falling in with an enactment, and justified by a theory—nothing less than a passion which works silently in all, and safely under the sanction of a law—could have effected such wide-spread destruction. Even humanity was enlisted by the Poor-law on the side of extirpation. As long as there was no legal provision for the poor, a landlord had some repugnance to drive them from every shelter; but the instant the law took them under its protection, and forced the landowner to pay a rate to provide for them, repugnance ceased: they had a legal home, however inefficient, to go to; and eviction began. Even the growth of toleration seems to have worked to the same end. Till the Catholics were emancipated, they were all—rich and poor, priests and peasants—united by a common bond; and Protestant landlords beginning evictions on a great scale would have roused against

---

3   See Introduction, pp. 12–14.

them the whole Catholic nation. It would have been taken up as a religious question, as well as a question of the poor, prior to 1829. Subsequent to that time—with a Whig administration, with all offices open to Catholics—no religious feelings could mingle with the matter: eviction became a pure question of interest; and while the priests look now perhaps, as much to the Government as to their flocks for support, Catholic landlords are not behind Protestant landlords in clearing their estates. English notions and English habits, without any reference to the causes of English greatness—which are not to be found in a Poor-law and farms of a particular size—impressed law-makers and the landlords of Ireland with a strong desire to enlarge and consolidate farms, and clear them of the squatters and subtenants, who had formerly been permitted, if not encouraged. With a Poor-law, that desire could be safely acted on, and so it supplies a temptation and the means to carry eviction extensively into effect.

The evictions were numerous before the potato rot. It was not that great calamity, therefore, that super induced them, it was the chief cause of the present desolation. The potato harvest and harvests of every kind have been lost many times before 1846, without reducing the people to their present misery. But that calamity threw the people at the mercy of the Government, and the Government used its power directly and indirectly, in accordance with the theory, to clear the land. Out-door relief was established in that season of distress, and relief altogether was coupled with the resignation of the land. The poor were required to give up their heritage, small though it were, for less than a mess of pottage. A law was passed, the 11 and 12 Vic. c. 47,[4] entitled, "An Act for the Protection and Relief of the Destitute Poor Evicted from the Dwellings," which provided a means of evicting them, subjecting the landlords to the necessity of giving notice to Poor-law guardians, and to the share of a common burden. Under such stimuli and such auspices, the clearing process has gone on in an accelerated ratio, and Ireland is now dotted with ruined villages, and filled with a starving population, besieging the doors of crowded workhouses, and creeping into the halls and chambers of the deserted mansions of the nobility and gentry. A gentleman's mansion turned into a poor-house, is a fit emblem of the decay that a mistaken policy has brought on all classes. The system intended to relieve the poor, by making the landlords responsible for their welfare, has at once made it the interest, and therefore the duty, of the landlords to get rid of them. Extirpation is accordingly going forward at a rapid rate; and the evidence of that is now placed before the eyes and the understanding of the readers of the ILLUSTRATED LONDON NEWS.

---

4   This act was intended to place some restrictions on evictions; it required seven days notice of eviction to the Poor Law Guardians and the tenant and made the practice of unroofing or demolishing houses set for eviction a misdemeanor.

SCALP OF BRIAN CONNOR, NEAR KILRUSH UNION HOUSE.

I will give you, by-and-bye, some notices of driving for rent, of land-owners impoverished by rates, and of bankrupt unions; but at present I must draw attention to some of the other Sketches I send. The Scalp of Brian Connor (here represented) has been already described; it is another illustration of the worse than pig-sty habitations of those who did live in the now roofless cottages.

There is something called a scalp, or hole dug in the earth, some two or three feet deep. In such a place was the abode of Brian Connor. He has three in family, and had lived in this hole several months before it was discovered. It was roofed over with sticks and pieces of turf, laid in the shape of an inverted saucer. It resembles, though not quite so large, one of the ant-hills of the African forests.

Another Sketch follows (of Miss Kennedy), which shows that, amidst this world of wretchedness, all is not misery and guilt. Indeed, it is a part of our nature that the sufferings of some should be the occasion for the exercise of virtue in others. Miss Kennedy (about seven years old) is the daughter of Captain Kennedy, the Poor-law Inspector of the Kilrush Union. She is represented as engaged in her daily occupation of distributing clothing to the wretched children brought around her by their more wretched parents.

MISS KENNEDY DISTRIBUTING CLOTHING AT KILRUSH.

In the front of the group I noticed one woman crouching like a monkey, and drawing around her the only rag she had left to conceal her nudity. A big tear was rolling down her cheek, with gratitude for the gifts the innocent child was distributing. The effect was heightened by the chilliness and dreariness of a November evening, and by the wet and mire in which the naked feet of the crowd were immersed. On Captain Kennedy being appointed to the Union, his daughter was much affected by the misery of the poor children she saw; and so completely did it occupy her thoughts, that, with the consent of her parents, she gave up her time and her own little means to relieve them. She gave away her own clothes—she was allowed to bestow part of her mother's—and she then purchased coarse materials, and made up clothing for children of her own age; she was encouraged by her father and some philanthropic strangers, from whom she received sums of money, and whose example will no doubt be followed by those who possess property in the neighbourhood; and she devoted herself with all the energy and perseverance of a mature and staid matron to the holy office she has undertaken. The Sketch will, I hope, immortalize the beneficent child, who is filling the place of a saint, and performing the duties of a patriot.

On all sides I hear praises of the amiable child and her excellent father, and this is not without a moral for the landlords. The public officers who are appointed to administer and control the relief of the poor, have it in their power to do much for the people. Mere kindness of manner, though they render no substantial assistance, endears them to the suffering crowd. Captain Kennedy is at once kind, charitable, and judicious. He is at the head of the

BRIDGET O'DONNEL AND CHILDREN.

Union. He fills for the people the most important office in the district. He is the great man of the place. It must be so in other districts. The funds are contributed by the landowners, but they are distributed by public officers. Thus the Poor-law, which disposes of the landowners' property, also deprives them of the pleasure and the burden of distributing it themselves. A public officer is made, in fact, to administer their estates, and he stands between them and their compulsory bounties, securing the respect and confidence which they might and ought to have. The more the subject is examined, the more, I have no doubt, it will be found that the poor-law is as injurious to the landlords as it is to the people.

Searching for Potatoes is one of the occupations of those who cannot obtain out-door relief. It is gleaning in a potato-field—and how few are left after the potatoes are dug, must be known to everyone who has ever seen the field cleared. What the people were digging and hunting for, like dogs after truffles, I could not imagine, till I went into the field, and then I found them patiently turning over the whole ground, in the hopes of finding the few potatoes the owner might have overlooked. Gleaning in a potato-field seems something like shearing hogs, but it is the only means by which the gleaners could hope to get a meal.

The Sketch of a Woman and Children represents Bridget O'Donnel. Her story is briefly this:—"I lived," she said, "on the lands of Gurranenatuoha. My husband held four acres and a half of land, and three acres of bog land; our yearly rent was £7 4s.; we were put out last November; he owed some rent. We got thirty stone of oats from Mr. Marcus Keane, for seed. My husband gave some writing for it: he was paid for it. He paid ten shillings for reaping the corn. As soon as it was stacked, one 'Blake' on the farm, who was put to watch it, took it away to his own haggard and kept it there for a fortnight by Dan Sheedey's orders. They then thrashed it in Frank Lellis's barn. I was at this time lying in fever. Dan Sheedey and five or six men came to tumble my house; they wanted me to give possession. I said that I would not; I had fever, and was within two months of my down-lying (confinement); they commenced knocking down the house, and had half of it knocked down

SCALPEEN OF TIM DOWNS, AT DUNMORE.

when two neighbours, women, Nell Spellesley and Kate How, carried me out. I had the priest and doctor to attend me shortly after. Father Meehan anointed me. I was carried into a cabin, and lay there for eight days, when I had the creature (the child) born dead. I lay for three weeks after that. The whole of my family got the fever, and one boy thirteen years old died with want and with hunger while we were lying sick. Dan Sheedey and Blake took the corn into Kilrush, and sold it. I don't know what they got for it. I had not a bit for my children to eat when they took it from me."

The last Sketch shows the **Scalpeen** of Tim Downs, at Dunmore, in the parish of Kellard, where himself and his ancestors resided on the spot for over a century, with renewal of their lease in 1845. He neither owed rent arrears or taxes up to the present moment, and yet he was pitched out on the roadside, and saw ten other houses, with his own, levelled at one fell swoop on the spot, the ruins of some of which are seen in this Sketch. None of them were mud cabins, but all capital stone-built houses.

I must conclude my present communication with an account of a great catastrophe, which has hurried 37 of the poor wretches that depended on the Union of Kilrush, with four other persons, into eternity. The Union will be relieved by an accident at which humanity mourns:—

"On the evening of Wednesday week intelligence reached the town of Kilrush that a large number of persons, most of whom were paupers, who had been seeking out-door relief at Kilrush, were drowned while crossing the ferry on their return to Moyarta. No less than 33 dead bodies were washed ashore on the northern side of the ferry. They were removed to an adjacent field, and the coroner, Mr. Frank O'Donnell, arriving soon after from Kilkee, an inquest was held on their wretched remains. It appeared upon the inquiry that no less than 43 or 45 persons (for they could not tell the exact number), were allowed to crowd into a crazy and rotten boat, which had been plying on this ferry for the last forty years. The boat moved on as far as the middle of the ferry, when a sea broke over her stern, and filled her at once, the wind blowing strong from the south-west at the time. She upset instantly, and her miserable living freight were immersed in the merciless waters, while four (who were eventually saved) clung to her until a boat from Captain Cox's men came to their assistance. The verdict of the coroner's jury was as usual in such cases, but imputing gross neglect, and attaching censure to the owners of the boat, for admitting such a number of persons into so frail a craft. With the exception of four, the victims were all paupers who had frequently come into the town in vain to seek out-door relief, and were returning that sad evening to their wretched hovels in the parishes of Moyarta and Kilballyowen."

Scalpeen: In a 15 December article Mahony described a scalpeen as: "A Scalpeen is a hole... It is often erected within the walls when any are left standing, of the unroofed houses, and all that is above the surface is built out of the old materials. It possesses, too, some pieces of furniture, and the Scalpeen is altogether superior to the Scalp."

Extracts from William Bennett, *Narrative of a Recent Journey of Six Weeks in Ireland* (London, 1847), 5, 7–8, 23–24, 26–28, 61–62, 127–28, 151–52

William Bennett was an English Quaker who worked on famine-relief efforts. He toured Ireland in the spring of 1847 recording his experiences and distributing turnip, carrot, and cabbage seeds to try to diversify Irish food sources.

The first evidence of the extreme distress of the times we witnessed was in the spectacle of a corpse exposed in the public road, death having apparently been the work of starvation. Not far from this, in an angle of the way side, under a low temporary erection of straw, was a poor family down in fever. We met along the road multitudes of emigrants, mostly on foot, with their bundles on their backs proceeding to Dublin. A few had more than they could thus carry; and it was an affecting sight to observe numerous whole families, with their worldly all packed up on a donkey-cart, attempting to look gay and cheerful, as they cast a wistful glance at the rapidly passing by coach-passengers; and thus abandoning a country which should have nourished them and their children. [...]

The word "Gombien," and the prevalence of the "Gombien system," was new to me; though I find it exposed and commented on in the able letters of the "Times Commissioner," No. 20. I cannot but think that it only requires to be fully brought out to the light, and generally known, to cease and exist altogether. The poor **cottier** having taken his plot of ground on **conacre**— that is, for the present crop, and no further interest in it—requires seed, and having no money to purchase it, he goes to a Gombien man. This man sells him potatoes, or oats, or whatever else it may be, on the credit of the harvest, taking his I.O.U. at 50, 70, and even 100 percent profit, according to the circumstance, on the current market value of the article. Under any accident or failure, or even in fair seasons, he is often unable to pay this exorbitant price when the time comes round....

While large tracts of land have been let on low terms, and underlet, or leases sold for lives renewable forever—so that the great proprietor has little interest in, or power over them—they get divided and subdivided, each at an increased rental, until the small holder pays those enormous rates we hear of under the conacre system. The average rent in Ireland at which arable land is let, is probably more than double the same in England; so that what with conacre rent for his land, and Gombien price for his seed, and ditto for his

cottier: In Ireland a cottier was a peasant who rented a cottage under a system whereby rent was determined by public competition. In practice this mean that many cottiers paid inflated rents.

conacre: A form of speculative short-term leasing of small strips of land.

food, while he tills the land, it is not surprising that the Irish peasant has been kept at the lowest verge of pauperism; for all inducement to industry, beyond the barest living, is in fact withdrawn. [...]

Belmullet

We now proceeded to visit the district beyond the town within the Mullet. The cabins cluster the road-sides, and are scattered over the face of the bog, in the usual Irish manner, where the country is thickly inhabited. Several were pointed out as "freeholders;" that is, such as had some wandering over the land, and "squatted" down on any unoccupied spot, owning no fealty, and paying no rent. Their neighbours had probably built them the cabin in four and twenty hours; expecting the same service in turn for themselves should occasion require it,—which a common necessity renders these poor people always willing to do for each other. Whatever little bit of ground they may reclaim around the cabin is necessarily done as much by stealth as possible; and the appearance of neglect and wretchedness is naturally carried out to the utmost; for should there be any visible improvement, down comes the landlord or his agent, with a demand for rent.... I mention it here not as peculiar to this district. It is an element pervading large portions of Ireland; entering into the very growth of a population ever—by habit and education—on the verge of pauperism, and of whom the landlord, rarely coming near the property, knows little, and unfortunately in many instances cares less. [...]

Many of the cabins were holes in the bog, covered with a layer of turves, and not distinguishable as human habitations from the surrounding moor, until close down upon them. The bare sod was about the best material of which any of them were constructed. Doorways, not doors, were usually provided at both sides of the bettermost—back and front—to take advantage of the way of the wind. Windows and chimneys, I think, had no existence ... we saw neither bed, chair, nor table, at all. A chest, a few iron or earthen vessels, a stool or two, the dirty rags and night-coverings, formed about the sum total of the best furnished.... And now language utterly fails me in attempting to depict the state of the wretched inmates. The scenes of human misery and degradation we witnessed still haunt my imagination, with the vividness and power of some horrid and tyrannous delusion, rather than the features of a sober reality. We entered a cabin. Stretched in one dark corner, scarcely visible, from the smoke and rags that covered them, were three children huddled together, lying there because they were too weak to rise, pale and ghastly, their little limbs—on removing a portion of the filthy covering—perfectly emaciated, eyes sunk, voice gone, and evidently in the last stage of actual starvation. Crouched over the turf embers was another form, wild, and all but naked, scarcely human in appearance. It stirred not, nor noticed us. On some straw, saddened upon the ground, moaning piteously, was a shrivelled old woman, imploring us to give her something,—baring her limbs partly, to show how the skin hung loose from the bones, as soon as she attracted our attention. Above her, on something like a ledge, was a young woman, with sunken cheeks,—a mother I have no doubt,—who scarcely raised her eyes in answer to our enquiries, but pressed her hand upon her forehead, with a look of unutterable anguish and despair. Many cases were widows, whose husbands had recently been taken off by the fever, and thus their only pittance, obtained from the public works, entirely cut off. In many the husbands or sons were prostrate, under that horrid disease,—the results of the long-continued famine and low living,—in which first the limbs, and then the body swell most frightfully, and finally burst. We entered upwards of fifty of these tenements.

On the Glenties poor-house

The building is well constructed and airy. It was satisfactory to find it in a fairly comfortable state as to food, cleanliness, and order: the greatest deficiency appeared to be the want of adequate instruction to the number of poor children there collected. But the distress without and disease within were fearful and increasing. The number of inmates was 500, of whom 102 were in the infirmary. But what was told us by the master of the poor-house, depicts most powerfully the wretched condition of the poor peasantry. He said, the crowds who were every day refused admittance for want of room, watched eagerly the daily deaths, for the chance of being received into the house.

Stay in Kenmare

We were beset immediately with the most terrific details of the want and sufferings of the people: indeed it could not be concealed. The sounds of woe and wailing resounded in the streets throughout the night. I felt extremely ill, and was almost overcome.

In the morning I was credibly informed that nine deaths had taken place during the night, in the open streets, from sheer want and exhaustion. The poor people came in from the rural districts in such numbers, in the hopes of getting some relief, that it was utterly impossible to meet their most urgent exigencies, and therefore they came in literally to die; and I might see several families lying about in the open streets, actually dying of starvation and fever, within a stone's throw of the inn.

Conclusions

To conclude, in the words of a late visitor to some of these districts, "Let us not consider our duty to Ireland fulfilled, by the effort to meet its present necessity. Its general and permanent condition is a subject in itself almost too dreadful to contemplate. Famine is there no new cry. It is a periodic disease. Every year there are districts where prevails somewhat of that misery that now rules the land. For a large portion of its population, all the great purposes of existence are forgotten in the struggle with death. I would not now discuss the causes of this condition, nor attempt to apportion blame to its authors; but of this one fact there can be no question, that the result of our social systems is, that vast numbers of our fellow-countrymen,—of the peasantry of one of the richest nations the world ever knew,—have not leave to live. Surely such a social result is not only a national misfortune, but a national sin, crying loudly to every Christian citizen to do his duty to remove it. No one of us can have any right to enjoy either riches or repose, until, to the extent of his ability he strive to wash himself of all share in the guild of this fearful inequality which will be a blot in the history of our country, and make her a bye-word among the nations."

DOCUMENT 15:

Extracts from Alexander Somerville, *The Whistler at the Plough; with Letters from Ireland* (Manchester, 1852), 437–39, 449, 485

> Somerville was a Scottish journalist and former soldier, known for his radical politics. In the spring of 1847 Somerville went to Ireland to report on conditions there for the Manchester newspapers, he later compiled and published these letters along with his larger volume on free trade, *The Whistler at the Plough*.

⁓

Dublin, 23d January 1847

The next thing that has struck me as remarkable in Ireland, previous to the present time, has been this—that rent was usually paid through the sheriff, his officers, the keepers put in possession of the pigs and potatoes, corn and cows, and the armed police who assisted the keepers to keep possession. The property distrained upon was sold by any one whom the landlord or his agent appointed; it being legal for a mere labourer to act as auctioneer, if so ordered. The agent of the landlord was usually himself the buyer, at least virtually so. He got legal possession of the crops by means of this **distraint** and by the aid of the armed police, and he sent the corn, pigs, potatoes, or whatever the property might be, to a seaport town for shipment to England. Arrived in England, they were sold readily. The landlord got his rent by their sale in England, not by their sale under the hammer in Ireland; and the people of England were pleased to find so much food coming from Ireland, though often wondering why the Irish people should be so poorly fed at home, as report said they were, when they sent so much food to England. That food left Ireland by the process I have described. Some landlords and some districts of the country might be exceptions; but in the south and west of Ireland, and in most of the midland counties, that has long been the method of collecting rents, and of exporting provisions to England.

The stranger could not get so far through the country, nor be so long in it as to understand this system of distraint, without seeing that the people were ragged to a degree of wretchedness not seen in any other country; that they were lodged with their pigs, the pigs not having a better lodging than a sty, and that the food of the people was potatoes, and only as many of them as the distraint system of getting rent left them. There being all the staff of sheriffs' officers, keepers, attorneys to sue out warrants, fees for warrants, attorneys to work on the other side to urge the tenant to **replevin**

distraint: The legal seizure of someone's property.

replevin: The restoration of confiscated property.

and resist, and so draw from the wretched man costs; there being all these to pay in addition to the rent, while the rent was paid by selling the crops at prices over which the tenant had no control, it is no wonder that the Irish tenantry were always poor and starving, or only kept from starving by a miserable diet of potatoes, while those who saw the Irish corn, cattle, and pigs coming to England, thought the Irish should be well-fed to have so much to spare.

This was rendered all the worse by the next characteristic of Ireland, namely, that those tenants thus distrained upon were tenants in the third or fourth degree. The head landlord was not the receiver of the rents. Some leaseholder was under him, both of them perhaps being non-resident. A person of some capital, of much energy, and little conscience, took a **townland** or other such portion of an estate. He let that out again at a rent which none of the peasantry who became his tenants could pay, which he knew they could not pay, but which, in the intense competition for land to keep in bare life, they engaged to pay; they not being able to get out of arrears at any time, could always be seized upon by him, and this has been his system—whenever they had anything. He was thus able at harvest or potato time, by the arrears due, to seize, sell, and send to England, or the certain stores to be ready for the English market, the corn and potatoes, before the producer of them eat too much. But this system of exacting engagements to pay rents which could not be paid, which never were expected to be paid, in order to have always the power of seizing the crops and selling them before the producers had time to eat them up stump and tump, was not confined to middlemen; it has been done by head landlords, and by many of them. As much was left to the miserable tenantry, but no more, than would keep them in life, with strength enough to put another crop in the ground.

But this system went farther. The enmity of Protestant and Catholic led the first, he being usually the landlord, to allow the latter, the potato-eating tenant, to get in **arrear**, that he might be at any time evicted by means of the law when a better tenant offered for the land. The Protestant landlord, having all the law on his side—all the officials being Protestants, from the lord-lieutenant to the hangman—he was seldom particular about the moral just of such cases. There were the armed police ever at hand to help the landlord, if the tenant did not yield possession, and betake himself to a ditch, to lie and die quietly. If he took vengeance into his own hand while in the ditch, or behind the hedge that skirted it and the high-way road, there was the hangman for him; that is, if they could catch him, and get the noose on his neck. But such a man was not easily caught in such a country, among such people. To be sure the pursuing law was not always particular about the right man; so as one or two or three were caught and hung up, the law, and the landlords, and the juries whom they employed were pretty well

townland: In Ireland a townland is the smallest administrative division of land.

arrear: Past due on rent.

satisfied; pretty well satisfied, unless a fourth or a fifth should be caught and sworn against; then the law was not satisfied until these were hanged by the neck also. And when the right man, the actual criminal, fell into the law's hands at least, he too must go as the two or three, the four or five innocent men charged with his crime, and found guilty by means which could only be found in a country corrupted by faction as Ireland has been;—he must go at last as they went before him.

Such was Ireland up to the time when the mysterious famine came, and, with a warrant more potent that that of all the sheriffs and sheriffs' officers of Ireland, (and they are no feeble band,) seized the crops and kept possession, from each and from all, Protestant and Catholic.

Clonmel, County of Tipperary, 29th January

As I had no pistols, powder, bullets, nor percussion caps, I was seriously warned on the Wednesday evening not to go out on the morning with the expedition to Dungarvan without them, particularly as it was not my intention to return with the military escort to Clonmel. Accordingly, as arming seemed the order of the day, I armed myself, and did it as follows:—I took one of my carpet bags and emptied everything of luggage kind out; took it to a baker's shop and purchased several shillings' worth of loaves of bread, and to a general dealer's shop, and purchased a piece of cheese. I put them in the bag, put the bag on the car by my side, ready, if any hungry Tipperarian or dweller on the Waterford mountains should present a blunderbuss at me, to put my hand into the bag, pull out, present, and throw to him a bullet of bread; not fearing but this style of defence would be more effective than a defence by powder and lead. Besides, it had this other advantage, that if bad roads, or bad weather, or other mischance detained me in the mountains, or if no inns or provisions shops could be met with on the road, I could begin and eat my ammunition; which if that ammunition had been gunpowder and leaden bullets, I could not have done.

Banagher, 19th February

A much greater breadth of land must come into cultivation now to supply the same amount of human subsistence as the total of 1,237, 441 acres of potatoes did. The cultivation is so generally defective, and soils so variable, that no attempt can be safely made to say how much land will require to be sown with oats to produce food in the place of potatoes. Some have said three acres of oats instead of one of potatoes. If the manure be applied to the oat crop or to some grain crop which would have been applied to the potatoes this will turn out an error of calculation. Three acres of grain should be more than equal to once acre of potatoes, unless the grain culture be very bad. Yet six acres of oats may be of less value than one acre of good potatoes.

The Irish agriculturists must grow root crops to feed cattle and produce manure. To effect this no plan will equal that of compelling them, by loans of money secured on the land, to employ a given number of men per hundred acres.

Extracts from Lord Dufferin and the Honourable G.G. Boyle, *Narrative of a Journey from Oxford to Skibbereen during the Year of the Irish Famine* (Oxford, 1847), 1–29

Frederick Temple Blackwood, Lord Dufferin (1826–1902) and George Frederick Boyle (1825–90) were students at Oxford when they journeyed to Skibbereen in County Cork to witness the famine. While there they distributed £50 that had been raised at Oxford and returned determined to raise more money on behalf of the poor.

e

S kibbereen was till this year a "comparatively" flourishing place; the shops were good, and the tradespeople very respectable; but now its wealth, trade, and prosperity, are completely prostrated. Almost the first thing we saw on entering the town were nine or ten deal coffins, of which before we had occasionally observed single specimens, ranged on end against the side of a house, just turned off from the maker's hands. Round the inn door were crowded numbers of the most wretched beings one had ever beheld, not so much clamouring for alms, as looking on in listless inactivity....

On enquiring for Mr. Townsend, we were told he was engaged at the Relief Committee; but presently meeting him on his return, we accompanied him to the Parsonage. On our way we introduced ourselves, and explained the object of our visit, begging of him to give us an account of how matters stood in the parish. To our enquiries he replied, that nothing could be worse; that the whole population was being destroyed; that the typhus fever had broken out, that two of his maid-servants had died from it; that from the frequency of deaths and the necessity of the dying, it was found impossible any longer to perform the accustomed rites of the Church, and that even the providing of coffins became a matter of difficulty....

We learnt, that the population of the parish is about 20,000; that the proportion of deaths has risen from 3 to upwards of 100; that the Union was crammed with far greater numbers than it was ever intended to contain; that generally there were three and four in each bed, a man recovering lying between two others in the height of raging fever; and that even still they were compelled to suffer multitudes to lie on the damp mud floor of their own cottages, the only alleviation being, that the frequency of deaths made continual room for new inmates. Some had even died in this uncared for condition, and their dead bodies had lain putrefying in the midst of the sick remnant of their families, none strong enough to remove them, until the rats and decay made it difficult to recognise that they had been human beings....

The cause of this is quite apparent; the small farmer upon the annihilation of his only support, unable to cultivate his patch of ground for want of immediate subsistence, is forced to resort to the public works, where he can at least earn **10d. a day**; while many of the larger farmers, the men who make the exports which astonish every one, and by the sale of their corn have alone flourished in the midst of the general calamity, are hoarding up their money in the Savings' Bank, withholding his due from the impoverished landlord, in order that they may on the first opportunity escape from the famine-stricken island to the unblighted harvests of America....

10d. a day: Half a stone of meal costs 1s. 8d. and is barely sufficient to afford a daily meal to a moderate family. (Footnote from original text.) Note: There were 12 pence (d.) in a shilling (s.), so the public works paid less than a shilling a day. Half a stone is seven pounds.

Conversing on these subjects, we reached a most miserable portion of the town; the houses were mere hovels, dark and dismal in the inside, damp and filthy to the most offensive degree. So universal and virulent was the fever, that we were forced to choose among several houses to discover one or more which it would be safe to enter. At length, Mr. Townsend singled out one. We stood on the threshold and looked in; the darkness of the interior was such, that we were scarcely able to distinguish objects; the walls were bare, the floor of mud, and not a vestige of furniture. The poor have pawned nearly every article of furniture which they possess, in order to obtain food; the number of tickets at the brokers is almost incredible; many have thus parted with the means of future subsistence, as in the case of some fishermen, who have pawned their boats and nets, and so deprived themselves of the power of deriving benefit from the fish, which abound along the coast. We entered another at no great distance: over a few peat embers a woman was crouching, drawing her only solace from their scanty warmth; she was suffering from diarrhoea: there seemed scarcely a single article of furniture or crockery in any part of the hut. The woman answered the enquiries of Mr. Townsend in a weak and desponding voice; and from what we could gather, there appeared to be several other human beings in different corners of the hovel, but in the darkness we were totally unable to distinguish them.

This case is cited, not as an instance of extreme destitution, but as proof of the miserable condition to which some, who were once in flourishing circumstances, have been reduced; for the woman, we were told, was the wife of a respectable tradesman, who but two months before was carrying on a thriving business; and the same reverse of fortune had been experienced by others likewise....

Our next visit was to the churchyard.... It was a very large grave-yard, and most of the graves had evidently long since been made; but in one corner there was about an acre of uneven and freshly-turned earth. This was the portion allotted to the late victims of famine and disease; by these graves, no service had been performed, no friends had stood, no priest had spoken words of hope, and of future consolation in a glorious eternity! The bodies had been daily thrown in, many without a coffin, one over another, the upper-most only hidden from the light of day by a bare three inches of earth, the survivors not even knowing the spot where those most dear to them lay sleeping....

Our tea at the Parsonage was sad and gloomy enough. Desirous of diverting the poor man's attention from the thoughts which were constantly preying on his mind, we tried a little general conversation; but though partially succeeding, we too often involuntarily returned to the pressing topics of the place. He told us, he was obliged to keep his outer gate locked, to prevent the influx of applicants who he could not relieve, and who might bring with them the infection. He distributes daily large supplies of bread, much of which is given to those found by the road side, unable from debility to proceed, or apply themselves to their work. One poor woman, sometime after the rest of the applicants had dispersed, was found lying on the ground in a pool of water before the windows, for when they have reached a certain state of hunger, food is often of no avail, and even fatal....

On our way, we called on Dr. Donovan, the zealous and indefatigable Physician of the place; he is night and day employed in ministering to the poor, and although he has visited every scene of death, and incurred every risk of infection, that merciful protection has hitherto extended to him, which so often shields the priest and the physician in the execution of their duties to the sick. He corroborated all Mr. Townsend's statements, and added an anecdote from his own knowledge. At some distance from Skibbereen there was a cottage, in which lay a man and his wife both sick of the fever; the woman died, and the husband had just sufficient strength to crawl out and bury the body in his garden. During the night he distinctly heard dogs scratching and howling over what he but too well knew was the lately made grave; he sent out his little girl to drive them away, but they only bit at her, and frightened her back into the cottage. The following day one of the neighbours brought back the head of the unfortunate woman, saying, "that his dog had brought it home!" [...]

We succeeded in hiring an outside jaunting car, to which an extra horse was attached. While this was being prepared, we sent out for an immense basket-full of loaves, intending to distribute them to the occasional starving beings we were sure to meet with by the way; but some of the people of the town had learnt our intention, and collected in a great crowd under the window to the number of 100 or 200, mostly women. It was a frightful sight to see those pale eager faces staring up at us, uttering all manner of entreaties. Of course there was no hope of carrying off the bread, indeed it would have been cruel to have made the attempt; the only question was, how to divide it. At first we sent it down to the door, but the rush was so great, that that scheme became impracticable; and it only remained, to throw it out of the window. One can never forget what followed; the fighting, the screaming, the swaying to and fro of the human mass, as it rushed in the direction of some morsel, the entreaties and gestures by which each one sought to attract our attention to herself, and above all the insatiable expression of the crowd as it remained unsatisfied and undiminished at the exhaustion of our loaves—for what were they among so many!

DOCUMENT 17:

Newspaper Coverage of Famine Diseases

> The largest cause of excess mortality during the famine years was not starvation but disease, which ravaged the weakened population. Typhus, cholera, and dysentery ran rampant across all of Ireland, and were particularly deadly in the close quarters of prisons and workhouses.

e

Nation, 13 March 1847

STATE OF THE COUNTRY—ARMAGH

It is stated that nearly 400 paupers have died in the Lurgan workhouse during the last eight weeks. In Armagh there is some dread that mortality will spread beyond its usual limits in the workhouse there. Typhus fever has appeared, and the medical attendant is at present ill of the disease. On Wednesday, the remains of fourteen of the paupers were lying in the dead-house.

London *Times*, 13 May 1848

DEATH OF LORD LURGAN

Another Victim to the prevailing contagion has fallen in the person of this much respected nobleman. The report of his Lordship's death was current here yesterday evening; but as the Belfast papers which reached last night had no confirmation of the rumour, it was hoped that it might prove unfounded ... obituary notice which appears in the *Newry Telegraph* of this day:—

"With unaffected sorrow we announce the demise of the Right Hon. Charles Brownlow, Baron Lurgan. The melancholy event, the effect of an attack of typhus fever, took place on Yesterday (Friday morning), at Lurgan Castle."

London Illustrated News, 6 April 1850

THE CHOLERA

The cholera has been committing ravages in the remote partof Kerry without attracting much attention elsewhere. The following return in the Cork Reporter, from Cahirciveen, shows the extent to which the epidemic has prevailed there:——"The total number of cases of cholera treated in hospital in Valencia, up to the 26th, 42; new cases none. Discharged cured, 15; died, 22; remaining under treatment, 5. Cahirciveen—total number treated for cholera in hospital since the 16th Jan., 168. Discharged cured, 174; died, 77; under treatment, 17.

Newspaper Coverage of Civil Unrest

As the famine took its toll, newspaper coverage noted increasing instances of civil unrest across Ireland. Peasants lashed out against the gentry and each other, towns were looted for food, and murders spiked.

e

London Illustrated News, 3 **October 1846**

RIOTING AND BLOODSHED AT DUNGARVAN

We regret to hear that serious riots have taken place in the town of Dungarvan, County Waterford, which it is feared will lead to loss of life. The particulars are contained in the following letter, dated:—

"Dungarvan, Tuesday Evening.

"Serious riots, I grieve to say, have taken place this town. Yesterday vast numbers of people, to the amount or eleven or twelve thousand, marched in here from the surrounding country, and proceeded to attack bakers' shops, from which they took quantities of bread. The mob were about to attack the stores of merchants and others, but, fortunately, a troop of dragoons, which had been ordered in consequence of the apprehension of riots, arrived from Kilmacthomas, and, with the co-operation of the military force already here, prevented further depredations. In the afternoon, however, in the dusk of some of the evening, some of the populace commenced throwing stones, and the dragoons had to charge them repeatedly. The people, however, still continued throwing stones, and the state of affairs began to look very serious. The dragoons were then ordered to fire; and, it is stated, about twenty shots were discharged. Two men were seriously wounded. They are still living; but several others, it is feared, were wounded more or less severely amongst the crowd, who fled subsequently to the firing. The town has been since perfectly free from disturbance; but dreadful excitement and alarm prevail amongst all classes here. It was owing to the commendable forbearance of the military that much more disastrous results did not ensue.

"These riots are attributable to discontent amongst the peasantry as to the amount of wages on the public works—no definite sum having been fixed as yet. In the first instance, eight pence a day was offered, but the people refused that rate as utterly insufficient. Ten pence was then offered, but also refused. In the course of yesterday, a written paper was handed from the people to the magistrates, requiring that their wages should be one shilling per day, and that they should be supplied with Indian meal at a corresponding price by the stone, to enable them to give sustenance to their families. My own impression is, that if those terms are complied with, we shall have no further disturbances."

London Illustrated News, 24 October 1846

RIOTOUS PROCEEDINGS AT MALLOW

The following letter from a Correspondent at Mallow, dated October 19, will give an idea of the temper of the peasantry in that part of the country:—"Early this morning a number of the peasantry, to the amount of 200 or 300 persons, entered the town for the purpose of seeking employment on the railroad now in progress between this and the city of Cork. On applying to the contractor they were informed that the work was impeded by a proprietor on the line, who refused to allow the road to pass through his lands until certain terms of his own were complied with, and that they could not be employed that day; whereupon they pillaged some bakers' shops, and proceeded, in military order, armed with spades, shovels, pickaxes, &c., to Mr. Flinn's residence, within a mile and a half of the town, and soon returned with him a prisoner, marched him through the main street, and compelled him to enter into such arrangements as to enable the work to proceed tomorrow. Mr. Flinn is an old man between 70 and 80; he was mounted on a horse in the midst of the mob, who were all on foot, and marched in quick time through the streets. They appeared to be of the lowest and most miserable class. They stopped at a baker's shop which escaped the plunder this morning, and compelled Flinn to buy them two or three pounds' worth of bread. Loaves were thrown in showers from the upper windows of the house to them, when the scene became awful though ridiculous. They then took him before the contractor."

London Illustrated News, 24 October 1846

THE LATE MURDER IN TIPPERARY

Gaynor, the poor man who was wounded in the shocking manner described in our paper last week, died in the most excruciating agony. A Coroner's Jury has found a verdict of "Death from gunshot wounds, inflicted by some person or persons at present unknown." The father of Gaynor is about ninety years of age, and rents a farm of one hundred acres, at ten shillings an acre.

London Illustrated News, 11 November 1846

ATTACK UPON THE GREAT SOUTHERN AND WESTERN RAILWAY

The Cork Examiner contains an account of an attack made on Monday morning on the works of this line in progress at Rathpeacon, about a mile and a half beyond Blackpool. A number of labourers, in all amounting to nearly 1,000, assembled on that morning, and immediately proceeded to Rathpeacon, where the works of this line commence. They attacked the men employed there to the number of 60 or 70, and compelled them to desist from work; they then destroyed the wheelbarrows, pickaxes, and other implements required in this description of work. It is said that the overseers were also maltreated. A military force was about to be dispatched to the scene of outrage, in order to prevent further aggression.

Freeman's Journal, 12 March 1847

STATE OF THE COUNTRY

Shinrone—On Friday night last, the soup kitchen of William Trench, Esq. of Cangort Park, was broken open, and a quantity of rice, Indian meal, and other articles stolen. Mr. Trench established the soup kitchen at his own private expense, and Mrs. Guy Atkinson benevolently devoted a large portion of her time to seeing the soup prepared.

London Times, 5 November 1847

ATROCIOUS ASSASSINATION

Another victim, selected from the landlord class, has perished by the arm of the … About 20 minutes past 6 o'clock, yesterday evening, as major Mahon … in the county of Roscommon, was returning to his residence, after a close day's attendance at a meeting of the Roscommon board of Poor Law Guardians, he was shot dead by an unseen hand when within about four miles from home. The event has created the utmost alarm, and the question "whose turn will be next" is heard from every side. The doomed gentlemen had made all the preliminary arrangements for giving employment to a vast number of labourers on works of drainage, and was on the day of his death engaged in the benevolent task of dismantling the Roscommon board from turning adrift a body of paupers for whom the workhouse accommodation was insufficient.

London Illustrated News, 8 January 1848

THREATENING NOTICES AGAINST THE ROMAN CATHOLIC

The Rev. Henry Brennan, parish priest of Kilglass, Roscommon, has addressed, through the Evening Post, a letter to the Lord Lieutenant, in which he states that he has received, through the Post-Office, a threatening letter, of which he supplies a copy. The letter contains a resolution, passed by twelve individuals calling themselves Protestants, binding them by oath to retaliate, by murdering the priests of the parishes in which any murder may be committed by the peasantry. Mr. Brennan adds:—"I understand similar ones have been sent to all the parochial Catholic clergy in this county. Your Excellency may perceive, by the description of paper, the scroll and style of writing, and the fact of its being posted in Dublin, that it must be the production of persons moving in a respectable sphere, and who evidently could do it better if they pleased. It is my firm conviction, and of those with whom I have been speaking on the subject, that they have been fabricated by a junta of rabid parsons, for the purpose of reviving religious bigotry and sectarian animosities, which every good man should deprecate."

London Illustrated News, 8 January 1848

ASSASSINATION

On Tuesday night last, between eight and nine o'clock, at Ballydine, within four or five miles of Cashel, a small farmer named Thomas Brown, was shot dead within a few yards of his own house, on the high road. He received five pellets in the breast, and his death was instantaneous.

PART 3

Government Responses
to the Famine

DOCUMENT 19:

Extracts from *Instructions to Committees of Relief Districts, Extracted from Minutes of the Proceedings of the Commissioners Appointed in Reference to the Apprehended Scarcity*, 1846

> The Poor Law Commission in Dublin sent out these instructions to local relief committees in early 1846 expressing how to respond to the emerging famine.

ei

Dublin Castle, 28 February 1846

The Commission having had under their consideration the necessity of establishing local committees, properly organised, in the several districts where destitution is likely to prevail, through whose superintendence the approach and progress of distress in such localities may be watched, and the means of relief administered according to the instructions of Government;

It is Resolved…

4. That a most important duty of the committee will be to promote, by every means in their power, the most profitable and most natural sources of employment in their district, by stimulating private enterprise; by urging the improvement and drainage of farms and estates, and by promulgating a knowledge of the facilities afforded by the Legislature for these objects, many of which are not under the consideration of Parliament, to meet the present emergency.…

5. That it is evident, and is also in strict accordance with the views and instructions of the Government, that the landholders and other ratepayers are the parties both legally and morally answerable for affording due relief to the destitute poor, and that the same parties are, from their local influence, and their knowledge of the situation and wants of the people in their

neighbourhood, best able to furnish such relief without waste or misdirection of the means employed.

That the measures to be adopted by the officers of Government are to be considered merely as auxiliary to those which it is the duty of the persons possessed of property in each neighbourhood to adopt.

That the local committee should, therefore, put themselves in communication with such persons, and should solicit subscriptions from them in proportion to their means, and to the extent of the distress in the locality to which they belong.

That where, notwithstanding such subscriptions, some assistance is likely to be required from the Government, a list of sums subscribed, together with a list of the landlords who do not contribute, should be confidentially brought under the notice of the Lord Lieutenant, who, after due consideration of the case, will determine on the sum to be contributed from the funds at this disposal in aid of the local subscription.

But those landlords are not to be considered in the list of persons refusing to contribute, who, by farm drainage, by other works of a more general nature on their estates, or by residence and employment, enable their tenants to meet the present emergency without an appeal to the public assistance.

In cases where there may arise a scarcity of food within a district, or the price of food may have been artificially raised, the Government will be prepared to transmit to the local committee, at cost price, including the expense of carriage, a quantity of food corresponding to the amount of the subscriptions paid in for that purpose, and to place that food in the hands of the local committee for the distribution, on their own responsibility, at cost price, or as wages of labour to destitute persons employed on local works, or when absolute destitution is united with inability to labour, in gratuitous donations....

7. That in cases wherein any assistance is afforded by Government, either in aid of local subscriptions, or otherwise, the following rules are to be invariably observed in the administration of relief:

1st: A task of work shall be required from every person capable of giving it, who applies for relief.

2nd: The payments for the work performed shall be made in food, and shall in every case be limited to such quantity of food as will be sufficient to support the workman and the helpless persons of this family.

3rd: If in any case it be impracticable to pay in food, the payments in money shall be limited to what is absolutely necessary for the above purpose.

4th: Gratuitous relief shall be afforded only to those persons who are entirely incapable of giving a day's work, and who have no able-bodied relative on whom they are dependent, and in these cases only in which their reception in the workhouse of the union to which they belong is, from want of room, impracticable: and, lastly,

5th: The works in which destitute persons are employed shall be in prosecution of some public improvement, approved by this commission, within or adjacent to the distressed locality, and shall be such as will be capable of being brought at once to a close when the circumstances of the people are improved.

8. That the committee should obtain townland lists, with minute reports of the circumstances of each family from whom application for relief may be made; that at their meetings, certificates or tickets should be given to such only as are ascertained to be without means of providing food for their families; that such certificates or tickets be the authority to the superintendent of the public works for receiving the persons to whom they are granted; and that a register of all certificates or tickets granted by the committee be preserved in a book to be supplied for that purpose by this Commission....

J.P. Kennedy, Secretary

Extracts from Speech by Earl Grey in the House of Lords, 23 March 1846, *Hansard*

Henry Grey, the 3rd Earl of Grey, was an influential member of the British political establishment and a member of the Liberal party, which was out of power at the time of this speech in March of 1846. Under the Acts of Union, Ireland was represented in the United Kingdom Parliament in both the House of Lords and the House of Commons, but its interests were generally subordinate to those of England.

ℰ

The state of Ireland is one which is notorious. We know the ordinary condition of that country to be one both of lawlessness and wretchedness. It is so described by every competent authority. There is not an intelligent foreigner coming to our shores, who turns his attention to the state of Ireland, but who bears back with him such a description. Ireland is the one weak place in the solid fabric of British power—Ireland is the one deep (I had almost said ineffaceable) blot upon the brightness of British honour. Ireland is our disgrace. It is the reproach, the standing disgrace, of this country, that Ireland remains in the condition she is. It is so regarded throughout the whole civilized world. To ourselves we may palliate it if we will, and disguise the truth; but we cannot conceal it from others. There is not, as I have said, a foreigner—no matter whence he comes, be it from France, Russia, Germany, or America—there is no native of any foreign country different as their forms of government may be, who visits Ireland, and who on his return does not congratulate himself that he sees nothing comparable with the condition of that country at home. If such be the state of things, how then does it arise, and what is its cause? My Lords, it is only by misgovernment that such evils could have been produced: the mere fact that Ireland is in so deplorable and wretched a condition saves whole volumes of argument, and is of itself a complete and irrefutable proof of the misgovernment to which she has been subjected. Nor can we lay to our souls the "flattering unction" that this misgovernment was only of ancient date, and has not been our doing. It is not enough in our own excuse to say, "No wonder this state of things exists: the Government of Ireland before the Union was the most ingeniously bad that was ever contrived in the face of the world; it was the Government of a corrupt minority, sustained by the superior power of this great country in oppressing and tyrannizing over the great body of the nation; such a system of government could not fail to leave behind it a train of fearful evils from which we are still suffering at the present day." To a certain extent, no doubt, this is true. No man has a stronger opinion than I regarding the iniquitous system of misgovernment in Ireland prior to the Union. But the Union is not an event of yesterday. It is nearly half a century since that measure passed. For nearly fifty years, now, Ireland has been under the immediate control of the Imperial Parliament. Since it has been so, a whole generation has grown up, and is now passing away to be replaced by another; and in that time, I ask you, what impression has been made upon the evils of Ireland? It is true some good has been done. I gladly acknowledge that many useful measures have been adopted, which have, I hope, contributed in some respects to the improvement of Ireland; but none of these measures have gone to the root of the social disease to which Ireland is a prey; in the worst symptoms of which no amelioration whatever can be observed: the wretchedness and misery of the population have experienced no abatement. Upon that point I can quote high authority. I find that the Commission presided over by a noble Earl, whom I do not now see in his place (the Earl of Devon), reported the year before last, that "improvement was indeed beginning to take place in agriculture; but there had been no corresponding advance in the condition and comforts of the labouring classes." By the Report of that Commission we are informed, that the agricultural labourers are still suffering the greatest privations and hardships, and still depend upon casual and precarious employment for their subsistence; that they are badly fed, badly clothed, badly housed, and badly paid for their labour; and the Commissioners conclude this part of their Report by saying—We cannot forbear expressing our strong sense of the patient endurance which the labouring classes have generally exhibited under sufferings greater, we believe, than the people of any other country have ever endured. This is an authentic statement, and comes from a Commission appointed only the other day to inquire into the state of the people of Ireland. It is a Report describing the state of things in that country before the failure of the potato crop, and the Commissioners tell you that the sufferings of the great mass of the people of that country are greater than those of the population of any other country in Europe. This is indeed a fearful statement, coming from such authority. But there is another symptom of the condition of Ireland, which seems to me even more alarming than the prevalence of distress—I mean the general alienation of the whole mass of the nation from the institutions under which they live, and the existence in their minds of a strong deep feeling of hostility to the form of government under which they are placed. This feeling, which is the worst feature in the case, seems to be rather gaining strength than to be diminishing. I am led to that opinion by what I heard two years ago fall from the Secretary of State for the **Home Department** in the House of Commons. I heard

Home Department: Government department in charge of internal affairs of the United Kingdom.

right hon. Gentleman: A
common honorific used in
Parliament; in this case Earl
Grey is referring to Sir James
Graham who was home
secretary to Sir Robert Peel
from 1841 until 1846. See
also Document 21.

that **right hon. Gentleman**—and it was a statement which made a deep
impression upon me—I heard the right hon. Gentleman, in answer to a
speech made by a noble Friend of mine, distinctly admit that we had military occupation of Ireland, but that in no other sense could it be said to be
governed; that it was occupied by troops, not governed like England. Such
was the admission of the Secretary of State for the Home Department. And
now, my Lords, I ask you, is that a state of things which ought to continue?
And I ask is not such a state of things, so clearly established by authorities
so high and indisputable, a good ground for inferring that there is something
wrong in the policy which has been hitherto pursued towards Ireland; and
that some measures different in character, and more effectual than those we
have been in the habit of trusting to, are necessary to meet the exigency?
That is the only inference which appears to me to follow from the premises
universally admitted. I cannot understand how any man with the use of
his reason could arrive at a different conclusion. I say, then, some change is
absolutely necessary; we are bound to endeavour to apply some remedy to
the evils of Ireland more efficient than any which have yet been attempted.

DOCUMENT 21:

Extracts from Sir Robert Peel, *Memoirs of the Right Honourable Sir Robert Peel* (London, 1857), 117, 121–23, 167–69

A British politician and member of the Conservative (Tory) party, Peel was prime minister of the United Kingdom in 1834–35 and from 1841–46. Lord Heytesbury was the Lord-Lieutenant of Ireland in 1845; while the blight had been reported in August of 1845, it was not until October, during the harvest, that the severity of the problem became apparent. Peel's response to the famine—to remove protectionist trade regulations (the Corn Laws) and import large quantities of cheap food—would eventually lead to a split in the Conservative Party, and Peel's own political downfall.

e

Letter to Peel from **Sir J. Graham**, 17 October 1845

I quite feel with you, that the most accurate and detailed information must be obtained from Ireland before we can venture to form a decision which, though arising from temporary circumstances, may produce momentous changes of a permanent character.

The suspension of the existing Corn Law on the avowed admission that its maintenance aggravates the evil of scarcity, and that its remission is the surest mode of restoring plenty, would render its re-enactment or future operation quite impracticable; yet if the evil be as urgent as I fear it will be, to this suspension we shall be driven.

I have entreated the Lord-Lieutenant to give us the most ample information. The real truth cannot be known until the digging is concluded: this will not be before the first week of November.

Sir J. Graham: James Graham, Secretary of the Home Department under Peel.

Letter to Lord Heytesbury, Lord-Lieutenant of Ireland, 15 October 1845

The accounts from Ireland of the potato crop, confirmed as they are by your high authority, are very alarming.

We must consider whether it is possible by legislation, or by the exercise of prerogative, to apply a remedy to the great evil with which we are threatened. The application of such remedy involves considerations of the utmost magnitude. The remedy is the removal of all impediments to the import of all kinds of human food—that is, the total and absolute repeal for ever of all duties on all articles of subsistence.

I believe that practically there would be no alternative. To remit the duty on Indian corn expressly for the purpose of averting famine, would make it very invidious to retain a duty on other species of corn more generally applicable to the food of man.

You might remit nominally for one year; but who will re-establish the Corn Laws once **abrogated** though from a casual and temporary pressure?

abrogated: Repealed.

I have good ground therefore for stating that the application of a temporary remedy to a temporary evil does in this particular case involve considerations of the utmost and most lasting importance.

You must therefore send us from time to time the most authentic information you can. There is such a tendency in Ireland to disregard accuracy and to exaggerate, that one is unwilling to give hasty credence to Irish statements. There can, however, I fear, be no reason to doubt that the failure of the potato crop will be very general.

Has the recent fine weather (which has, I presume, extended to Ireland) had a favourable effect? What is the price of potatoes in the different markets? Is that price rapidly increasing?

I fear the lowness of price—even if it exist—might be no indication of abundance. There might be an undue quantity of inferior potatoes sent for sale, for fear of rapid decay if they were kept on hand.

Can you employ any persons to collect information to be relied on, in the chief potato growing districts in Ireland?

Would a person of intelligence specially sent to Galway, Cork, &c. &c., have better means of ascertaining the facts and the prospects of the failure than can be derived from written reports from stipendiary magistrates or others?

The private letters which reach me are very discouraging. Still action in this case, on the authority of the Executive, is so important a matter, that it ought to be grounded on nothing short of moral certainty of its necessity.

At what period would the pressure be felt? Would it be immediate if the reports of the full extent of the evil are confirmed, or is there a stock of old potatoes sufficient to last for a certain time?

I need not recommend to you the utmost reserve as to the future, I mean as to the possibility of Government interference. There could be none without summoning Parliament, to adopt measures or confirm those of the Executive.

In this section of his memoirs Peel reflects on his response to the political crisis posed by the Famine.

It was not difficult indeed to find such reasons, and not unsafe to insist on them. There was the full assurance of support from powerful majorities in each House of Parliament well-disposed to the maintenance of the Corn

Laws. I was not insensible to the evil of acting counter to the will of those majorities, of severing party connections, and of subjecting public men to suspicion and reproach and the loss of public confidence; but I felt a strong conviction that such evils were light in comparison with those which must be incurred by the sacrifice of national interests to party attachments, and by deferring necessary precautions against scarcity of food for the purpose of consulting appearances and preserving the show of personal consistency. I felt, too, that the injury to the character of public men, the admitted evil of shaking confidence in their integrity and honour, would be only temporary; that if a public man resolved to take a course which his own deliberate judgement approved—if that course were manifestly opposed to his own private and political interests—if he preferred it with all its sacrifices to some other, the taking of which would exempt him from personal responsibility, would enable him to escape much obloquy, and to retain the goodwill and favour of his party—I felt, I say, a strong conviction that no clamour and misrepresentation, however sustained and systematic, would prevent the ultimate development of the truth, the ultimate acknowledgement that party interests would not have been promoted—the honour of public men would not have been maintained—the cause of Constitutional Government would not have been served, if a Minister had at a critical period shrunk from the duty of giving that advice which he believed to be the best, and from incurring every personal sacrifice which the giving of that advice might entail.

DOCUMENT 22:

Extracts from Speech by Lord John Russell in the House of Commons, 17 August 1846, *Hansard*

After Sir Robert Peel was forced to resign in June of 1846, Lord John Russell, the leader of the Liberal Party, became prime minister; he would remain in office until 1852. In this speech early in his term he outlined his plan for responding to the famine. Russell's plan relied on a system of public works, as opposed to importing cheap food.

ev

Sir, it has, therefore, become our duty to consider in what manner we should propose to Parliament to make provision for some employment for the labouring people of Ireland—proposing that to Parliament for which we require the direct sanction of Parliament, and at the same time affording to the Government a discretion to take such measures as any emergency may in their opinion render necessary, of which measures they would afterwards give an account to Parliament. Sir, it has appeared to us, with regard to the first measure to be adopted, that while there ought to be public works, and those public works ought to be undertaken under due control, we should not, with regard at least to the general measures proposed, defray the cost of those works by means of grants, but by loans, to be repaid by the baronies and the counties in the districts for which they are granted. We, therefore, propose to introduce a Bill to this effect, that the **Lord Lieutenant** shall have power, on recommendation made to him, to summon a **barony sessions or a county sessions** for works for relief of the poor. When those sessions shall been assembled, they will be empowered and required to order such public works as may be necessary for the employment of the people and for their relief. I say, "empowered and required," because it is intended that it shall be incumbent on them, on being summoned to those sessions, to order those works. The choice of the works will be left to them, and they will be put in execution by the officers of the Board of Works. When I say that the choice will be left to them, I mean that they shall point out the works which they consider necessary, but the approbation of the Government will be required, that is to say, of the Board of Works, before those works can be finally undertaken. It is further proposed, that advances shall be made from the Treasury, for the purposes of those works, to be repaid in ten years at 3½ per cent interest, the lowest rate ever taken for works of this kind. The whole amount so advanced by the Government will, however, have to be repaid. I should also state that in levying for the repayment of the money, and for

Lord Lieutenant: By August of 1846 the Lord-Lieutenant was John Ponsonby, the Earl of Bessborough.

barony sessions or a county sessions: A local administrative body meeting for a fixed term.

the interest, those levies will not be made according to the assessment for the county rate, but according to the assessment for the poor rate....

Having already stated the evils which have in practice arisen from interference by the Government with the supply of the public food, I have only to add that we do not propose to interfere with the regular mode by which Indian corn and other kinds of grain may be brought into the country. We propose to leave that trade as much at liberty as possible. But there may be particular cases, as there were in 1836 and 1839, where, in consequence of the part of the country where the famine prevailed being very inaccessible, it became necessary to employ the commissariat officers. As a general rule, however, we still take care not to interfere with the regular operations of merchants for the supply of food to the country, or with the retail trade, which was much deranged by the operations of last year....

Sir, as I stated at the commencement, this is a special case, requiring the intervention of Parliament. I consider that the circumstances I have stated, of that kind of food which constitutes the subsistence of millions of people in Ireland, being subjected to the dreadful ravages of this disease, constitute this a case of exception, and render it imperative on the Government and the Parliament to take extraordinary measures for relief. I trust that the course I propose to pursue will not be without its counterbalancing advantages; that it will show the poorest among the Irish people that we are not insensible, here, to the claims which they have on us as the Parliament of the United Kingdom; that the whole credit of the Treasury and means of the country are ready to be used as it is our bounden duty to use them, and will, whenever they can be usefully applied, be so disposed as to avert famine, and to maintain the people of Ireland; and that we are now disposed to take advantage of the unfortunate spread of this disease among the potatoes, to establish public works which may be of permanent utility. I trust, Sir, that the present state of things will have that counterbalancing advantage in the midst of many misfortunes and evil consequences. I know not that I need detain you any longer, than to assure the Committee and the House, that we consider that our predecessors in office did show a very laudable anxiety to meet the evil—that the remedies they applied were suited to the occasion—that we shall endeavour to imitate the spirit in which they acted, while we shall endeavour to take advantage of their experience to correct errors which were inevitable in consequence of such unforeseen difficulties.

DOCUMENT 23:

Extracts from *Correspondence Explanatory of the Measures Adopted by Her Majesty's Government for the Relief of Distress Arising from the Failure of the Potato Crop in Ireland* (London, 1846), 25–26, 1, 217–19

The earliest government response to the famine consisted of importing and distributing large quantities of Indian corn. There were unforeseen challenges in introducing a new and unfamiliar food to people who subsisted on boiled potatoes. The Irish did not know how to prepare cornmeal, and it tended to cause stomach problems.

ev

Commissary-General Hewetson to Sir Robert Peel, Southampton, 5 November 1845

Trusting the subject of this communication will apologise for my presumption in addressing the first minister of the Crown, I beg leave most respectfully to bring under your notice, with reference to the want to be apprehended among the labouring classes in the country and Ireland, arising out of the disease so generally fatal to the potato crops, that a cheap, nutritious, and excellent substitute for the potato, viz., Indian corn meal, can be procured in great abundance in the United States of America, at a cost, in comparison with other substitutes, exceedingly low. My long residence in North America as a public officer enables me to state, with great confidence, that should Her Majesty's Government contemplate the formation of magazines in this country and Ireland for the supply, in the course of the winter, of food to the destitute classes, Indian corn meal would be the cheapest substitute for the potato, equally, if not more substantially, nutritious, and as simple in its mode of preparation. Its use in the United States is most universal among the peasantry and labouring people. Should its introduction by Her Majesty's Government into this country, for this specific purpose, be deemed expedient, by prompt and secret measures, it can be cheaply and readily purchased to any extent and shipped from the ports of New York and Baltimore, so as to arrive here in January, 1846; the arrangement would, of course, be temporary, to meet an emergency, and should such an emergency be proved, I have no hesitation in adding that Indian corn meal in every point of view, with great economy as a leading feature, is one of the best descriptions of supply that can be laid in for gratuitous distribution. Whatever prejudices, if any, may exist, as to its use as an article of food in this country, will, I should say, on trial, with simple directions for its preparation, immediately cease.

Respectfully soliciting to apologise for intruding this letter.

Sir Robert Peel's Reply, Whitehall, 9 November 1845

Sir Robert Peel presents his compliments to Mr. Heweston, and is much
obliged by the communication which Mr. Heweston has very properly
addressed directly to Sir Robert Peel.

Letter from Mr. Charles Trevelyan to **Sir Randolph Routh**, Treasury,
3 February 1846

Sir Randolph Routh:
A British Army officer,
from 1845 to 1848 he was
supervising the distribution
of Famine relief in Ireland.

I feel satisfied that you will concentrate your whole energies on the direct
and practical measures for the relief of the suffering to be anticipated from
the impending scarcity.

Whether we regard the possible extent of that suffering, the suddenness
with which it may come upon us in various points, or the fearful consequences of its not being promptly relieved, the subject is one which calls
for all of our foresight and power of arrangement.

That indirect permanent advantages will accrue to Ireland from the
scarcity, and the measures taken for its relief, I entertain no doubt; but if we
were to pursue these incidental objects to the neglect of any of the precautions immediately required to save the people from actual starvation, our
responsibility would be fearful indeed.

Besides, the greatest improvement of all which could take place in
Ireland would be to teach the people to depend upon themselves for devel-
oping the resources of their country, instead of having recourse to the
assistance of the Government on every occasion. Much has been done of
late years to put this important matter on its proper footing; but if a firm
stand is not made against the prevailing disposition to take advantage of
this crisis to break down all barriers, the true permanent interests of the
country will, I am convinced, suffer in a manner which will be irreparable
in our time.

Up to the present date, nothing has, so far as I am aware, been done
which should prevent a perfectly sound line from being taken, and one
which will bear looking back upon, after the excitement arising from present
circumstances shall have passed away.

Your official letter of the 1st instant, and its enclosure, are of such a
thoroughly practical character that, by taking upon the several paragraphs
seriatim, and commenting freely upon them, I shall be able to come to a
satisfactory understanding with you on every point.

seriatim: One after another.

I continue to be of opinion that we ought to rely upon the organized establishments and active discipline of the constabulary and revenue forces, for the person to be employed in responsible, though subordinate situations, such as the charge of detached depots. The officers, and others of the police and coast guard acquitted themselves, I believe, greatly to their credit in charge of the oatmeal stations on the coast of Donegal, under Sir J. Hill, in 1836; and it is reasonable to expect that persons whose prospects in life depend entirely upon their giving satisfaction in the public departments to which they belong, will exert themselves more, and be more trustworthy, than those who have been suddenly called from private life, and may therefore be tempted to make the most of the opportunity to lay up a store for future use....

You may therefore consider this outline as so far settled, and remaining to be filled up at such times, and to such extent, as the progress of events may require; it being of the utmost importance that our measures should not precede the actual necessity of the case.

Letter from Sir Randolph Routh to Mr. Charles Trevelyan, Dublin Castle, 31 July 1846

As the scene of our operations during the last active service in Ireland is now drawing to a close, I think it will be desirable as a reference, and perhaps as a guide, to lay before you for the information of the Right Honourable my Lords Commissioners of Her Majesty's Treasury a trace of the course we have pursued.

I received their Lordship's instructions in November last, to proceed to Dublin, where I was appointed a member of a Relief Commission to inquire into the scarcity arising from the loss of the potato crop, and of which the Right Honourable **E. Lucas** was chairman.

E. Lucas: Edward Lucas of Castle Shane, County Monaghan, was an Irish politician and member of the Relief Commission.

At an early period in the autumn of 1845, the general blight in the potato crop throughout the south and west districts, and detached parts of the north and east, excited so much alarm, that though it did not exaggerate the fact, the apprehension was so great that it antedated the period when the supply would fail. The crop was unusually large, and early in December a very severe frost set in, and appeared partially to arrest the progress of the disease under certain circumstances, and in certain situations. There was also a marked capriciousness in the disease itself, leaving particular fields untouched and healthy, whilst others in their immediate vicinity were almost a mass of corruption.

None of the remedies suggested for the preservation of this crop were successful, but that which most assisted this object, was the plan adopted by the peasantry amongst themselves, of leaving the potatoes in the ground until they were required for use.

I have not been able to obtain any satisfactory explanation of this calamity, which has spread simultaneously over the greater part of Europe and America, and in every diversity of climate, and it is as difficult to decide whether the fungus is the cause or effect of the disease. Those who advocate the latter, and that a sound plant is only to be raised by renovation from the seed, have not succeeded in their experiment, the result being nearly an equal division between sound and diseased plants. The plants raised from the seed did not produce one sort only, but exhibited promiscuously every variety of the potato.

As soon as the rains set in towards the end of January and until March, the partial suspension of the disease gave way, and reappeared with greater virulence, not only amongst the potatoes already tainted but manifesting itself amongst the sound pits in districts which had hitherto resisted it.

These variations in climate and the effects they produce, first in diminishing the anxiety and apprehension in the fall, and subsequently in confirming all these fears, will account for the diversity of opinions which prevailed in relation to the extent of the scarcity....

The quantity of Indian corn and Indian corn meal imported from America into Cork through the house of Messrs. Baring Brothers and Co., somewhat exceeded eight thousand tons.

No individual could have undertaken it, for the duty was a prohibition, and being a new article of food untried, and of doubtful success, it was altogether out of the sphere of mercantile speculation on the large scale on which only it could have the desired result....

Having procured a great variety of **receipts** for the use of Indian corn meal from the United States, I embodied them in a small pamphlet which was distributed through the country.

receipts: Recipes.

It should be very much cooked or baked; and when used as bread, it is much improved by mixing the yeast with one-sixth of wheaten flour,[1] using hot water, and after it has arisen, to add the five parts of Indian meal.

But the mush, or **stirabout**, seems to be the favourite preparation in Ireland, of which a large quantity is made at once to economize the fuel, and then eaten cold, or cut in slices and repassed through the oven.

stirabout: Porridge.

It has become so popular, that the oatmeal which we have in store is seldom asked for, though offered at a low price.

The Indian meal is so nutritious, that one meal in the morning supports the labourer throughout the day; and it has been remarked by the peasantry that where it has been used, fever has been less prevalent, or has entirely disappeared.

---

1 Flour was beyond the means of most potato-dependent Irish poor.

The great object which now presented itself was to postpone the assistance of Government to the latest possible period, and to enforce the necessity of self-exertion as a claim to that assistance, for once commenced this aid could not be suspended or withheld without danger to the public peace. The uncertainty of the demand to be made upon us, of which it was impossible to frame any calculation, and the limited quantity in store in comparison with the exigencies for the whole country, made it an important object to postpone the commencement of the issue, until it was indispensable, so that the resources within the reach of the community might be first applied to their wants, before the depots in reserve were opened for their supply. The expectation and certainty, of it, when the great pressure arrived, satisfied the people in the midst of many sacrifices, and induced in the meanwhile a proportionate activity and outlay amongst the landed proprietors....

One of the main objects in these instructions went to establish, that the aid of the Government should be only auxiliary to the efforts of the people, and the large amount subscribed, and much of that in small sums from 6d. to 10s., afford a gratifying proof of the good feeling of the proprietors.

DOCUMENT 24:

Bill to Make Provision for the Punishment of Vagrants and Persons Offending against the Laws in Force for the Relief of the Destitute Poor in Ireland, 15 April 1847

Vagrancy was regarded as a serious problem by Poor Law Commissioners who feared that it would undermine the Poor Law structure. Begging was widespread during the famine and strict laws such as this were meant to discourage it. However, this legislation does not seem to have been regularly enforced.[2]

e

Whereas it is expedient to make further provision for the punish-ment of Beggars and Vagrants and persons offending against the laws in force for the relief of the Destitute Poor in Ireland; Be it therefore enacted by the Queen's most Excellent Majesty, by and with the Advice and Consent of the Lords Spiritual and Temporal, and Commons, in this present Parliament assembled, and by the Authority of the same, that so much of an Act passed in the second year of Her present Majesty, intituled, "An Act for the more effectual Relief of the Destitute Poor in Ireland," as provides for the punishment of persons deserting and leaving their wives or any children whom such persons may be liable to maintain, so that such wives or children should become destitute and be relieved in the workhouse of a Union, shall be repealed.

And be it enacted, that every person who shall desert or leave his wife or any child whom he may be liable to maintain, so that such wife or child shall become destitute and be relieved in or out of the workhouse of any Union in Ireland, shall, on conviction thereof before any Justice of the Peace, be committed to the common gaol or house of correction, there to be kept to hard labour for any term not exceeding Three Calendar Months.

And be it Enacted, That every person wandering abroad and begging, or placing himself in any public place, street, highway, court or passage to beg or gather alms, or causing or procuring or encouraging any child or children so to do, and every person who, having been resident in any Union in Ireland, shall go from such Union to some other Union in Ireland for the purpose of obtaining relief in such last-mentioned Union, shall, on conviction thereof before any Justice of the Peace, if such Justice shall think fit, be committed

---

2   Kinealy, *This Great Calamity*, 198.

to the common gaol or house of correction, there to be kept to hard labour for any time not exceeding one calendar month.

And be it enacted, that it shall be lawful for any person whatsoever to apprehend any person whom he shall find offending against this Act, and to take and convey such offender, as soon as may be reasonably practicable, before any Justice of the Peace, to be dealt with as is herein before provided, or to deliver him to any constable or other peace officer of the county or place wherein he shall have been apprehended to be so taken and conveyed as aforesaid; and it shall be the duty of every constable or peace officer to take into his custody every such offender so delivered to him, as well as every person whom he shall find offending against this Act, and to take and convey them respectively before a Justice of the Peace, as soon as may be reasonably practicable, to be dealt with as is directed by this Act.

DOCUMENT 25:

Extracts from C.E. Trevelyan, *The Irish Crisis* (London, 1848), 108, 151–54, 184–86, 201

Charles Trevelyan was a British civil servant who served as assistant secretary of the Treasury during the famine, in which capacity he oversaw official famine relief efforts. In private correspondence Trevelyan was known to express contempt for the people of Ireland. Publically he was a strong advocate of laissez-faire economics and did not believe that government should intervene in the economy. Whichever belief motivated his actions, as director of official famine relief efforts he is frequently blamed for the slow and inadequate response to the crisis. His book *The Irish Crisis* published in 1848 was meant to vindicate his and the government's response to the famine.

∾

The consequences of depending upon the potato as the principal article of popular food, had long been foreseen by thinking persons.... The relations of employer and employed, which knit together the framework of society, and establish a mutual dependence and good-will, have no existence in the potato system. The Irish small holder lives in a state of isolation, the type of which is to be sought for in the islands of the South Sea, rather than in the great civilized communities of the ancient world. A fortnight for planting, a week or ten days for digging, and another fortnight for turf-cutting, suffice for his subsistence; and during the rest of the year, he is at leisure to follow his own inclinations, without even the safeguard of those intellectual tastes and legitimate objects of ambition which only imperfectly obviate the evils of leisure in the higher ranks of society. The excessive competition for land maintained rents which left the Irish peasant the bare means of subsistence; and poverty, discontent, and idleness, acting on his excitable nature, produced that state of popular feeling which furnishes the material for every description of illegal association and misdirected political agitation....

It has been a popular argument in Ireland, that as the calamity was an imperial one, the whole amount expended in relieving it ought to be defrayed out of the Public Revenue. There can be no doubt that the deplorable consequences of this great calamity extended to the empire at large, but the disease was strictly local, and the cure was to be obtained only by the application of local remedies. If England and Scotland, and great parts of the north and east of Ireland had stood alone, the pressure would have been severe, but there has been no call for assistance from national funds.

The west and south of Ireland was the **peccant** part. The owners and holders of land in those districts had permitted or encouraged the growth of the excessive population which depended upon the precarious potato, and they alone had it in their power to restore society to a safe and healthy state. If all were interested in saving the starving people, they were far more so, because it included their own salvation from the desperate struggles of surrounding multitudes frenzied with hunger. The economical administration of the relief could only be provided for by making it, in part at least, a local charge. In the invariable contemplation of the law, the classes represented by the rate payers have to bear the whole burden of their own poor; the majority of the British community did so bear it throughout this year of distress and besides fulfilling their own duties, they placed in the hands of the minority the means of performing theirs, requiring them to repay only one half. [...]

Three things had become apparent before the close of the year 1846: the first was, that if these gigantic efforts were much longer continued, they must exhaust and disorganize society throughout the United Kingdom, and reduce all classes of people in Ireland to a state of helpless dependence; the second was, that provision ought to be made for the relief of extreme destitution in some less objectionable mode than that which had been adopted, for want of a better, under the pressure of an alarming emergency; and the third was, that great efforts and great sacrifices were required to provide another and a better subsistence for the large population which had hitherto depended upon the potato. Upon these principles the plan of the Government for the season of 1847–8, and for all after time, was based.

Much of the larger portion of the machinery of a good Poor Law had been set up in Ireland by the Irish Poor Relief Act (1 & 2 vic. c. 56), which was passed in the year 1838. The island had been divided into unions, which were generally so arranged as to secure easy communication with the central station; and these had been subdivided into electoral districts, each of which appointed its own guardian, and was chargeable only with its own poor, like our parishes. A commodious workhouse has also been built in each union by advances from the Exchequer, and rates had been established for its support. No relief could, however, be given outside the workhouses, and where these buildings once became filled with widows and children, aged and sick, and others who might with equal safety and more humanity have been supported at their own homes, they ceased to be either a medium of relief or a test of destitution to the other destitute poor of the union. To remedy this and other defects of the existing system, three Acts of Parliament were passed in the Session of 1847, the principle provisions of which were as follows: Destitute persons who are either permanently or temporarily disabled from labour, and destitute widows having two or more legitimate children dependent upon them, may be relieved either in or out of the workhouse, at the discretion of the guardians. If, owing to want of room, or to the prevalence of fever or any infectious disorder, adequate relief cannot be afforded in a workhouse to persons not belonging to either the above-mentioned classes, the Poor Law Commissioners may authorize the guardians to give them outdoor relief only.... Relieving officers and medical officers for affording medical relief out of the workhouse are to be appointed; and in cases of sudden and urgent necessity, the relieving officers are to give "immediate and temporary relief in food, lodging, medicine, or medical attendance," until the next meeting of the guardians. After the 1st November 1847, no person is to be relieved either in or out of the workhouse, who is in the occupation of more than a quarter of an acre of land. No person is to be deemed to have been resident in an electoral division so as to make it chargeable with the expense of relieving him, who shall not during the three years before his application for relief have occupied some tenement within it, or have usually slept within it for thirty calendar months.... Public beggars and persons going from one district to another for the purpose of obtaining relief are rendered liable to one month's imprisonment with hard labour. [...]

Those who object to the existing Poor Law are bound to point out a more certain and less objectionable mode of relieving the destitute and securing the regular employment of the poor. The principle of the Poor Law is, that rate after rate should be levied for the preservation of life, until the landowners and farmers either enable the people to support themselves by honest industry, or dispose of their property to those who can and will perform this indispensable duty.

The fearful problem to be solved in Ireland, stated in its simplest form, is this. A large population subsisting on potatoes which they raised for themselves, has been deprived of that resource, and how are they now to be supported? The obvious answer is, by growing something else. But that cannot be, because the small patches of land which maintained a family when laid down to potatoes are insufficient for the purpose when laid down to corn or any other kind of produce; and corn cultivation requires capital and skill, and combined labour, which the cotter and conacre tenants do not possess. The position occupied by these classes is no longer tenable, and it is necessary for them either to become substantial farmers or to live by the wages of their labour. They must still depend for their subsistence upon agriculture, but upon agriculture conducted according to new and very improved conditions. Both the kind of food and the means of procuring it have changed. The people will henceforth principally live upon grain, either imported from abroad or grown in the country, which they will purchase out of their wages; and corn and cattle will be exported, as the piece-goods of Manchester are, to provide the fund out of which the community will be maintained under the several heads of wages, profits, and rents. [...]

Having thus furnished as clear a sketch as the variety and complexity of the incidents would allow, of this remarkable crisis in our national affairs, when the events of many years were crowded into two short seasons, and a foundation was laid for social changes of the highest importance, it may be asked, what fruits have yet appeared of this portentous seed-time, and what the experience is which we have purchased at so heavy a cost?

First, it has been proved to demonstration, that local distress cannot be relieved out of national funds without great abuses and evils, tending, by a direct and rapid process, to an entire disorganization of society. This is, in effect, to expose the common stock to a general scramble. All are interested in getting as much as they can. It is nobody's concern to put a check on the expenditure. If the poor man prefers idling on relief works or being rationed with his wife and children, to hard labour; if the farmer discharges his labourers and makes the state of things a plea for not paying rates or rent; if the landed proprietor joins in the common cry, hoping to obtain some present advantage, and trusting to the chance of escaping future repayments, it is not the men, but the system which is in fault. Ireland is not the only country which would have thrown off its balance by the attraction of "public money" à discretion. This false principle eats like a canker into the moral health and physical prosperity of the people. All classes "make a poor mouth," as it is expressively called in Ireland. They conceal their advantages, exaggerate their difficulties, and relax their exertions. The cotter does not sow his holding, the proprietor does not employ his poor in improving his estate, because by doing so they would disentitle themselves of their "share of the relief." The common wealth suffers both by the lavish consumption and the diminished production, and the bees of the hive, however they may redouble their exertions, must soon sink under the accumulated burden....

Another point which has been established by the result of these extensive experiments in the science, if it may be so called, of relieving the destitute, is that two things ought to be carefully separated which are often confounded. Improvement is always a good thing, and relief is occasionally a necessary thing, but the mixture of the two is almost always bad; and when it is attempted on a large scale without proper means of keeping it in check, it is likely to affect in a very injurious manner the ordinary motives and processes by which the business of society is carried on. Relief, taken by itself, offers, it if is properly administered, no motive to misrepresent the condition of the people; and being burdensome to the higher, and distasteful to the lower classes, it is capable of being carefully tested and subjected to effectual control. But when relief is connected with profitable improvements and full wages, the most influential persons in each locality become at once interested in establishing a case in favour of it, and the higher are always ready to join with the lower classes in pressing forward relief works on a plea of urgent distress, which it may be impossible to analyse and difficult to resist. Relief ought to be confined as much as possible to the infirm and helpless. Wages, by means of which improvements are carried on, should be given by preference to the able-bodied and vigorous. Relief ought to be on the lowest scale necessary for subsistence. [...]

Now, thank God, we are in a different position; and although many waves of disturbance must pass over us before that troubled sea can entirely subside, and time must be allowed for morbid habits to give place to a more healthy action, England and Ireland are, with one great exception, subject to equal laws; and, so far as the maladies of Ireland are traceable to political causes, nearly every practicable remedy has been applied. The deep and inveterate root of social evil remained, and this has been laid bare by a direct stroke of an all-wise and all-merciful Providence, as if this part of the case were beyond the unassisted power of man. Innumerable had been the specifics which the wit of man had devised; but even the idea of the sharp but effectual, remedy by which the cure is likely to be effected had never occurred to anyone. God grant that the generation to which this great opportunity has been offered, may rightly perform its part, and that we may not relax our efforts until Ireland fully participates in the social health and physical prosperity of Great Britain, which will be the true consummation of their union.

DOCUMENT 26:

Papers Relating to the Proceedings for the Relief of Distress, and the State of Unions and Workhouses in Ireland (London: William Clowes and Sons, 1848), 67, 364, 579, 40, 1–3

The existing Poor Law structure in Ireland quickly proved inadequate to the scale of the distress occasioned by the potato blight. The reports received by the Poor Law Commission from unions across Ireland illustrate the challenges many areas faced in responding to a crisis on this scale.

e

Lieutenant Hamilton, Temporary Inspector at Ballina, to the Commissioners: 4 December 1847

I attended the weekly meeting of the Board of Guardians yesterday, as usual. The proceedings were retarded by certain members who were anxious to have everything their own way, consequently there was a very small amount of business transacted; a great deal of talking, and a great deal of important business left undone, owing to the day having been wasted in fruitless discussions.

I am exceedingly sorry to trouble the Commissioners with so unpleasant a report, particularly as there are several Guardians on the Board who are most anxious to act, in accordance with the Commissioner's instructions; but in a Union like this, it is impossible to transact the necessary business with justice both to the rate-payers and the applicants for relief, unless all co-operate and make the best use of the one day in the week, which is appropriated to business.

In my last report, I alluded to the increasing pressure on the workhouse, and I stated my intention of consulting Mr. Bourke, Poor Law Inspector, as to the best mode of meeting it. We agreed to make the workhouse continue to bear the pressure until the next Board day, and then to urge on the Guardians the immediate necessity of providing additional accommodation, which you will perceive by the minutes has been authorised.

store: A storehouse or warehouse.

This morning, in company with three of the Guardians, I hired a **store** for 50 guineas a-year, capable of containing 300 paupers, which number will be this day removed from the workhouse. This will, for the present, prevent the having recourse to extreme measures at this early period; but it is impossible to say how long this will be adequate for the increasing applications. There is another small store, which I am in hopes of being able to obtain.

I have now been through the greater portion of my district, and I have little hesitation in stating that, although very great destitution exists among certain classes and to an extent which it is very questionable whether the present powers of the Guardians can effectually meet much longer, yet up to this period, it is by no means general, and there is a considerable portion of the population who may safely be left to their own resources, for some months to come. There is another portion, who are subsisting almost exclusively on turnips, who will very soon either from disease or the exhaustion of their stock, have to be provided for; the remaining portion, who are subsisting either by plunder or begging, are still holding on in the hope that out-door relief must be granted; and there are many who encourage them in such a hope.

It is evident to me, from what I have seen, that no system of relief can be carried out in this district without considerable abuses, and the more extensive the relief, the greater will be the abuses; consequently, if the Commissioners should, from the amount of distress of the classes to which I have alluded, be obliged to issue an order for out-door relief, I am afraid that the present machinery of the Poor Law will prove quite inadequate, as a sufficient check upon the imposition which will be attempted, and which, if not properly checked, will require funds to an amount of which no estimate can be formed.

So far, I have alluded only to the portion of the Union which is in my district; but the state of the district of Erris has been so repeatedly before the Guardians (the majority of whom seem inclined to treat it as a distinct district), that I think it right to call the attention of the Commissioners to the embarrassing position in which the Inspector there is placed; thrown on his own resources, and loaded with a responsibility which I am sure, it is not the Commissioners' intention should be exclusively borne by him.

The Vice-Guardians of Ballinrobe Union to the Commissioners: 13 December 1847

We have the honour of informing you that on our arrival at Ballinrobe, on Thursday morning, we found, at least, 1000 individuals at the door of the workhouse claiming admittance, and a more wretched or desolate group it would be difficult to imagine; the rain was descending in torrents, accompanied by a fierce wind, both sufficient to destroy the whole body, if left long exposed to their influence. Fortunately some influential persons were in the Board-room, whose assistance we engaged in urging the crowd to depart to their homes, with an assurance that they should receive immediate relief, and also that every properly qualified person should be placed on the relieving officer's lists for out-door relief. It was a most harrowing exhibition, and many and great efforts were required to pacify their clamorous appeals, and persuade them to depart.

Rev. Eugene O'Sullivan, Parish Priest, to the Commissioners: 6 December 1847

Since I had the honour of receiving your letter of the 25th ultimo, I waited on the Board of Guardians of the Caherciveen Union, and endeavoured to impress on them the absolute necessity of giving out-door relief to the persons referred to in your letter, in order to save them from immediate death by starvation.

I regret to state that I could not make any impression on the Board. It is needless for me therefore, to state, that no language can convey an adequate idea of the frightful condition of the poor in the electoral division in this parish attached to the Caherciveen Union. As it is totally out of the question that disabled and infirm persons could walk to the workhouse, I requested of the Board to give funds to the relieving officer which would enable him to procure carts for their conveyance, but in this I was equally unsuccessful.

I respectfully beg leave to call the attention of the Commissioners to these facts, and to request that something be done to save the lives of the people.

It is totally inexpedient that the Killorglin Dunkerron electoral division should be attached to the Caherciveen Union, because the distance between the workhouse of the Union and the electoral division is too great, being, in some instances 35 miles.

Now it is quite plain, that even an able-bodied person with five or six children, some of whom he must convey on his back, would not now accomplish in the depth of winter, through a most dreary and desolate country, so long a journey.

If this electoral division were attached to the Killarney Union, the average distance from the workhouse would be about 12 miles. It is obvious then that the greatest convenience would result if it was attached to the Killarney Union, besides the interests of the division cannot be so well attended to if it remains attached to the Caherciveen Union, because the distance is so great, that neither will the ex-officio or the elected Guardians attend the sittings of the Board. I think it right to remark, that this subject was brought under the consideration of the Commissioners.

Mr. D'Arcy to the Commissioners: 4 January 1848

Referring to the discovery of the body of Thomas Robinson, and the verdict of the coroner's jury thereon, I have to submit the following report:—The deceased, with his mother, brother, and sister had been admitted to the Ballyshannon workhouse upon the 23rd of October, 1847, and continued in it until the 12th of December following, when they requested their discharge, that they might look after some bedding and articles of furniture which remained in their house at Canakeel, which is commonly called Callagheen, and is a townland of the electoral division of Inismacsaint, and not of Boho, situate about two miles off the high road and in the hills.

On visiting the spot, I found the body had been discovered in a standing posture under a bush in a ditch; and it appeared that the deceased had there taken shelter from the storm and rain, which was very violent upon the day he is supposed to have died, which was Friday the 17th; the discovery of the body by the police having taken place on the 18th of December.

About 12 o'clock on the 17th of December, his mother had sent him with one penny to purchase its value in meal, which he had done, and in addition, received from the person selling it, some turnips as a gratuity, and was returning when his weakness and the remarkable severity of that day occasioned his death: there can be no doubt entertained he died from weakness and destitution, hastened by the inclemency of the weather.

Anne Robinson, the mother of Thomas Robinson above referred to, with a son and daughter, are at present in the workhouse. Last evening, on my return from Canakeel, I went there to ascertain the dates of their previous admission and discharge, and found she had been re-admitted provisionally upon the 31st of December ultimo. I questioned her, and received the same information I had previously from the peasantry in the vicinity of the spot his death took place.

Employment of Able-Bodied Paupers in receipt of Out-Door Relief-Circular of Instructions to Boards of Guardians of Unions to which an Order for Out-relief to the Able-bodied has been Issued. Poor Law Commission Office, Dublin, 1848

The Commissioners for administering the Laws for Relief of the Poor in Ireland desire me to call the especial attention of the Guardians of Union to that part of the order of the Commissioners, authorizing the Guardians to afford out-door relief to able-bodied persons in food, which requires that every able-bodied male person so relieved, shall perform a task of work during eight hours at least of every day for which he receives relief....

Most of the suggestions which have been made to the Commissioners have reference to the supposed advantage of obtaining productive labour in return for the relief afforded; and many of them involve the proposal of employing the able-bodied applicants for relief in the cultivation of land, on the best terms which can be obtained by the Guardians, from the parties occupying or owning such land.

To every proposal of this nature the Commissioners consider objections to exist which are insurmountable, and they do not contemplate giving their approval to such proposals under any circumstances whatsoever. One obvious objection is, that such proceedings might interfere with the operation of the legislative measures expressly provided to facilitate the improvement of landed property in Ireland; under which measures, labour will be employed and paid in the ordinary course, without any disturbance of those relations which naturally subsist between the employer and the employed, and which it is of the utmost consequence to maintain as far as possible undisturbed....

With these views, the Commissioners recommend the Guardians to establish a system of breaking stones by measure, as the most suitable employment for able-bodied males requiring relief. The advantages of stone-breaking are, that it is easy to superintend and regulate as task work,—that the materials are generally available, the implements of labour few and simple,—and, above all, that it is less eligible to the labourer than most other employments, provided that it be vigilantly superintended, and that a full day's labour be rigorously exacted from each recipient of relief....

In every electoral division, therefore, in which the Guardians find it necessary to avail themselves of the power to give rations to the able-bodied, it is their imperative duty, in discharge of the trust which they have received from the rate-payers, to provide a rigid system of task-work, and to appoint a sufficient number of superintendents of labour, under that branch of the order which authorises them to appoint such officers....

The justice of this arrangement stands on the following basis:—The food is given, not as the price of labour, but as the relief of destitution. The Labour given in return is the condition of receiving that relief; and if the necessities of the recipient and his family are wholly relieved, it is just that he should give in return the full value of his labour whatever that may be.

PART 4

Non-Government Responses to the Famine

DOCUMENT 27:

Public Opinion in the Press

Public opinion on the government's response to the famine varied considerably. Irish nationalist newspapers such as the *Nation* and the *Freeman's Journal* frequently charged the British government with attempting to exterminate the Irish people, while English newspapers such as the London *Times* and *Punch* frequently expressed dismay at Irish ingratitude for the aid they had received.

Economist, 10 October 1846

THE PUZZLE OF IRELAND

The rulers of Ireland are not men to be envied, either at this juncture or at any other. Their position is one of singular and unexampled difficulty. They are men to be sincerely compassionated—charitably judged—gently censured when they err—zealously and generously supported in their efforts to go right. They are hemmed in with perplexities on every side. There is unquestionably great distress in Ireland: there is as unquestionably a disposition to make an unfair use, and take an ungenerous advantage of that distress. Many of the peasantry, it cannot be doubted, are destitute and starving; many more are resolved to avail themselves of this undoubted destitution and starvation, to evade exertion, to extort relief, to create confusion, and to violate all law and order. Mobs—composed of ten men who are starving, and fifty who are dissolute, turbulent, and lazy—rifle baker's shops, and threaten them with murder if they do not sell food at half the price they gave for it; forgetting that bakers will soon cease to bake for such customers and under such compulsion. Other mobs, similarly composed, apply vehemently to the committees and Government commissaries for employment; and when work is offered to them, refuse it, except at their own wages, and on their own terms—which terms are

presentment sessions:
Local administrative bodies
that considered grants for
public works.

**"the Saxon and the
stranger":** Reference to an
editorial by Lord Frederick
Cavendish (1777–1856).
Cavendish founded a
newspaper, the *Connaught
Telegraph*, and used it to
advocate for the lower class.
In an editorial he wrote in
1833 he said, "Though milk
and honey still abound in
Ireland, they flow for the
Saxon and the stranger and
not for the natives of the
land."

generally half work and double pay. Crowds of labourers—with the distinctive taste of Irishmen, who would always rather beg for a halfpenny than work for a penny—leave important and productive works, when they can earn 1s 6d a day on task-work; leave railroads and works for improving the navigation of the Shannon; nay, we are informed, even leave crops unreaped upon the ground, in the west of Ireland, to flock to the artificial Government undertakings, where they receive 9d and 10d a day, and give nothing that deserved the name of labour in return for it. While in many counties the **presentment sessions** are voting the outlay of enormous sums of money, with a wild and panic-struck profusion under the false impression (in direct contradiction to the letter of the law, and the positive declaration of the Government) that the land will not be called upon to repay it, but that they are in fact voting away the money of **"the Saxon and the stranger."** In the meantime, the Ministers—oppressed and apparently confused, by the fearful weight of responsibility which both England and Ireland unfairly concur in casting upon them, and hampered by the first false step of their predecessors—are doing that, against their judgement, against their intentions, against their public declarations, which, while it may alleviate the present, must aggravate future distress; and will assuredly confirm the Irish people in those very habits of laziness, jobbing, improvidence, and reliance upon others instead of themselves, which lie at the root of their permanent wretchedness....

Our people [the English], as well as the Irish, are obliged to resort to oatmeal and Indian corn, in lieu of the potatoes which have failed them; but they do this naturally, and without either murmur or distress. Why this marvellous difference? We have explained it fully in our last three articles on this subject, and can only repeat here, that it is because the English have long ceased to be dependent solely on the cultivation of the soil, or to subsist upon its lowest, cheapest, easiest, laziest produce; because the English have diligently devoted themselves to those manufactures which the Irish have driven from their shores; because the English have not, like the Irish, resisted, even unto blood, the attempts of their well-wishers to introduce among them improved modes of culture, and habits of industry, economy, and forethought; because, last, though not least, the upper classes among the English have not, like the upper classes among the Irish, so completely or so long abdicated and abjured the sacred duties of their station. These are harsh observations, and delivered in uncourteous language; but they are just, they are strictly true, and they are very necessary; for Irish misery will never be cured, or even materially alleviated, until Irishmen have learned to look for its causes in their own character and their own conduct, instead of stupefying their sense and drugging their consciences by the old, habitual, false chorus in which they are accustomed to attribute it all to Protestant bigotry—to English injustice—to Government oppression.

London *Times*, 1 January 1847

IRISH DISTRESS

To the Editor of the Times.

Sir,—It is argued that the present distress in Ireland may be more equitably and more effectually relieved by the government out of the produce of the taxes than it could be by individuals by means of funds raised by private subscriptions....

In the first place, many persons may wish to contribute towards the relief of the famishing multitudes in Ireland in a greater proportion than that which they contribute to the general taxation of the country, and it is right that persons so disposed should have every practicable facility given them for carrying their benevolent intentions into effect.

The Government cannot give gratuitous relief.

When the present fears and necessities of the Irish people, and their habitual dependence upon, and exaggerated notions of, the power and resources of the government are considered....

This is the point at which it is desirable that a private subscription should come to the aid of the public resources, the money raised by the subscription being exclusively appropriated to the assistance of those who cannot maintain themselves by labour.

Punch, vol. xii, 1847, 183

A WORD OF ADVICE

What can be done with Ireland? Kindness, judging from the speeches of Young Ireland, is thrown away upon her. Every sympathy is shown to her distress, that charity can devise and money execute; but it all goes for nothing. She rejects the sympathy, and only keeps the money. Instead of saying "Thank you," she does nothing but heap abuses on the hand that relieves her. We wonder what will satisfy Ireland! We think the best plan to bring her to her senses will be to let her shift for herself for a twelvemonth. After a year's punishment, with such ministers as **O'BRIEN and MEAGHER**, she will be too glad to go down upon her knees, and say; in all bitterness, "I am sorry for what I have done; I will never do so any more." We truly hope there will be no occasion to carry the punishment into effect.

O'BRIEN and MEAGHER: William Smith O'Brien and Thomas Francis Meagher were Irish nationalists and members of the Young Ireland movement; O'Brien was also a member of Parliament. They were later convicted and exiled for their part in the Rebellion of 1848.

Quarterly Review, vol. 79, March 1847, 476–79

OUT-DOOR RELIEF

Mr. Poulett Scrope:
George Julius Poulett Scrope (1797–1876) was an English geologist, political economist, and member of Parliament.

Giraldus Cambrensis:
Gerald of Wales, a Norman clerk and historian, wrote *Topographia Hibernica* (Topography of Ireland) in 1188.

Romish: Derogatory term for Roman Catholics or Roman Catholic ideas.

We give **Mr. Poulett Scrope** credit for most sincere humanity; but he is a man of lively imagination, and the extent to which he has become blind to the plainest facts in this case is truly lamentable. In direct opposition to this gentleman, we must say it is absolutely necessary to keep our eyes fixed on the great and hitherto unquestioned fact, that the root of all the misery of Ireland is the aboriginal idleness of the people—that hatred of regular labour which has always characterised them ever since history began. More than five centuries ago **Giraldus Cambrensis** thus described them:—"Given they are to idleness above all things: they count it the greatest riches to take no pains, and count it to the most pleasure to enjoy liberty." … We can hardly conceive how this state of things should have survived—if it had not been for the introduction and abuse of the potato. Fatal has been the facility with which masses of men could this obtain the means of animal existence. Most pernicious has been the boon that prolonged exemption acknowledge that the **Romish** clergy, with rare exceptions, have during the pressure of this great calamity acquitted themselves in an admirable manner; but we must not on that account forget for a moment the unhappy results of their general practice in forwarding, not discouraging, one of the most fatal of all the sources of misery and guilt among the poor of Ireland.

A poor law should be administered in a spirit of charity. But charity is not indiscriminating. Establish a rule of out-door relief, and in spite of all ingenuities of subordinate regulation, you will speedily find that you have confounded all distinctions between the honest and the vicious, the industrious few and the idle many, among the Irish poor. The evil of such a rule is too well known in England to require exposure; but it ought to be kept in mind that the rule which was law and tradition amongst us is as yet unknown to Ireland. Legislation had to reform it here: there it will have to impose it upon a people on whom its influence will be still more prejudicial. To create a right to out-door relief in Ireland, is to allure one-half of the rural population into pauperism—it is to pronounce agrarian outrage legitimate—it is to create offices, which will be well paid, for incendiaries—it is to convert the whole face of the country in many districts into, not a workhouse, for work will not be done, but into haunts of laziness and vice—it is to demand of every man, honest enough to withstand spoliation, that he shall hold his life forfeit to the assassin in any moment that finds him unarmed and unguarded—it is to arrest civilization in its progress, to oppose the manifest purpose of God, that Irishmen shall be raised to the common lot of labour; and to reduce a people to that state, the worst and darkest of all, in which honest industry had no hope, and idles no apprehension for the future. The workhouse makes a distinction between the pauper and the poor—it serves too as a main drain or great receptacle, into which elements unfavourable to the moral wholesomeness of rural life are discharged. The profligate and the pilfered, as well as the incorrigible beggar, can be forced within its shelter, and society at large lightened of their presence....

It seems to be expected by many that the terrible lesson of this famine will of itself be sufficient to generate a universal and permanent distrust of the potato system even in Ireland. We wish we could partake in this expectation. Our anticipation, on the contrary, is, that the potato disease will prove a visitation as transitory as the cholera, and its warning be as soon forgotten by the poor; that the diminution of the population will but place new facilities at the command of survivors disposed to renew and prolong the ancient slothfulness of that ruinous barbarity; that the potato gardens will flourish again, and no such paradise wants either its woman or its devil; that the thinned swarms will very speedily be denser than ever; and, finally, that the only permanent change produced will be the addition, in the form of an extended poor law, of an enormous stock of hitherto unknown temptation to the indulgence of the national hatred of toil.

London *Times*, May 1847

THE IRISH RELIEF

To the Editor of the Times

Sir,—It is with feelings of no slight satisfaction that I see now daily evidences through the English press, that the English people are beginning rightly to appreciate the true cause of the "poverty" of the Irish. It is a satisfaction to me, because I may pardonably hope that the seed which, when in Ireland, I laboured to sow through your columns is at last beginning to bring forward fruit.

For some days past letters have appeared in your columns from many clergymen of the Church of England expressing feelings of indignation that they should again be called upon to solicit alms from their congregations on behalf of "the poor and starving Irish."

To have refused **eleemosynary** relief to a distressed people when those amongst them who were in want could not obtain food by law from a community of those who had enough to spare, whilst the law punished them as criminals if they took that food by force, would have been a manifest cruelty and injustice.

eleemosynary: The process or act of giving alms, a charitable effort.

Punch, 1849

IRISH USES FOR ENGLISH MONEY

suffragan: An assistant or subsidiary bishop.

Archbishop McHale and his **suffragan** Bishops have addressed a pastoral letter to their flocks, in which, after bitterly complaining of Irish destitution, and utterly ignoring the efforts of English charity to relieve it, they urge those addressed to subscribe, out of their necessity, in order to afford an independence to the Pope. "And afterwards," concludes the document, "we will have your bounty carried to Rome."

Parliament is called upon to vote £50,000 for the relief of Irish famine, and this grant—as Goodness knows it is not the first, so neither will it be the last of a series. We are to give Ireland, who cannot feed herself, but can subsidize the Pope, £50,000, and more.

THE ENGLISH LABOURER'S BURDEN;
Or, THE IRISH OLD MAN OF THE MOUNTAIN. [See *Sinbad the Sailor*.

Nation, 9 October 1847

THE EXTERMINATION OF THE IRISH PEOPLE

To be sure, "out-door relief" will not poison men by arsenic. In the dungeons called poorhouses murder by the knife is not actually committed. But, were out-door relief for all possible it is not, for an idle nation cannot sustain itself—it will and must swallow up all properly, without creating more—but suppose that "out-door" system possible for all thrown on it, can millions, I ask you, live in health and sturdy manhood, for any length of time, on enforced beggary, and pauper diet scantily given?

Nation, 29 September 1849

MORE EVICTIONS IN CLARE

Sir—The effects of the "Clearance" system, and the meaning of the word "Extermination" are now so fully demonstrated to the wretched people of this unhappy country, as to render it perfectly clear and concise, even to the dullest comprehension, that they are merely relative terms for "robbery" and "murder." But, from the frequent application of the system, people look on it with that sluggish indifference which they bestow on matters of *everyday* occurrence; and it is rarely the subject of remark, except in cases which are particularly distinguished by their magnitude, or peculiar acts of oppression....

Freeman's Journal, 22 October 1850

WHAT IS EXTERMINATION?

The Kilrush Inquiry

The word "extermination" has become as familiar to men's ears that it falls on them without exciting a passing thought, much less suggesting an inquiry as to the fearful realities which that word denotes when applied to the process now in operation against the peasantry of the south and west. Men seem either to have become monotonised by the frequent repetition of the word, or to have calmed their emotions and stopped inquiry by the assumption that "extermination" is a figurative phrase used by imaginative writers to express their dislike of some salutary economic change which is being effected in opposition to their own peculiar theories. Upon some such supposition alone can we account for the fact that human nature does not revolt against the system, and demand that instant measures be taken to stay the murderous process which annually slays its thousands and tens of thousands of a patient and long-suffering people.

It is time, however, the public should awake from this monotony to a full and clear understanding of what extermination means. When farmers speak of having exterminated the rats which fed upon their corn, and point to the heaps of slain in testimony of the prowess of their favourite vermin hunters, they do not speak in figures but plainly, as matter-of-fact men who detail a matter-of-fact deed. When the shipmaster, describing the process by which he exterminated the vermin that infested his barque, tells us how he poised a plank over her broadside, cleared his decks, fumigated her hold with brimstone, and saw the vermin drop in twos, and threes, and tens, overboard, we distinctly understand that the exterminated rats were driven into the sea and destroyed.

Now, it is this same process, as applied to men, that we call extermination. The process is as much a matter of fact in one case as in either of the other two. The bailiffs do not, 'tis true, worry the hunted peasants to death, as do the farmer's terriers the rats, and heaps of mangled corpses do not, therefore, bear equally distinct testimony to the efficient action of the one, as they do to that of the other. But nevertheless, the evicted people whose homes are levelled are no less surely destroyed. It would be almost consistent with humanity to regret that there is this difference in the two processes, for one great human **battue**, with its corpse-heap of exterminated peasants, would end the system for ever. But such a process of extermination would not be a bloodless murder, and would not be according to law. The prevailing process is, therefore, more like to that adopted by the shipmaster, in which nor blood, nor corpse, but only the cleared decks bear testimony to the event. The peasantry are "smoked out," their cabins are levelled with the ground, and they themselves, assailed equally by hunger and by cold, perish in the ditch side, or pass into the poorhouse—to them the ante-chamber to the grave—and are heard of no more.

battue: Wholesale slaughter of unarmed crowds.

Nation, 8 May 1852

The nationalist weekly newspaper the *Nation* here argues that the famine was a force of extinction. This is similar to John Mitchel's portrayal in his 1861 book *The Last Conquest of Ireland (Perhaps)*.

But there is another sort of persecution which I can well understand where millions are shut up in workhouse graves or workhouse prisons, or banished for ever to foreign climes. I can imagine that the religion of a country is in danger when a church and a nation are in process of speedy extinction—when; under pretense of the rights of property, a small class of men exercise unbounded power over hundreds of thousands. Have those who are zealous for the faith considered that there is not a landlord in Ireland who, if he set about it in right earnest, could not make his tenants, in nine cases out of ten, apostates?

DOCUMENT 28:

Extracts from William Henry Smith, *A Twelve Months' Residence in Ireland, during the Famine and the Public Works, 1846 and 1847* (London: 1848), 55–57, 57–59, 79–81

William Henry Smith was an English engineer employed on public works schemes that were established in 1846. Supported by the prime minister, John Russell, the public works proposed to allow the Irish poor to earn public assistance by working on improvement projects. Most projects primarily focused on building new roads.

e

Often in passing from district to district have I seen the poor enfeebled labourer, young and old alike, laid down by the side of the bog or road, on which he was employed, too late for kindness to avail, nevertheless giving his dying blessing to the bestowers of tardy relief.

It was objected to employ persons who were known to have either stock or money; thus the industrious man, too honest to deny what were his means, frequently lost the earning of an entire life; and the fifty or hundred pounds which should have gone to till his land, and provide for future years, went to support his family. To avoid this, as I have before stated, numbers emigrated, and those who remained in hopes of some change for the better, were too frequently, before the close of the year, brought to the same resource as the most improvident.

I consider that all who sought employment should have had it, for surely men who would accept work at 5s. per week, a sum equivalent to 3s. in seasons of plenty, surely such men could not be too opulent for employment. This I, at the time, strongly advocated, and had it been adopted, would, I doubt not, instead of being an increased expense, have proved a saving. By making a favour of employment all tried to succeed, and sooner or later most did so; but by making it general, it would no longer have been sought after, by those who really could avoid it. […]

Labourers: Duties

This class were at first generally employed by day-work; afterwards, a system of Task was adopted, each gauger and his men having allotted to them a portion of a road to cut away, for which they were given a certain price per cube yard, as it was removed; the maximum rate being 1s. 6d. per diem. This system was obviously most difficult and led to much scheming and imposition. In the first place, it was frequently impossible to find a sufficient number of persons competent to measure up work, and even where these persons were obtained, a correct system of task-work could not, in many cases by adopted.

Labourers: Remarks

For instance, supposing a hill required to be cut down, and two gangs placed at equal distance from the top, on the opposite ascents; the men are to cut twenty yards forward, and one yard deep, at 6d. per yard, the road being ten yards in breadth; to all appearances, this work will be fairly and equally allowed; yet, on the one side they might earn 2s. or 2s. 6d. per diem, and on the other, they would not make 6d. This arises from the difference of stratification; on one side might be found nothing but sand, or sand and gravel, whilst on the other, large blocks of boulders might appear that would require breaking, or even blasting up, ere they could be removed; nor could this be remedied, as was suggested by first breaking into the ground; every yard might vary from rock to sand, as is frequently the case. No contractor, even on the largest scale, can be certain of his prices; he will lose on some, and gain upon others, and frequently the difference of 1d. in the yard in heavy earthworks, such as docks, or sea embankments, would suffice to make a fortune, or a bankruptcy. […]

The Public Works were conceived and carried out in a hurry, and to meet an emergency, otherwise much improvement might have been introduced in the mode of labour. In my experience the Board of Works always paid every attention to suggestions, but to adopt an important change would have been to re-organize a system. It would have been impossible in the existing state of the country. A course of procedure was resolved upon, which there was scarcely time or assistance to put into operation, much less to re-model....

Where the mistake arose was not in commencing at road improvements, but in keeping the people there too long, on what were no longer improvements; in not preparing works of drainage or agricultural improvement, whilst they were occupied on the roads. They were thus literally "in the lanes when they should have been in the fields."

It is not in my experience that the people, except in one instance, refused to work upon the lands; had they done so, when required by the landlords, and offered the same prices as on the public works, they should have been immediately dismissed; and the responsibility would have rested with the engineer, and not with the proprietors, as some have said. Indeed, I fear that this was too often advanced by those who were without power, or perhaps the will, to cultivate their estates: although it could not but be expected that men on the verge of starvation, many with helpless families to support, would make every effort to obtain the highest possible wages for their labour, and sacrifice to the emergencies of the present moment all consideration for that future which they scarcely expected, and many never did reach.

DOCUMENT 29:

Extracts from James H. Tuke, *A Visit to Connaught in the Autumn of 1847* (London, 1848), 23–25

An English Quaker and businessman, James Hack Tuke (1819–96) became deeply involved in relief efforts in Ireland following his visit to Connaught in 1847. Tuke's interest in Ireland did not end with the famine and he remained involved in Irish philanthropy during the failure of the potato crop in 1885. In this excerpt he records his observations on workhouses, Poor-Law Unions, and the land system.

✑

I will here refer, although somewhat out of place, to the condition of the Union-houses of Connaught. I have already stated that owing to the want of funds, great difficulty exists in many of the Unions in providing for the inmates, but I am happy in being able to state that a large number are well managed, and are in an improved condition, as compared with last year. The Union-houses of Sligo and Boyle are in beautiful order. The worst which I visited was that of Carrick-upon-Shannon: it was in a miserable state, and the doors were closed against further admissions; and although built for seven hundred, had but two hundred and eighty inmates; the gates were besieged by seventy or eighty wretched beings who in vain implored for admission. Numbers of them were in various stages of fever, which was terribly prevalent in the neighbourhood, and the fever sheds over-crowded. Two months before my visit, the doors of the poor-house were opened and the inmates expelled, entailing upon them most dire misery. Stern necessity has, in a considerable degree, overcome the strong prejudices of the poor people to enter these houses, and they are now generally full.

Nearly two-thirds of the inmates of the Union-houses of Connaught are, as may be expected, children, many of them orphans. The neglected condition of the children in the Union-houses is a subject which often struck me as deserving serious attention. In many Unions, owing to their bankrupt state, there are no books, and no means whatever for providing the necessary books and school requisites; and thus we may see hundreds of children wholly idle and unemployed, where a few pounds expense would enable them to be taught....

The enormous size of the Unions of Connaught is also a subject which deserves attention; I have before mentioned that Leinster, which contains nearly the same area and population, has nearly double the number of Unions, and, of course, Union-houses. The Union of Ballina (county Mayo) is about 60 miles in width by 30 in breadth, or nearly three times the size of Middlesex, containing an area of 509,154 acres, with a population of 120,797 persons, and a net annual value of £95,774. Let us suppose an Union stretching from London to Buckingham or Oxford in one direction and from London to Basingstoke in another, with a poor-house at St. Albans, and we shall have a good idea of the extent of the Ballina Union. A consideration of these facts, or a glance at the map, will convince anyone how impossible it is for the wretched paupers of the extreme or even central portions of this mammoth Union to receive relief which, by law, is designed for them. Look to the parish of Belmullet in the barony of Erris, itself as large as the county of Dublin, and conceive for a moment the hardships of those who travel 50 miles or more to the poor-house at Ballina. The barony of Erris alone is clearly large enough for one Union, and ought to have its poor-house at Belmullet.

I must be allowed to dwell at some length upon the peculiar misery of this barony of Erris, and the parish of Belmullet, which I spent some days examining…. This barony is situated upon the extreme north-west coast of Mayo, bounded on two sides by the Atlantic Ocean. The population last year was computed at about 28,000; of that number, it is said, at least 2,000 have emigrated, principally to England, being too poor to proceed to America; and that 6,000 have perished by starvation, dysentery, and fever. There is left a miserable remnant of little more than 20,000; of whom 10,000, at least, are, strictly speaking, on the very verge of starvation. Ten thousand people within forty-eight hours' journey of the metropolis of the world, living, or rather starving, upon turnip-tops, sand-eels, and sea-weed, a diet which no one in England would consider fit for the meanest animal which he keeps. And let it not be supposed that of this famine diet they have enough, or that each of these poor wretches has a little plot of turnips on which he may feed at his pleasure. His scanty meal is, in many cases, taken from a neighbour hardly richer than himself, not indeed at night, but, with the daring of absolute necessity, at noon-day….

After some miles ride I found a resting place for my horse, and leaving him to bait, explored, in the mountains, a village upon the property of Sir R. Palmer, a **non-resident proprietor**, who is said to have an income of many thousands from this county, but is doing nothing to improve his estate, or to give employment to this starving portion of his tenantry. Most of the inhabitants of this village were owing a year and a half's rent, for their "sums" of land (uncertain quantities), for which they generally paid from £3 to £8 per year. The condition of the people was deplorable; and the last year had not left them the means of meeting this demand. The landlord's "driver" was pursuing his calling, seizing almost every little patch of oats or potatoes, and appointing keepers whose charges, amounting to 45s. for the fifteen

non-resident proprietor:
In other words an absentee landlord.

days allowed between seizure and sale, are added to the rent, and unless the tenant can raise a sum sufficient to satisfy the landlord and his bailiff, his whole crop is liable to be "**canted**" and himself and family to be evicted.

canted: Disposed of by auction.

One poor widow with a large family, whose husband had recently died of fever, had a miserable patch of potatoes seized, and was thus deprived of her only resource for the ensuing winter. What could she do? The poor-house was thirty miles distant, and it was full. Though many of these ruined creatures were bewailing their cruel fate, I heard nothing like reproach or reflection upon the author of their misery, and the bailiff told me that he had no fear of molestation in pursuing his calling....

Although so much has already been said about evictions, I can hardly omit to mention one instance connected with that system of extermination which many Irish landlords think themselves justified in adopting. The extreme western portion of Erris is a narrow promontory, called the "Inner Mullet:" upon this wretched promontory, a proprietor named Walsh, residing in another part of the country, has an estate, from which he was desirous of ejecting a number of tenants. As no less than one hundred and forty families were to be turned out, and cast forth to beg or perish (for the poor-house was fifty miles distant, and could not have contained them), it was natural to expect some resistance, even to the preliminary process, from persons with such prospects. The landlord, therefore, summoned the sheriff to his assistance—the stipendiary magistrate was requested to call out the police: but a maddened tenantry might overcome a handful of police; and as it was thought the "kindest" way to prevent bloodshed by showing superior power, fifty soldiers headed by the commanding officer of the district, were added to the force. Surely to the minds of these poor ignorant people, law, police, military, magistracy and proprietary must have seemed alike confederated against them....

The rent which has usually been obtained from these little tenants has never left them more than the barest means of subsistence upon potato diet; the corn which they may have grown and the pig which they have fed have always gone to the owner of the soil, and yet the loss of these little plots of land has been and still is a question of existence. Miserable as is the usual condition of the little farmer or cottier, yet when he loses his little holding he is thrown into a condition in comparison of which his former position was highly privileged. The mere labourer, where there are no employers, is an utter outcast, driven to beggary in a country in which the only givers are the poor cottiers or farmers, from whose state he has fallen. It may be said, that this extraordinary visitation presses as heavily upon the owner as the occupier; and we freely admit that the well-disposed owner, who is in many cases the heir to a deeply-encumbered estate—the result perhaps of a long-continued system of the most reckless extravagance—is truly an object of our sympathy; nevertheless, the consequences of their ancestors' course must be considered as part of their entail. And, where land has been held for generation by tenants who have paid all which they could raise beyond a bare subsistence, is not the land-lord morally liable for the risk of extraordinary providences? In a country labouring under such complicated evils, it may fairly be doubted whether the ordinary exercise of the rights of property, as practiced in England, can be equitably and morally carried out.

DOCUMENT 30:

Extracts from *Report of the British Association for the Relief of the Extreme Distress in Ireland and Scotland* (London, 1849)

The British Relief Association, founded in 1847, was one of the most prominent private charities founded to address the potato famine. Its subscribers included Queen Victoria, the royal family, notable politicians, aristocrats, and bankers. The association worked closely with the British Government, including Charles Trevelyan, to coordinate their activities.

ev

At the expiration of two years from the commencement of their labours, the Committee of the British Relief Association find the funds entrusted to them expended, and their operations consequently brought to a close. It remains for them to present a statement which will show the application of the money subscribed, and the results which that application has secured....

The Committee laid down the following general rules for their guidance in making grants from the fund.

1. That all grants should be in food, and not in money.
2. That no grant should be placed at the disposal of an individual for private distribution.
3. That the grants from the fund should be exclusively for gratuitous distribution.

It was in some cases found difficult to adhere strictly to the first rule; for, although the Committee were at this time sending large supplies of food to Ireland, and establishing depots round the coast, and also had permission to draw, to a certain extent, from the Government stores, still there were many applications from districts so situated in the interior as to rend it impossible for the applicants to obtain provisions from any of those stations. These applications it was found impossible to refuse, and in such instances, small amounts of money were voted....

Such being the system on which it was determined to grant assistance, and the conditions on which it was to be afforded, the Committee proceed to detail the steps which were taken to relieve, as far as possible, the horrible misery prevailing in the sister kingdom:—The article of subsistence almost exclusively relied on by the great bulk of the people of that country was gone. Nor was this deficiency supplied by any other article of human sustenance. Grain had reached a famine price, and a very limited quantity only was to be found in the markets. The Committee felt that their first great object must be to assist in supplying the country with the provisions which it would be their duty to dispense.

At the period referred to there was no absolute want of money in Ireland; the Local Relief Committees had raised during the season from subscriptions 199,470 l. to which Government had added 189,000 l. in donations from the public purse. The amount of money which was flowing into the country from other channels cannot accurately be estimated, but it is well known to have been very considerable. Various charitable associations were distributing with a liberal hand. The clergy were making great exertions among their wealthier English friends. A case is recorded of a Clergyman labouring in a parish of 10,000 souls, in the south-west of Ireland, who received privately 1,000 l. supplied by benevolent Englishmen. In more than once instance wealthy families in this country had taken an entire parish under their especial care; and many Clergymen were known to be remitting sums of 20 l. or 30 l. weekly, from collections amongst their congregations, to districts and to brother Clergy in the sister island. In addition to this, the poor, who were employed on the public works in great numbers, were receiving wages from the public purse. At this time 570,000 persons were in receipt of such wages, a number which gradually increased in the month of March to no less than 734,000. The wages received by these labourers were higher than the average rate of wages in the country. What was wanted was food, and more especially cheap food. To this subject the Committee directed their earliest attention. A Sub-Committee ... was appointed, to regulate the purchase and shipment of provisions, and the formation of depots round the coast and in the interior of the country....

In the same documents will be found an account of the arrangements that were made for the relief of this extreme destitution. Cargoes of provisions were despatched by the Committee to the various ports on the coast; and the Government depots were strengthened as far as possible, in order to meet the calls of the Association....

The new Government measure of relief was gradually superseding the old system. By it relief was afforded to the distressed in food. A Relief Committee was appointed in every electoral division to superintend its action, and a Finance Committee was required to control the expenditure of each Union. Lists were made out by the Electoral Division Committees, of the persons requiring relief, and those lists were transmitted for revision by Inspecting Officers appointed by the Relief Commissioners to watch over the affairs of the Union. The tests applied were, the personal attendance at the place of distribution by all parties requiring relief, and the issue to them of cooked food.

On the 5th May, **Count de Strzelecki** reported that the Act was in full operation in every Electoral Division of the Westport Union, and that he considered it advisable that relief of the Association to the Union should be discontinued. By the Government measure of relief every really destitute person was entitled to daily rations; and, therefore as the Act gradually came into operation in the distressed Unions of the west of Ireland, the necessity for the intervention of the Association ceased to exist....

The Government had determined to abandon the system of relief through the public works, and to try the efficacy of a more extended and vigorous administration of the Poor Law. The transition from the one system to the other, it was obvious, would be attended with considerable difficulty, out of which much additional pressure of a temporary character might probably arise. The attention of the Committee was now directed to this new cause of distress, and it was strongly urged upon them that their remaining funds could in no other way be so beneficially employed as in the effort to alleviate the difficulties and sufferings which might be connected with the change in the system of Government relief.

Mr. (now **Sir Charles**) Trevelyan wrote to the Chairman of the Association, on the 20th of August, "I recommend that you should not form any new independent machinery, which you might find difficult to manage, and which would produce the impression that the lavish charitable system of last season was intended to be renewed; but that you should select, through the Poor Law Commissioners, a certain number of Unions in which there is a reason to believe that the ratepayers will not be able to meet their liabilities, and that you should appropriate from time to time such sums as the Poor Law Commissioners may recommend for the purpose of assisting in giving out-door relief in certain districts of these Unions, the expenditure for this object being under the special superintendence of the Assistant Poor Law Commissioners, who would take care that no misappropriation took place. This plan is substantially the same as that which was last recommended by Count de Strzelecki, and it would be attended with the double advantage of limiting the relief afforded by the Association to those parts of the country which are undoubtedly the most distressed, and of supporting and strengthening the administration of the Poor Law, which is the great point of all. The further condition should be annexed, that the Poor Law Commissioners should be able to certify that the ratepayers were making such exertions as could reasonably be expected from them; and then I think every practicable security will have been taken that the bounty of which the Association is the organ will have been bestowed aright." [...]

Having thus traced the various measures of relief adopted, the Committee have only to place this statement of their labours before their subscribers. It has been their object to render a clear and faithful account of the manner

Count de Strzelecki: A Polish geologist who became a British subject, Strzelecki was the association's agent supervising County Sligo and County Mayo.

Sir Charles: Charles Trevelyan was knighted in April of 1848.

in which they have endeavoured to satisfy the benevolent intentions of the Subscribers to the Fund.

Assuredly, evils of greater or less degree must attend every system of gratuitous relief; but the Committee feel confident that, in the application of this fund, any evils which may have accompanied its distribution have been far more than counterbalanced by the great benefits which have been conferred upon their starving fellow-countrymen. If ill-desert has sometimes participated in this bounty, a vast amount of human misery and suffering has been relieved; if an isolated instance can be shown of idleness engendered, there can be also no doubt, real and permanent good has been effected amongst the poor, and amongst the rising generation more especially. If, indeed, the single good result had been that which the Poor Law Commissioners have deliberately put on record, "that thousands have by this means been saved from starvation," the Committee will have reason to rejoice in the belief that their labour has been far from vain.

Extracts from Thomas Carlyle, *Reminiscences of My Irish Journey in 1849* (New York, 1882), 76, 176–77, 179–80

Thomas Carlyle was a Scottish writer and philosopher who toured Ireland in 1849. In the sections below he records his observations on workhouses. The idea behind the workhouse system was for the poor to work at frequently menial tasks in exchange for the minimal support they received in the workhouse. Workhouses were meant to be miserable places so that only the desperate would call upon their relief. During the famine workhouses were frequently overcrowded and riddled with disease.

ℰℯ

Description of the Westport Workhouse

O'Shaughnessy's subsidiary poorhouse (old brewhouse, I think), workhouse being filled to bursting: with some eight thousand (?) paupers in all. Many women here; carding cotton, knitting, spinning, etc. etc.; place and they very clean; "but one can," bad enough! In other Irish workhouses saw the like, but nowhere ever so well. […]

Human swinery has here reached its acme, happily: 30,000 paupers in this union, population supposed to be about 60,000. Workhouse proper (I suppose) cannot hold above three or four thousand of them; subsidiary workhouses, and out-door relief the others. Abomination of desolation; what can you make of it! Out-door quasi-work: three or four hundred big hulks of fellows tumbling about with shares, picks, and barrows, "levelling" the end of their workhouse hill. At first glance you would think them all working; look nearer, in each shovel there is some ounce or two of mould, and it is all make-believe; five or six hundred boys and lads, pretending to break stones. Can it be a charity to keep men alive on these terms? In face of all the twaddle of the earth, shoot a man rather than train him (with heavy expense to his neighbours) to be a deceptive human swine. Fifty-four wretched mothers I saw rocking young offspring in one room. […]

Westport Union has £1100 a week from government (proportion rate-in-aid), Castlebar has £800, some other has £1300, etc., etc.; it is so they live from week to week. Poor-rates, collectible, as good as none (**£28,14,0** say the books): a peasant will keep his cow for years against all manner of **cess**-collection. Spy-children; tidings run, as by electric wires, that a cess-collector

£28,14,0: Currency at the time was pounds, shillings, pence.

cess: A tax or rate levied by local authorities for local purposes.

is out, and all cows are huddled under lock and key—unattainable for years. No rents; little or no stock left, little cultivation, docks, thistles; landlord sits in his mansion, for reasons, except on Sunday: we hear of them "living on the rabbits of their own park." Society is at an end here, with the land uncultivated, and every second soul a pauper. "Society" here would have to eat itself, and end by cannibalism in a week, if it were not held up by the rest of our empire still standing afoot!

DOCUMENT 32:

Extracts from "The Famine in the Land—What Has Been Done, and What Is to Be Done," *Dublin University Magazine*, xxix, April 1847, 501–14

Founded in 1833, Dublin University Magazine was an independent literary and political magazine. Generally Protestant and Unionist in its political leanings, the magazine also had a keen interest in promoting Irish culture and literature.

ে৴

Ireland is now, in one sense, in the midst, in another sense, we fear, in the beginning of a calamity, the like of which the world has never seen. Four millions of people, the majority of whom were always upon the verge of utter destitution, have been suddenly deprived of the sole article of their ordinary food. Without any of the ordinary channels of commercial intercourse, by which such a loss could be supplied, the country has had no means of replacing the withdrawal of this perished subsistence, and the consequence has been, that in a country that is called civilized, under the protection of the mightiest monarchy upon earth, and almost within a day's communication of the capital of the greatest and richest empire in the world, thousands of our fellow-creatures are each day dying of starvation, and the wasted corpses of many left unburied in their miserable hovels, to be devoured by the hungry swine....

In the autumn of 1845, it was discovered that a disease had attacked the potato in Ireland, and in other parts of the world. Of the actual existence of such a disease there was no doubt. Its extent was, like most questions in Ireland, made a party one—and, we grieve to say, the Tory party were in the wrong. Some of the journals in Ireland, supposed most to represent the aristocracy, persisted in vigorously denying the existence of any failure to more than a very partial extent. The question of the **corn laws**, then pending, gave this question an imperial interest. The potato famine in Ireland was represented as the invention of agitators on either side of the water. So far was party feeling carried, that the conservative mayor of Liverpool, honestly, we are sure, refused to convene a meeting for the relief of Irish distress. A committee which sat at the Mansion House, in Dublin, and at first declared their belief in the approach of an overwhelming calamity, were stigmatized as deluding the public with a false alarm. Men's politics determined their belief. To profess belief in the fact of the existence of a formidable potato blight, was as sure a method of being branded as a radical, as to propose to destroy the Church....

corn laws: Trade legislation which imposed tariffs on imported grain.

It was, however, the misfortune of famine-stricken Ireland, and a deep misfortune almost all men in Ireland now feel it to be, that party combinations ... removed from office the man [Sir Robert Peel] who had shown himself alone, perhaps, of living statesmen, alive to the exigencies of the crisis, and capable of boldly and efficiently meeting them ... and with the removal of Peel from office he lost the power of even assisting to obviate the danger, which, we do believe, had he remained in office, he would successfully have met....

What can be more absurd, what can be more wicked, than for men professing an attachment to an imperial Constitution to answer claims now put forward for state assistance to the unprecedented necessities of Ireland, by talking of Ireland being a drain upon the English treasury? ... If the Union be not a mockery, there exists no such thing as an English treasury. The exchequer is the exchequer of the United Kingdom. Its separation into provincial department is never thought of when imperial resources are to be spent, or imperial credit pledged, for objects principally or exclusively of interest to the English people. Ireland had been deprived by the Union with England of all separate power of action. She cannot do now, as in the days of her parliament she might have done—draw upon her own resources, or pledge her own credit, for objects of national importance. Irishmen were told indeed that in consenting to a Union which would make them partners with a great and opulent nation, like England, they would have all the advantages that might be expected to flow from such a Union.

DOCUMENT 33:

Extracts from the Central Relief Committee of the Society of Friends, *Distress in Ireland, Extracts from Correspondence* (Dublin, 1847), 9, 12–13, 23

The Society of Friends, commonly known as the Quakers, were one of the first groups to mobilise in response to the emerging famine. Quakers, whose religion promoted total human equality, were frequently involved in social justice campaigns such as the anti-slavery movement. The Quakers were successful at raising funds internationally in support of their relief efforts. Below is some correspondence from the United States in support of their efforts and a reply sent by the Quakers detailing some of their efforts.

e

Letter from the Irish Relief Committee of New York, 24 February 1847

Christian Friends,

Our fellow-citizens of every name and creed, deeply sympathizing with the distresses of the Irish people, have, with the greatest alacrity, come forward to contribute their **mite** towards the alleviation of a misery which we fear no human aid can reach in all its depths and recesses.

mite: A small contribution of money to a cause or charity, which is as much as the giver can afford.

You will see from the public papers of this city what has been done. As a part of the fruits of the contributions of our people, we enclose Grinnell, Minturn and Co.'s first of exchange of the 23rd instance, on, Baring Brothers and Co., London, at sixty days, for Three Thousand Pounds sterling, payable to our treasurer, and by him endorsed to your order as secretaries of the Central Committee of Friends in Dublin.

This contribution together with such others as we may send, is intended to be applied by your impartial Committee towards the alleviation of the misery of the famishing poor of Ireland. Our people generally prefer sending bread-stuffs, or other provisions; but the committee supposed that a speedy remittance in this form might give you notice of our zealous co-operation in your labours, and furnish a little aid which might be found useful before a cargo of provisions could reach you.

Letter from Boston, 26 February 1847

Liberator: An abolitionist newspaper founded and run by William Lloyd Garrison, the author of this letter.

Esteemed friend,

You will see by the ***Liberator***, that your letters, communicating some particulars of the unparalleled destitution in Ireland at the present time, have been laid before the American public. The first one has been extensively copied into the newspapers, and has been the means of creating much sympathy, and securing considerable pecuniary aid for your suffering countrymen. From one end of the vast country to the other, the people are now pretty well informed as to the famine; for there is not a newspaper, whether religious or political, whether literary or scientific, among the multitude printed among us, which has not communicated to its readers the awful tidings, and called upon them, in tones of earnest entreaty, to contribute of their substance to send across the Atlantic the needed relief. The number of public meetings that have been held on this subject is too great to be chronicled in this letter. Cities, towns, villages—whether near or remote—have been deeply stirred, and are coming to the rescue in the spirit of universal brotherhood. I should judge that at least £50,000 had already been contributed in money, to say nothing of donations in the shape of food and clothing; and these, I trust, are only the first drops of a coming shower. I wish I could say that all will be done that ought to be done; but enough will be given to indicate a strong and wide-spread sympathy for the multitudes in your land who are crying for bread, or for anything that will sustain life....

Our city has led the way in the performance of noble deeds, and I trust she will more than maintain her high character in this instance. A petition has gone on from our merchants to Congress, asking that body to allow one of the sloops of war, now lying in our harbour, to sail for Ireland, freighted with provisions that are ready to be contributed for this charitable purpose. It would be a strange use for such a vessel, but not more strange than beneficent.

Our friend Francis Jackson has had something like a thousand dollars put into his hands, within a few days, almost exclusively by our little band of abolitionists, which sum he will transmit to Dublin by the Cambria on Monday next.

My heart aches to think of the destitution that abounds throughout your naturally beautiful and fertile island. The poverty and wretchedness which I saw during my ride from Portadown to Drogheda, afflicted me beyond description; and yet they were nothing compared to what exists in a large portion of your country. What is to be the end of these things? Are the millions to be left to perish, or left to subsist on the uncertain, inadequate charities of others, always on the verge of starvation? Surely this is not the will of God. The famine may not be laid to his charge. He never made the human family, or any portion of it, to live on a particular root, or to die of starvation in case that root should be suddenly blighted.

Continue to make such suggestions as may occur to you, from time to time, through the medium of the *Liberator*, in aid of your country. I am thankful that having a press under my control, I am able to address many thousands of the people, and to exert some little influence for the relief of suffering humanity. The shocking condition of Ireland shall at no time be forgotten by me.

Ever faithfully yours,
Wm. Lloyd Garrison

57, William-Street, 26th of **Third Month**, 1847

The extensive reduction, now in progress, of labourers hitherto employed on the public works, has claimed the attention of this Committee.

It is apprehended that many who are dismissed will not immediately find means of procuring food, by wages earned elsewhere, and that the measures of relief provided under the **Act 10 Vic. cap. 7**, cannot in all cases be brought to bear so quickly as may be required.

In order to encourage and enable them to work on their own allotments of land, some immediate steps for supplying food under careful regulations, to the discharged who are engaged in measures of public relief, to endeavour to mitigate the increased suffering which may be expected during the transition from old to new arrangements, with vigour and promptitude.

This Committee is desirous to encourage well directed efforts for this object, by renewing their grants on a scale proportioned to the means at their disposal, in cases where local funds are insufficient.

They would especially recommend those who have received from them grants of rice, for distribution in a cooked state, to be prompt and liberal in their disposal of it. Care must be taken, however, that none but the real destitute receive it gratuitously. In connexion with the treatment of diseases now so fearfully prevalent, and the preservation of health of those who have heretofore been insufficiently supplied with food, or consuming unwholesome kinds, it is strongly urged on all who provide food for the poor, to consider where they can serve them more effectually, than by promoting the consumption of properly cooked rice.

In offering additional grants of money and food, where they may be thus required, it is to be clearly understood:—

1st. That parties applying for renewed assistance should furnish proof of former supplies having been faithfully and judiciously distributed; and

2ndly. That there are not available local resources to meet the exigency.

Third Month: March: Quakers generally did not use traditional calendar names. They objected to days of the week and months that were named for pre-Christian gods and traditions.

Act 10 Vic. cap. 7: The 1847 Poor Relief (Ireland) Act.

It is proper to state that this Committee has been chiefly prompted to make this offer of co-operation and help, in the present emergency, in consideration of considerable additional means being now entrusted to them by their friends in America, and through the munificence of the citizens at large in many parts of the United States, for whose seasonable assistance, under Divine Providence, it will doubtless be felt that the grateful acknowledgements of the suffering poor of Ireland are eminently due.

DOCUMENT 34:

Extracts from *Transactions of the Central Relief Committee of the Society of Friends during the Famine in Ireland in 1846 and 1847* (Dublin, 1852), 53–54, 56, 452–54

The Quakers ran an extensive network of soup kitchens, the basic operation of which is detailed below, along with some related correspondence between Sir Charles Trevelyan and Jonathan Pim (1806–85), the Irish philanthropist and politician who served as secretary for the Quaker Relief fund during the famine.

e

The first step adopted by us, to alleviate this widely-spreading destitution, was the establishment of a soup-shop in Dublin, both as a means of directly relieving the poor of this city, and as a model for similar establishments elsewhere. Premises were taken for the purpose in Charles street, Upper Ormond-quay, and the institution was opened under the care of a sub-committee, on the 23rd of **First-month**, 1847. Several of the committee attended in rotation, twice every week-day, to superintend the distribution. The soup was sold at one penny per quart; or, with a piece of bread, at three half-pence. Tickets were also sold at the same price to those who wished to distribute them gratuitously. In consequence of the prevalence of bowel-diseases, occasioned in a great degree by the use of unwholesome food, the sub-committee, in Third-month, introduced the use of cooked rice. Their report expresses their belief that considerable benefit was derived from its use. The quantity of soup sold averaged about 1,000 quart per day. After the Temporary Relief Act came into operation, the demand gradually decreased, so that on the 22nd of Seventh-month, 1847, the sub-committee recommended that the establishment should be closed. This soup-shop appears to have accomplished, to a great degree, both the objects which were contemplated at its formation; for it not only afforded considerable relief to a large number of the poor of Dublin, but it was visited by many persons who were connected with similar establishments throughout the country. [...]

The distribution of relief throughout the rural districts was a far more difficult undertaking. The first object was to obtain the co-operation of suitable local agents.... Wherever it appeared practicable, we tried to procure the establishment of soup-shops, and for this purpose made several grants of boilers, and of sums of money for their outfit. At first we were anxious to engage, as far as possible, the assistance of local committees; but the residents in the most distressed districts were so few and so scattered,

First-month: January.

that it soon appeared necessary, in the great majority of cases, to trust to individual correspondents. Many of these exerted themselves assiduously and zealously, for the distribution of relief to their distressed neighbours; and their proceedings were in general as satisfactory as those of committees, and often more so. A very large proportion of grants were made to ladies, who were found to be our most efficient **almoners**. [...]

almoners: People responsible for giving out alms, or poor relief.

Letter from Sir Charles Trevelyan to one of the Secretaries of the Central Relief Committee, Treasury, London, 2 June, 1849

Lord John Russell: Prime minister at this time.

Lord John Russell has desired me to enquire from you, what plan the Relief Committee of the Society of Friends is now pursuing for the relief of the serious distress which still prevails in some of the western districts of Ireland; and to express to you his willingness to contribute one hundred pounds towards the object. I do this with much satisfaction, as besides the good that would be done, it affords a proof of his lordship's continued and, I must add, well deserved confidence in your society.

Reply to Trevelyan, Dublin, 5th of Sixth-month, 1849

I waited for a meeting of our Relief Committee, before acknowledging thy kind letter of the 2nd instant, enquiring on the part of Lord John Russell, what plan we are now pursuing for the relief of the serious distress which still prevails in some of the western districts of Ireland, and expressing his willingness to contribute one hundred pounds towards this object. Our Committee met this day, and have desired me in the first place to convey their warm acknowledgements to Lord John Russell, for this second and valued proof of his confidence.

The subject brought before them by thy letter has engaged their long and anxious consideration; and in endeavouring, in accordance with their directions, to answer Lord John Russell's enquiry as to what plan we are now pursuing, I feel I must trespass on thy time, by explaining our position and views at some length.

When the potato crop of 1846 failed, there were no sufficient legal arrangements to meet the calamity which ensued. There was also an absolute dearth of food, especially in the western districts, and prices were enormously advanced as compared with former years. Under these circumstances, the exertions of private relief associations and the raising of contributions appeared the only means of meeting a great, and, as we then hoped, a temporary calamity, which might be expected to terminate with the next harvest.

On this idea, our Relief Committee and also the other Relief Associations acted, and our exertions and the benevolence of those who confided their contributions to our care, were efficiently seconded by many residents of all classes in the various distressed districts of Ireland. Their feelings excited by the distress prevailing around them, and sustained by the hope of effectually relieving at least some portion of it—they devoted themselves in very many cases to the work with self-denying energy and singleness of purpose; neglecting their domestic comforts, and giving up almost their whole time to the work of charity.

Exertions of this character could not last. The work was too great, and those qualified to labour far too few. Moreover, it became hopeless. The evils of continued almsgiving became apparent. The constant sight of misery blunted their sensibility. They began to feel the burden of their own affairs, and could no longer spare the time to attend to those of others; and, in many cases, became distressed themselves, their own families needed that relief which they had at first assisted in distributing to their neighbours. Yielding to these and other causes, many of our best and most trusted assistants in the work dropped off one by one; and it became evident to us that if we continued our distribution of grants, we must act in many cases through inferior channels. Concurrently with this, the Imperial Parliament thought it right to extend the provisions of the Poor Law so as to meet the cases of all destitute persons; and we felt the extreme difficulty of a private association guarding against abuses, when attempting to relieve distress which was at the same time under the care of a legally organized body; a difficulty which, it is worthy of remark, was evidently so felt by the British Relief Association, as to induce them to dispense the chief part of the balance then remaining in their hands through the agency of the **Poor Law Guardians**; in fact, to devote their funds to the same purpose as the rates levied off the property of the unions.

Poor Law Guardians: Elected officials who oversaw poor relief in each Poor Law Union, under the Poor Law of 1838.

We endeavoured at first to avoid this difficulty, by confining our grants to classes who were not the objects of adequate poor-law relief, by assisting schools, by distributing seeds, and by cultivating ground by spade labour; and at length decided on bringing our system of almsgiving to a final close, and on devoting the balance then remaining to objects which might encourage the industry of the country. In pursuance of this decision, we have for the past nine months expended very little money, except in the completing of some objects previously undertaken; in some operations for the encouragement of the fisheries; in loans for the cultivation by spade labour; and in some considerable loans to encourage the cultivation and improved preparation of flax in the county of Mayo. We have also appropriated a sum of £12,000, being nearly the whole of our available balance, to the purpose of conducting a model farm and agricultural school in the county of Galway.

About a month since, our Dublin Committee had the opportunity of consulting many of our country friends, who have taken an active part in relief operations. The question was then again considered, whether the great and increasing distress prevailing in many parts rendered it advisable to make renewed efforts for affording gratuitous relief, and the conclusion adopted was in the negative. We felt that even if we asked for another contribution, the utmost amount we could expect would be utterly insufficient; that even with ample funds, we could no longer hope for that active and self-denying co-operation in the distressed districts, on which we had formerly relied, and without which we could not work usefully; in short, that our plan of acting was no longer practicable alongside of the Poor Law, and that the relief of destitution, on any extended scale, must in future be trusted to those arrangements which the Imperial Parliament has provided for that purpose. Seeing that the difficulty was so far beyond the reach of private exertion, and that the only machinery which it was practicable to employ was that under the control of the public authorities; and believing that the Government alone could raise the funds, or carry out the measures necessary in many districts to save the lives of the people, we feared that if we ventured to undertake a work for which our resources were so inadequate, we might, through our incompetency, injure the cause of those whom we desired to serve.

Under these circumstances, we are not now in a position to undertake the distribution of charitable relief; and we are truly sorry that it is therefore out of our power to offer ourselves as the distributors of Lord John Russell's bounty to our suffering fellow-countrymen.

I trust thou wilt excuse this long explanation of our views.

Signed: Jonathan Pim

DOCUMENT 35:

Reactions in the United States

> During the years of the famine, international reaction was broadly
> sympathetic to the plight of the Irish. In New York the Irish American
> community organized aid societies to send assistance, and they organized in
> opposition to British government policy towards Ireland.

e

New York Herald, 6 June 1848

THE FRIENDS OF IRELAND IN NEW YORK TO THE IRISH PEOPLE:

Friends in Ireland Across the seas, we have watched in silence and with
attention the course of events in your island, until the instincts of our
common humanity are no longer to be repressed. In the fullness of our
hopes and fears, we hasten to renew the relations of Sympathy and succor
which early and long have existed between America and Ireland.

Five years ago, this month of June, when Nature was kindling into
summer verdure and beauty, Ireland, too, seemed bursting into the fullness
of life. The quickening impulse was felt throughout this land, and from the
Mississippi and the great lakes to the Atlantic, the whole country pressed
forward with its encouragement and aid....

New York Herald, 6 June 1848

Hon. Benjamin F. Butler, who addressed the meeting in the following language:—Mr. President and Fellow citizens:—The duty has been assigned
to me to propose a resolution and support it with a few remarks in its
spirit, but I can't stop to read it. My Irish blood runs too fast. That blood
which gives me my name will not allow me to stop to read the resolution.
I tell you why it is; I wish to get at it—to speak of the accumulated wrongs
which have been heaped upon Ireland by Britain, and to say that they are
unequalled in the history of tyranny and oppression, and I believe every
word of it and so do you.... But what was England when she commenced
her oppressions towards Ireland. They acknowledged the same system of
faith—they professed to worship, not only the same God, but they recognized
the same Judge and the same head of the church—and yet from the time

of Henry the Second, the rule of England over Ireland was by intolerant laws, as unjust as it afterwards became when great differences of religion rose between them. For the last two hundred years what has been the rule of England over Ireland, and how has that tyranny been aggravated by the fact that during the whole period England has stood at the head of civilization of science, of letter, and in her professed love for liberty? And yet, with a rule of iron has she oppressed that people. And Why?

New York Herald, 21 June 1848

GREAT IRISH MASS MEETING TO SYMPATHIZE WITH JOHN MITCHEL

JOHN MITCHEL: Irish nationalist convicted and exiled for his role in the 1848 rebellion. Author of *The Last Conquest of Ireland (Perhaps)* (1861).

Mr. G.: Presumably Horace Greeley, founder and editor of the *New York Tribune*.

He (**Mr. G.**) would, however, take this occasion to say something in reference to Ireland, and the duty of Americans towards her in her present situation, the case of John Mitchel. (No sooner was the name uttered, than the loudest roars and thunders of deep sensation arose, and reverberated from the lofty dome of the building. There was something terrible in the sound. This demonstration of feeling continued some time.) The case of John Mitchel, continued Mr. Greeley has been brought before us and has waked up many an American mind, hitherto quiescent on the subject of Ireland, to deep thought, and feeling on the subject. We are, said Mr. G., so accustomed in this country to scrutinize, and comment with the most boundless freedom, upon the conduct of government, that it appears to us a strange thing, when we hear of a free man being brought before a packed jury, and sent away from his native land before us a transported felon, to distant climes, for merely speaking the words of truth and soberness concerning the government of his country.

DOCUMENT 36:

Bishop John Hughes, *A Lecture on the Antecedent Causes of the Irish Famine, Delivered at the Broadway Tabernacle March 20th, 1847* (New York, 1847)

John Hughes (1797–1864), sometimes called "Dagger John," was born in County Tyrone, Ireland. He was the son of a tenant farmer and immigrated to the United States in 1817. He was named Bishop of New York in 1842, and later Archbishop when New York was elevated to an archdiocese in 1850. In this position he dealt with the massive influx of famine immigrants from Ireland as well as the anti-Catholic and **Nativist** reactions to their arrival. Hughes's 1847 lecture on the causes of the famine was delivered as part of a fundraising campaign by the General Committee for the Relief of the Suffering Poor in Ireland.

Nativist: An anti-immigration political movement in the United States, in the 19th century nativists greatly opposed mass Irish immigration as a result of the famine.

e

I have not come here to enlarge upon the feelings of sympathy that have been aroused in our own bosoms, nor yet on those of gratitude that will soon be awakened in the breasts of the Irish people. I come, not to describe the inconceivable horrors of a calamity which, in the midst of the nineteenth century, eighteen hundred and forty-seven years after the coming of Christ, either by want or pestilence, or both combined, threatens almost the annihilation of a whole Christian people. The newspapers tell us, that this calamity has been produced by the failure of the potato crop; but this ought not to be a sufficient cause of so frightful a consequence: the potato is but one species of the endless varieties of food which the Almighty has provided for the sustenance of his creatures; and why is it, that the life or death of the great body of any nation should be so little regarded as to be left dependent on the capricious growth of a single root? Many essays will be published; many eloquent speeches pronounced; much precious time unprofitably employed, by the State economists of Great Britain, assigning the cause or causes of the scourge which now threatens to desolate Ireland. I shall not enter into the immediate antecedent circumstances or influences, that have produced this result. Some will say that it is the cruelty of unfeeling and rapacious landlords; others will have it, that it is the improvident and indolent character of the people themselves; others, still, will say that it is owing to the poverty of the country, the want of capital, the general ignorance of the people, and especially, their ignorance in reference to the improved science of agriculture. I shall not question the truth or the fallacy of any of these theories; admitting them all, if you will, to contain each more or less of truth, they yet do not explain the famine which they are cited to account for. They are themselves to be accounted for, rather as the effects of other causes, than as the real causes of effects, such as we now witness and deplore: for in the moral, social, political, and commercial, as well as in the mere outward physical world, there is a certain and necessary connection between cause and effect, reaching from end to end, through the whole mysterious web of human occurrences. So that, in the history of man, from the origin of the world, especially in his social condition, no active thought, that is, no thought which has ever been brought out into action or external manifestation, is, or can be isolated, or severed from its connection with that intricate universal, albeit mysterious, chain of causes and of consequences, to which it is, as it ever has been, the occupation of mankind to add new links every year, and every day.

If the attempt, then, be not considered too bold, I shall endeavor to lay before you a brief outline of the primary, original causes, which, by the action and reaction of secondary and intermediate agencies, have produced: the rapacity of landlords, the poverty of the country, the imputed want of industry among its people, and the other causes to which the present calamity will be ascribed by British statesmen. I shall designate these causes by three titles; first, incompleteness of conquest; second, bad government; third, a defective or vicious system of social economy. Allow me first, to say a word of the country itself.

Ireland, as you know, is not larger in its geographical extent, than two-thirds of the State of New York. An island on the western borders of Europe, its bold coast is indented with capacious bays and safest harbors. For its size it has many large and navigable rivers; and it is said that no part of the island is more than fifty miles from tide-water. Its climate is salubrious, although humid with the healthy vapours of the Atlantic; its hills (like its history) are canopied, for the most part, with clouds; its sunshine is more rare, but for that very reason, if for no other, far more smiling and beautiful than ever beamed from Italian skies. Its mountains are numerous and lofty; its green valleys fertile as the plains of Egypt, enriched by the overflowings of the Nile. There is no country on the globe that yields a larger average of the substantial things which God has provided for the support and sustenance of human life. And yet, there it is that man has found himself for generations in squalid misery, in tattered garments often as at present; haggard and emaciated with hunger; his social state a contrast and an eye-sore, in the midst of the beauty and riches of nature that smile upon him, as if in cruel mockery of his unfortunate and exceptional condition.

The invasion of Ireland took place toward the close of the twelfth century, under the Anglo-Norman King, Henry II. An Irish chieftain had been expelled from his country by the virtuous indignation which a flagrant act of immorality had aroused against him, in the minds of his countrymen and of his own subjects. He had recourse to the British monarch: the king merely gave him letters patent, authorizing such adventurers as were so disposed, to aid him in recovering his estates. Such adventurers were not wanting. They embarked and landed under the banner of invasion, upheld by the criminal hand of an Irish traitor. They succeeded in effecting a partial conquest. The native population were driven out of that portion of the country which stretches along the east and southeastern coast, which afterwards became known in history as the **English Pale**. This portion of the kingdom, less than one-third—may be considered as having been really conquered by the adventurers; but the rest of the island continued as before, under its ancient princes and proprietors; some of them having simply recognized the monarch of England as their superior lord, by agreeing to pay a mere nominal tribute. Here is the real point in history, at which the fountain of Ireland's perennial calamities is to be placed. Many a tributary streamlet of bitterness came afterwards, to swell the volume of its poisoned waters; but this is the fountain which supplied and gave its direction to the current. The king displayed, when he visited Ireland, an authentic or a **forged document from the Pope**, authorizing the invasion. There is no evidence, however, except what rested on the royal testimony, that such a document had been granted; but whether or not, it had no more effect in the success of the invasion, than if it had been so much blank Parchment....

The conquest was thus cut short, almost at the opening of the book; and the calamities that have resulted to Ireland, from that time until our own days are but so many supplements, many of them bloody ones, to complete the volume. The invaders were pleased to consider themselves as having conquered the Irish nation; and as having acquired right of supreme dominion over the Irish soil. The king divided the lands of the whole kingdom into ten sections, or regions, and bestowed them upon as many of his principal followers. Having flung this apple of discord between the old and new race of the Irish people, he sailed back to England,—had the emerald gem of **Erin's** sovereignty set among the jewels of his crown, and called himself Lord of Ireland. The consequence of his distribution was, from this time that every portion of the Irish soil, every estate, had two sets of owners; the one, owner by justice, hereditary title, and immemorial possession; the other, owner by assumed right of conquest, and the **sign manual** of Henry II. If Henry had conquered the country, he might have made these grants a reality; but as it was, they were simply as royal letters-patent, authorizing the iniquities and disorders of all kinds which make up the history of the relations between the Irish people and what was called the English Pale.

The invaders regarded the natives as illegal occupiers of the soil—as barbarians, who stood between them and the peaceable possession of their

English Pale: The area surrounding Dublin, the only area of Ireland under effective English control in the Middle Ages.

forged document from the Pope: *The Laudabiliter* was a papal bull issued by Adrian IV in 1155 which authorized Henry II to invade Ireland. No original copy of this bull has ever been found so its existence is disputed.

Erin's: English derivative of the Irish word for Ireland (Éirinn).

sign manual: A signature, particularly that of a sovereign used to authenticate a document.

property. To attempt to dispossess the native population, however, by force, would have been a dangerous experiment; and it makes one shudder to see the persevering ingenuity with which the aid of inhuman legislation was invoked, with which laws for the protection of cruelty and treachery of every description were enacted, to accomplish by piecemeal and by fraud the complete conquest which they were too feeble or too politic to refer, once for all, to the more humane decision of the battle-field.

If we look at the legislation of the Pale for the entire period of four hundred years, we will find the tone of its enactments to be always in harmony with this purpose—**laws against** intermarriages with the natives—laws against their language—laws against their manners and customs—and even laws making criminal for a liegeman of England to allow a native horse to graze on his pasture. In the minds of the invaders,—in the acts of Parliament,—in royal proclamations, during all those centuries down to the reign of Queen Elizabeth, the natives are designated as aliens and Irish enemies. No part of the soil of their country was recognized as theirs. They were denied all share in the benefits of English laws; the iniquities of the royal grant, supported by the iniquities of legislation, made it lawful for the invaders to kill or rob "the mere Irish," as the accidents of opportunity, or the caprice of expediency, might direct. If any of the natives appealed to the law for redress, it was enough for the defendant to prove, that the would-be plaintiff was a mere Irishman, and did not belong to any of the five families to whom the protection of the British laws had been, by special favor, extended. This plea arrested all farther proceedings in the court. Frequently, during this long interval, had the natives petitioned and implored to be admitted into the Pale, and under the protectorship of the laws; but as often was their petition rejected. On the other hand, their own sovereignty was paralyzed and rendered impotent by the invasion, and the disorders which resulted from its incompleteness. They were broken up and divided, so that they were deprived of all opportunity for social or physical improvement, by any legislative organization of their own. This sketch conveys a faint idea of the condition of Ireland, during nearly four hundred years after the invasion.

The English Pale, meantime, instead of enlarging its boundaries, had often been obliged to curtail them; and as late as the reign of Henry VIII, it was restricted to only four counties out of the whole kingdom. Enough has been said, I think, to illustrate the principle with which I set out, that to assume the fiction of a conquest; to accomplish it by halves; to leave it incomplete; to repair its deficiency, which must be repaired, by other means, which must be fraudulent, is the most cruel policy, as well as the most injurious to both, that a strong nation can employ in the subjugation of a weak one. If it must be done at all, it will be mercy to do it thoroughly so that the sword shall have determined, to the conviction of all parties, the

laws against: The reference here is most likely to the Statutes of Kilkenny, issued in 1366 to discourage English nobles in Ireland from adopting Irish customs.

reality of the new relations that have sprung up, by its decision, between the conquerors and the conquered. The bad policy of the incomplete conquest of Ireland had to be repaired, or rather completed, in the sixteenth century, by commencing the work anew: for, it was only under Queen Elizabeth, who was no half-way ruler, but who, whatever else she may have been, was, I had almost said, a king every inch of her, that Ireland was finally crushed, if not conquered.

It would have been, however, too humiliating to British sovereignty to supply the original defect, under the original name, of conquest. It was, therefore, now to be accomplished under the title and form of "reducing insubordinate and rebellious subjects"—although it required the help of a strong legal fiction to regard as rebels, those who had hitherto been repulsed from the protection of the law. But even this reduction could not be accomplished, it seems, without cruelties, for which the annals of mankind, in the most barbarous ages of the world, furnish no parallel. It is a singular coincidence and full of admonition, that in this second conquest, British statesmen recommended—and military officers employed—and lords deputies approved of—FAMINE as their most effectual instrument and ally in the work of subjugation.

The occupation of the troops, from year to year, was to prevent the cultivation of the land, to destroy the growing crops already planted, for "famine," says the English historian who records the fact, "was judged the speediest and most effectual way of reducing the Irish." The consequences were, that whole provinces were left desolate, without an inhabitant, except in the towns and villages; that those whose misfortune permitted them to escape the sword, sometimes offered themselves, their wives and children, to be slain by the army, rather than for that slow, horrid, death of famine and starvation, which had been reserved for them; for we can all conceive that, compared with the deliberate use of this instrument of war, against a rural and scattered agricultural population, the Indian's tomahawk becomes a symbol of humanity. Meantime, the old chieftains of clans, the owners of the soil, the leaders of the people, the "great rebels," as they were called, were becoming fewer and fewer. Some perished on the battle-field—they were the most fortunate; others gave themselves up on the word of honor and protection, and were then impeached and executed. Some were slain at the festive board of the invading commander, whose invitation to the banquet they had accepted, thinking foolishly, that the laws of truce and hospitality made of their rights not only secure, but even sacred, under the tent of a true soldier; and thus, in few years, the Irish aliens, the Irish enemies, or the Irish rebels if you will, were indeed reduced; and now there was a prospect of the invaders being permitted to enter into peaceable possession of those estates which, by right of conquest, as they understood it, had been theirs from the first invasion.

Elizabeth proposed to colonize the whole province of Ulster with English settlers, but she did not live to accomplish her project.

The plantation of Ulster remained to be carried into effect by her successor, James I. He secured to himself a new and better title; he confiscated to the crown sixteen counties of Ulster, in one day; and parceled them out, chiefly among his Scotch, rather than his English friends, the native, the hereditary population having been, of course, sent adrift. The king and his ministers congratulated themselves, and compared this act of his Majesty to the conduct of a wise and thrifty husbandman, who transplants his trees according to the soil in which they will grow best. After James came Charles I, and the civil wars in England. When other resources failed the monarch, the fragments of property, real and personal, that still remained to the Irish people, were strained into the supply of his empty coffers. He obtained from them, by royal promise, £120,000 sterling, for what was called "**Graces**;" the principal of which was, what every American inherits by birthright—liberty of conscience.

Graces: Concessions promised to Irish gentry both Catholic and Protestant in exchange for the £120,000. The graces needed to be confirmed by the Irish Parliament, and the king evaded confirming them by not summoning Parliament.

He pocketed the money, but I am sorry to say he refused the "Graces." His deputy in Ireland projected and carried out a system for the confiscation, in detail, of private estates, under a "Commission" for inquiry into defective titles. The jury that refused to find a verdict for the crown, under this system, was punished and ruined; and as to the judges, the lord deputy writes to his royal master, that he had got them to attend to this business, as if it were their own personal affair, by promising four shillings in the pound to the judge who presided at the trial, out of the first year's income from all confiscated estates. Under the Commonwealth, Ireland is the scene of new exterminations,—new confiscations,—new foreign settlers, amidst the wrecks and ruins of the native population. On the Restoration, the loyalists of England and Scotland were reinstated in their rights; but in Ireland, the loyalists were abandoned by the crown; and the followers of Cromwell confirmed in their possessions. Nay, James II came in on the **title of a Cromwellian**, and appropriated to himself, in one instance, no less than from 70,000 to 140,000 acres, that had been confiscated by Cromwell to punish the fidelity of its rightful owners for adhering to the cause of that miserable James' unfortunate father. Finally, that Country which had been conquered so often, submitted at last to William III, successor to James on the English throne—submitted, but still not to the sword of a conqueror, but to the faith of a king, stamped on a written instrument, mutually agreed upon by him and the last representative of unconquered Ireland, called the "Treaty of Limerick." But every article of it, autograph, royal seal, and all, was repudiated the moment it was safe to do so.

title of a Cromwellian: Reference to the monarchy's policy after the Restoration of 1660 to not reverse the titles and lands granted by Oliver Cromwell in Ireland, as they did in the other kingdoms.

The enactment of the entire penal code, soon afterwards, is evidence of the entire and deliberate violation of all the articles of the treaty of

Limerick. By that code, the inhabitants of Ireland were again divided into two classes; the one consisting of those whose conscience we allow them to take the State oath, on the subject of religion: to them high privileges were secured. But penalties were enacted against those who could not, or would not, swear that oath. The great overwhelming majority of the Irish people refused the test; and the penal law came quickly to punish them, even in their family relations and domestic circle. It invested any child, who might conform to the test prescribed, with the rights of property enjoyed by his father. It invested the wife with rights of property over the husband. If any of those who had refused to swear, purchased an estate for any amount of money, any of the others, who had taken the oath, could dispossess him without paying one shilling for such estate. If any of the former class owned a horse worth fifty or one hundred pounds, any of the latter class had a right, by law, to tender five pounds and tell him to dismount. If any of the former class, by his skill and industry in agriculture, raised the value of his land, so as to yield a profit equal to one-third of the rent, any of the latter could enter on the Profits of his labor, and take possession of his land. These laws continued for between eighty and ninety years, down to the period of American Independence. And in this enactment we see what a penalty was inflicted on the agricultural industry of the Irish—what a premium was held out to encourage that indolence which British statesmen now impudently complain of.

The same system has been continued to the present day: as if some cruel law of destiny had determined that the Irish people should be kept at the starving point through all times; since the landlord, even now claims the right, and often uses it, of punishing the industry of his tenant, by increasing the rent, in proportion to the improvement the tenant makes on his holding. If then it be true, that the Irish are indolent, which I deny, the cause could be sufficiently explained by the penalties which a bad government has inflicted upon them, in their own country, for the crime of being industrious. Then, if it be said, as a reproach, that the Irish are ignorant, let it be remembered that this same code of penal laws closed up the schools of popular education; that the schoolmaster was banished for the crime of teaching, and if he returned he was liable to be treated as a felon. If ignorance of the people, then, be the cause of the famine, enough has been said to point out the cause of the ignorance itself.

The melancholy training of so long a period of oppression served to bring out, in the shades of adversity, virtues which perhaps would not have bloomed or borne fruit in the sunnier atmosphere of national prosperity. Filial reverence, domestic affections, always congenial to the Irish heart, had here ample opportunity of proving themselves, and were never found wanting. The law put it in the power of any son, by declaring himself a

Protestant, to enter immediately upon the rights of property enjoyed by his father and his family; but no son of Irish parents was ever known to have availed himself of the law. As a matter of expediency, it was customary for the Catholic proprietor, for the protection of his property, to vest the legal title in some Protestant neighbor, and again it is consoling to know that, notwithstanding the temptations presented by these iniquitous laws, there is no instance of that private confidence having been violated. These laws originated at the close of the seventeenth century, and continued in force until two years after a British general, Burgoyne, turned the point of his sword to his own breast, and presented the hilt to the hand of his conqueror, after the **battle of Saratoga**. Then came the only brief, bright period of Ireland's history: the period of her volunteers, of her statesmen and orator—her illustrious **Grattan** rousing the patriotism of his country, and emancipating her long enslaved Parliament. The period of her **Bushe**, her **Flood**, her **Curran**, and the other great names that have made Irish eloquence as immortal as the Anglo-Saxon tongue. But the sun of her brief day soon declined and set, shrouded in clouds of blood, for it closed by the banishment or martyrdom of her patriots—her noble-hearted **Emmets** and **Fitzgeralds**. It was brought to an end by a new policy, conducted in the old spirit. A rebellion had been deliberately fomented by the agents of a foreign government, until it reached the desired point of and then it was crushed with promptness and with cruelty. Martial law for the people, gold for the senate—a bayonet for the patriot who loved Ireland, and a bribe for the traitor who did not, led to the Act called the Unions in which the charter of Irish nationality was destroyed, but I trust not forever.

The rest you are all acquainted with; it has occurred in our day, and within our memory. It will be manifest from what has been said that the causes which have prevented the prosperity of Ireland, the development of her material resources, the cultivation of her mind, have existed from an early date; and, under one form or another, have been in perpetual activity. She has hardly been permitted to enjoy repose sufficient even for a fair experiment of improvement. During the first four hundred years after the invasion, her people were outlawed because they were mere Irish. Afterwards, when the English laws were extended to her, in 1610, her people were again outlawed or worse, not now because they were Irish, but because they were Catholics. By adhering to their old religion, their rulers supposed them to have shipwrecked their hopes of happiness in another world, which would have been misfortune enough, without inflicting punishments for their mistake so well calculated to destroy their prosperity here. At the commencement of these changes the law required them to attend the church and service of the State religion; if they attended, did not understand a syllable of that service, which was conducted in the English language: if they did not attend, their

battle of Saratoga: On 7 October 1777 British General John Burgoyne surrendered to General Horatio Gates during the American Revolution.

Grattan: Henry Grattan (1746–1820) was an Irish politician who campaigned for the legislative independence of the Irish Parliament in the late eighteenth century.

Bushe, Flood, Curran: Gervase Parker Bushe, Henry Flood, John Philpot Curran were all political allies of Grattan.

Emmets: Prominent Irish patriots in the late eighteenth century. Thomas Addis Emmett was a member of the United Irishmen. Robert Emmet led a failed rebellion against British rule in 1803.

Fitzgeralds: Lord Edward Fitzgerald was a prominent leader of the United Irishmen; he died in 1798 from wounds sustained while being arrested for his part in the 1798 rebellion.

property was seized by fines for their nonattendance, £20 a Sunday. Then, either by grants or confiscations, under Charles the First, to whose cause they were loyal, their property was still diminished. Under Cromwell, they were punished and plundered both as idolaters, and because they had been faithful to their king. Under the Restoration, all preceding iniquities as regarded the ownership of property were confirmed. Under William III and his successors, the penal laws were applied in the same way, not to the body politic at large, but with an ingenuity of detail, to every joint, and sinew and muscle, as if the object were to paralyze all effort at national amelioration. Just in proportion as the struggle of these colonies for independence was successful, in that proportion did the policy of the British government relax the pressure of this weighty bondage of the Irish people.

We sometimes hear comparisons instituted between the prosperity, industry, and moral, or at least, intellectual condition, of the Scotch, and the poverty of all kinds of the Irish; and the conclusion is generally adverse to the latter, either on the score of national character or of religion. Some even assert that the Catholic religion is in reality the cause of the poverty and degradation of Ireland. I have said enough to show that it has been at least an occasion; but I am willing to go farther, and admit that in one sense it has been a cause too; for I have no hesitation in saying that if the Irish, by any chance, had been Presbyterians, they would have, from an early day, obtained protection for their natural rights, or they would have driven their oppressors into the sea. The Scotch escaped nearly all the calamities I have described; they were never conquered; their soil was never taken from beneath their feet; they merged themselves spontaneously at their own time, and on their own terms, into the State of England. They kept also, the property of their old religion for their own social and religious use. Already, before the change, parish schools were established in Scotland; after the change these were multiplied, improved, and endowed out of the old church property.

But in Ireland, everything was the reverse: church buildings, monasteries, **glebes**, tithes, from year to year, all went by the board: all were subtracted from the aggregate of the national wealth. And even in modern times, we read of incumbents appointed to ecclesiastical livings, entering on their **cure or rather sinecure**, penniless, and after a few years, by the probate of their own wills, leaving to their foreign heirs, in some instances, as much as three, and four, hundred thousand pounds sterling, if they ventured to suggest a defective or vicious system of social and political economy as the other great cause of Ireland's peculiarly depressed condition. By social economy I mean that effort of society, organized into a sovereign state, to accomplish the welfare of all its members. The welfare of its members is the end of its existence—**"Salus populi, suprema lex."** It would be a reproach to say

glebes: A portion of land assigned to a clergymen.

cure or rather sinecure: A cure is an ecclesiastical office that involves the spiritual care of parishioners; a sinecure is an office that does not involve such responsibilities.

Salus populi, suprema lex: Roman saying, "Let the good of the people be the supreme law."

that Christianity conceived a meaner or a lower idea of its obligation. This idea, it may not, perhaps, be possible to realize fully in practice under any system; but it should never be lost sight of. The system which now prevails has lost sight of it, to a great extent. It is called the free system,—the system of competition,—the system of making the wants of mankind a regulator for their supplies.

It had its origin in the transition of society from that state of mitigated slavery which was called feudalism and serfage, as they prevailed in England. As regards the mere physical position, food, clothing, lodging, of the entire people of England, there is no doubt that the old system provided better for it than the present one. The old Barons never allowed their serfs to die of a hunger which they were not willing to share. As the latter emerged from serfdom, and before they were able to take their ranks with advantage, in a more honorable sphere of free labor, the church property, of its great means constituted a Providence of protecting for this class. When the church property was distributed among the nobles of England this resource failed, and then it was that Poor Laws were enacted, and taxes began to be levied by the State, from the poor, for the support of the pauper. Until then, the aggregate physical comfort, if not the aggregate wealth, of the English people, taking them altogether members of one State, was greater than it ever has been since, or so far as we can see, is likely ever to be again. There were not, indeed, those colossal individual fortunes which now exist, but neither were there on the other hand those abysses of physical and moral destitution, which are now yawning on every side for the new victims, whom the pressure of the present system is pushing, every day, nearer and nearer to their fatal brink. By this system England has, I admit, become the richest country on the globe; but riches are by no means synonymous with prosperity, when we speak of the social condition of a whole people. And this system, though it may work well, even for national prosperity, in certain given times and circumstances, yet carries within it, in the palmiest days of its success, a principle of disease, which acts first on the lower extremities of the social body; and with the lapse of time will make itself felt, at the very heart and seat of life. It is an appalling reflection that out of the active and productive industry of Great Britain and Ireland, provision must be made for the support of between four and five millions of paupers. This number will be increased by every depressing crisis in commerce and in trade; by every blight of sterility which Providence permits to fall on the fields of the husbandman; and the experiment of Sir Robert Peel, in imposing on the wealthy an income tax, may be regarded as a premonitory warning that, although the time may not yet have arrived, it is approaching, and, perhaps, at no very remote distance, when the mountains of individual wealth in England shall be made comparatively low, and the valleys of pauperism will be partially filled up. I am aware that in speaking on this subject, I will go as it were in opposition to the almost universal sentiment of this age, but for the expression of my opinion I will offer you this apology, that provided you do me the honor to hear, I will not ask you to coincide in so much as one of the conclusions at which my mind has arrived in regard to it.

I know that no living man is accountable for the system of which I am about to complain; it is older than we are, it is the invisible but all-pervading divinity of the fiscal, the unseen ruler of the temporal affairs of this world. Kings and Emperors are but its prime ministers, premiers and parliaments but its servants in livery; money is the symbol of its worship, we are all its shows, without any power to emancipate ourselves; the dead and the dying in Ireland are its victims.

It will not be disputed, I presume, that the present system of social and political economy resolves itself, when analyzed, into a primary element of pure selfishness. The principle that acts, the mainspring that sets all its vast and intricate machinery in motion is self-interest; whether that interest assume a national form in the commercial rivalship of States, or an individual form in the pursuits, the industry, and enterprise of private persons. The conqueror, indeed, carries off great spoils from the contest; but his enjoyment of them would be disturbed if he could only hear the cries of the wounded and the dying who have fallen in the battle.

The true system, in my opinion, would regard the general interest first, as wholly paramount, and have faith enough to believe that individual interest would, in the long run, be best promoted by allowing it all possible scope for enterprise and activity within the general limits. Then individual welfare would be the result and not the antecedent, as it is when the order is reversed. The assumption of our system is, that the healthy antagonisms of this self-interest, which, as applied to the working classes, its advocates sometimes designate pompously "the sturdy self-reliance of an operative," will result finally in the general good. I am willing to admit, that in the fallen condition of human nature, self-interest is the most powerful principle of our being, giving impulse and activity to all our individual undertakings, and in that way, to the general operations of life. But unfortunately this system leaves us at liberty to forget the interest of others. The fault which I impute to it, however, is that it values wealth too much, and man too little; that it does not take a large and comprehensive view of self-interest; that it does not embrace within its protecting sphere, the whole entire people, weak and strong, rich and poor, and see as its first and primary care, that no member of the social body, no man shall be allowed to suffer or perish from want, except by the agency of his own crime. The fault that I find with it, is, that in countries of limited territorial surface and dense population, by a necessary process it works down a part of the community, struggling with all their might to keep up, into a condition not merely of poverty, but also of destitution; and then treats that poverty, which itself had created, as a guilt and an infamy.

The fault that I find with it, is that whilst it allows, and properly so, competition to be the life of trade, it allows it also to be, oftentimes, the death of the trader. The premier of England is reported to have said not long since, "that nothing prevented him from employing government vessels to carry bread to a starving people, except his unwillingness to disturb the current of trade." Never was oracle of a hidden and a heartless deity uttered more faithfully, or more in accordance with the worship of its votaries, than in the language here imputed to the British minister, who may be fairly regarded as the living high priest of political economy. To put public vessels in competition with merchantmen, in the low business of mere trade, would indeed have been wrong and unworthy of a great ruler; but if the profits of trade had been curtailed in the proportion of three or four per cent per annum, during this crisis of the famine, it would have saved many lives, and yet not have inflicted a wound or a scar on the health of commerce.

The fault that I find with the system, then, is, that it not only allows but sanctions and approves of a principle, which operates so differently in two provinces of the same State, divided only by a channel of the sea. It multiplies deposits of idle money in the banks on one side of that channel, and multiplies dead and coffinless bodies in the cabins, and along the highways, on the other.

The fault that I find with it is, that it guarantees the right of the rich man to enter on the fields cultivated by the poor man whom he calls his tenant, and carry away the harvest of his labor, and this, whilst it imposes on him no duty to leave behind at least food enough to keep that poor man alive, until the earth shall again yield its fruits. The fault that I find with it, is, that it provides wholesome food, comfortable raiment and lodgings for the rogues, and thieves, and murderers, of its dominions, whilst it leaves the honest, industrious, virtuous peasant, to stagger at his labor through inanition, and fall to rise no more! O! if this system be all in all, why did he not, in his forlorn state, entitle himself to its advantages? Why did he not steal or commit murder? For then the protection of our modern Christian governments would be extended to him, and he would not be allowed to die of want.

I may be told that I avail myself unfairly of an extraordinary calamity to prove the defects of our present system; I may be told that the famine in Ireland is a mysterious visitation of God's providence, but I do not admit any such plea. I fear there is blasphemy in charging on the Almighty, what is the result of his own doings. Famine in Ireland is, and has been for many years, as the cholera in India, indigenous. As long as it is confined to a comparatively few cases in the obscure and sequestered parts of the country, it may be said that the public administrators of social and political economy are excusable, inasmuch as it had not come under their notice; but in the present instance, it has attracted the attention of the whole world. And yet they call it God's famine! No! no! God's famine is known by the general scarcity of food, of which it is the consequence; there is no general scarcity, there has been no general scarcity of food in Ireland, either the present, or the past year, except in one species of vegetable. The soil has produced its usual tribute for the support of those by whom it has been cultivated; but political economy found the Irish people too poor to pay for the harvest of their own labor, and has exported it to a better market, leaving them to die of famine, or to live on alms; and this same political economy authorizes the provision merchant, even amidst the desolation, to keep his doors locked, and his sacks of corn tied up within, waiting for a better price, whilst he himself is perhaps at his desk, describing the wretchedness of the people and the extent of the misery; setting forth for the eye of the first lord of the treasury, with what exemplary patience the peasantry bear their sufferings, with what admirable resignation they fall down through weakness at the threshold of his warehouse, without having even attempted to burst a door, or break a window.

Such conduct is praised everywhere; even Her Majesty, in a royal speech, did not disdain to approve of it; and it is, in truth, deserving of admiration: for the sacredness of the rights of property must be maintained at all sacrifices, unless we would have society to dissolve itself into its original elements; still the rights of life are dearer and higher than those of property; and in a general famine like the present, there is no law of Heaven, nor of nature, that forbids a starving man to seize on bread wherever he can find it, even though it should be the loaves of proposition on the altar of God's temple. But, I would say to those who maintain the sacred and inviolable rights of property, if they would have the claim respected, to be careful also and scrupulous in recognizing the rights of humanity. In a crisis like that which is now passing, the Irish may submit to die rather than violate the rights of property; but on such a calamity, should it ever happen, which God forbid, the Scotch will not submit; the English will not submit; the French will not submit; and depend upon it, the Americans will not submit. Let us be careful, then, not to blaspheme Providence by calling this God's famine. Society, that great civil corporation which we call the State, is bound so long as it has thy power to do so, to guard the lives of its members against being sacrificed by famine from within, as much against their being slaughtered by the enemy from without. But the vice which is inherent in our system of social and political economy is so subtle that it eludes all pursuit, that you cannot find or trace it to any responsible source. The man, indeed, over whose dead body the coroner holds the inquest, has been murdered, but no one has killed him. There is no external wound, there is no symptom of internal disease. Society guarded him against all outward violence; it merely encircled him around in order to keep up what is termed the regular current of trade, and then political economy, with an invisible hand, applied the air-pump to the narrow limits within which he was confined, and exhausted the atmosphere of his physical life. Who did it? No one did it, and yet it has been done.

It is manifest that the causes of Ireland's present suffering have been multitudinous, remote, and I might almost say, perpetual. Nearly the whole land of the country is in the ownership of persons having no sympathy with its population except that of self-interest—her people are broken down in their physical condition by the previous calamities to which I have directed your attention. Since her union with England, commerce followed capital, or found it in that country, and forsook the sister island. Nothing remained but the produce of the soil. That produce was sent to England to find a better market, for the rent must be paid; but neither the produce nor the rent ever returned. It has been estimated that the average export of capital from this source has been equal to some 25 or perhaps 30 millions of dollars annually, for the last seven and forty years; and it is at the close of this last period, by the failure of the potato, that Ireland, without trade, without manufactures, without any returns for her agricultural exports, sinks beneath the last feather, not that the feather was so weighty, but that the burthen previously imposed was far above her strength to bear. If it be true that the darkest hour of the night is that which immediately precepts the dawn, may we not indulge the hope that there are better days yet in store for this unfortunate people. They have been crushed and ruined in all the primary elements of their material happiness, but yet they have never forfeited any of the higher attributes of a noble, generous nature. They might, perhaps, have shared with the other portions of the empire in the physical comforts and improvements of modern civilization, if they had renounced their religion, at the period when the others saw fit to change theirs; but after the present famine shall have been forgotten, the high testimony which the Irish people bore to the holiness of conviction within their soul, at all risks, and through all sacrifices, will be considered an honor to humanity itself. They believed, whether rightly or not is not now the question, they believed that to profess religion which had no hold on their contraction, would offend God, and involve them in the double guilt of falsehood and hypocrisy—that it would degrade them in their own minds, that it would entitle them to the contempt of the world—and sooner than do this, they submitted to everything besides. There was this one sovereignty which they never relinquished—the sovereignty of conscience, and the privilege of self-respect. Their soul has never been conquered; and if it was said in Pagan times that the noblest spectacle which this earth could present to the eye of the immortal gods, was that of a virtuous man bravely struggling with adversity; what might not be said of a nation of such men who have so struggled through entire centuries? Neither can it be said that their spirit is yet broken. Intellect, sentiment, fancy, wit, eloquence, music and poetry, are, I might say, natural and hereditary attributes of the Irish mind and the Irish heart; and no adversity of ages was sufficient to crush these capacities and powers; who will say that such a people have not, under happier circumstances, within themselves a principle of self-regeneration and improvement, which will secure to them at least an ordinary portion of the happiness of which they have been so long deprived? The charity of other countries, and among them preeminently of England herself; the sympathy of distant and free states, on this occasion, in themselves have an effect. They will show Ireland that she is cared for; they will inspire her with the pleasing hope that she is not to be always the down-trodden and neglected province, the outcast nation among the nations of the earth.

PART 5

Effects of the Famine

DOCUMENT 37:

Extracts from William Steuart Trench, *Realities of Irish Life* (London, 1868), 101, 122–23

William Steuart Trench spent most of his career working as a land agent beginning in 1841. He left the profession upon the publication of *Realities of Irish Life*, his first book, in 1868. In these excerpts he describes his first encounter with the blight in 1846 and later recounts his role in the eviction of Kenmare in Country Kerry in 1850 on behalf of his employer **Lord Lansdowne**. The reality of migration was far harsher for the tenants than Trench assumes it will be.

Lord Lansdowne: Henry Petty-Fitzmaurice, 4th Marquess of Lansdowne (1816–66).

ᥱᥱ

On August 6, 1846,—I shall not readily forget the day,—I rode up, as usual to my mountain property, and my feelings may be imagined when, before I saw the crop, I smelt the fearful stench, now so well-known and recognized as the death sign of each field of potatoes. I was dismayed indeed, but I rode on: and, as I wound down the newly engineered road, running through the heart of the farm, and which forms the regular approach to the steward's house, I could scarcely bear the fearful and strange smell, which came up so rank from the luxuriant crop then growing all around; no perceptible change, except the smell, had as yet come upon the apparent prosperity of the deceitfully luxuriant stalks, but the experience of the past few days taught me that all was gone, and the crop was utterly worthless. [...]

I therefore resolved to put into practice a scheme which I had meditated for a long time previously, namely, to go myself to Lord Lansdowne at **Bowood**, to state to him the whole circumstances of the case, and to recommend him to adopt an extensive system of voluntary emigration as the only practicable and effective means of relieving this frightful destitution.... The broad sketch of the plan I laid before him was as follows: I showed him by the poor-house returns, that the number of paupers off his estate and receiving relief in the workhouse amounted to about three thousand. That

Bowood: Lansdowne's estate in England. Like many Irish landlords, Lord Lansdowne was an absentee landowner who entrusted the running of his estate to agents like Trench.

I was wholly unable to undertake the employment of these people in their present condition, on reproductive works; and that if left in the workhouse, the smallest amount they could possibly cost would be 5*l.* per head per annum, and thus that the poor-rates must necessarily amount, for some years to come, to 15,000*l.* per annum, unless these people died or left, and the latter was not probable. I stated also, that hitherto the people had been kept alive in the workhouse by grants from the rates in aid and other public money; but that this could not always go on. That the valuation of his estate in that district scarcely reached 10,000*l.* per annum; … I explained further to him, that under these circumstances, inasmuch as the poor-rates were a charge prior to rent, it would be impossible for his lordship to expect any rent whatever out of his estate for many years to come.

The remedy I proposed was as follows: That he should forthwith offer free emigration to every man, woman, and child now in the poor-house and chargeable to his estate. That I had been in communication with an emigration agent, who had offered to contract to take them to whatever port in America each pleased, at a reasonable rate per head. That even supposed they all accepted this offer, the total, together with a small sum per head for outfit and a few shillings on landing, would not exceed from 13,000*l.* to 14,000*l.*, a sum less than it would cost to support them in the workhouse for a single year. That in the one case he would not only free this estate of this mass of pauperism which had been allowed to accumulate upon it, but would put the people themselves in a far better way of earning their bread hereafter; whereas by feeding and retaining them where they were, they must remain a millstone around the neck of the estate, and prevent its rise for many years to come; and I plainly proved that it would be cheaper to him, and better for them, to pay for their emigration at once, than to continue to support them at home.

DOCUMENT 38:

Newspaper Coverage of Evictions

Many Irish peasants leased their farms from large landowners. During the famine evictions became commonplace as Irish farmers who fell behind on their rent were unceremoniously evicted by landowners and their agents.

e

London Illustrated News, 4 April 1846

EVICTION OF TENANTRY IN ROSCOMMON

A writer in The Freeman's Journal (a Dublin paper), gives an appalling account of the evictions of tenantry in the counties of Roscommon and Galway, from the estates of a lady named Gerrard. After giving some account of the property, the writer says:—"But let us proceed to the scene of ruin. Leaving Newtown Gerrard, you pass along to the left of the river Sheeven. On the road to Mount-Bellew, and about a mile from that pretty little town, the first sight of the recent scene of desolation presents itself to view. The village of Ballinglass, parish of Kilasobe, and barony of Killyon, county of Galway, was situate here, and was built on the confines of a bog, which, in a great measure, had been reclaimed by the tenants; the land, particularly at the rear of where the houses once stood, presenting an appearance of high cultivation, which was produced by the patient and hard industry of the tenants, who are now scattered over the country, without a resting-place for their weary and time-worn limbs, save that supplied by the broad canopy of Heaven, and the charity of a few poor people in the neighbourhood and in Mount Bellew. About a quarter of a mile from the main road, the houses were clustered together in groups of three or four, and so continued at short distances apart; they were in number 61. Not one of those habitations is now standing, save one; and you shall presently see the reason that this solitary dwelling is still permitted to remain. I went through, or I should rather say walked over, the ruins of all; and, from what I saw and heard, I concluded that they were all comfortable, clean, and neatly-kept habitations, with snug kitchen gardens either before or behind them. In corroboration of this, I have had the evidence of Mr. Mathew Donovan, of Ballygar, by whom I was accompanied, and who afforded me most important information on this inquiry.

"Mr. Donovan, who witnessed the scene which took place on Friday, March 13, 1846, describes it as the most appalling he had ever witnessed— women, young and old, running wildly to and fro with small portions of their property, in order to save it from the wreck; the screaming of the children, and wild wailings of the mothers driven from home and shelter; their peaceful homes, hallowed by a thousand fond recollections, all combined to form a picture of human misery such as the darkest imagination alone could realise. At an early hour on the morning of Friday, the 13th ult., the Sheriff, accompanied by a large force of the 49th Regiment, commanded by Captain Brown, and also by a heavy body of police, under the command of Mr. Cummings, proceeded to the place marked out for destruction. The people were then, according to the process of law, called on to render possession, and forthwith the bailiffs of Mrs. Gerrard commenced the work of demolition. In the first instance the roofs and portions of the walls were only thrown down: the former, in most instances, lie on the side of the road. It was stated that a child had been killed by the falling of a beam, as the bailiff would not wait until the boy came out of the house, but I am happy to inform you that this is a mistake. The boy was certainly hurt, but not severely, and, it appears, he was son to one of the bailiffs, not to a tenant, and that the transaction was purely accidental.

"Mr. Donovan and myself walked through the ruins of every house, and counted them to the number you have above. Great pains must have been taken to demolish the houses, as the walls were very thick, and composed of an umber clay, and when the inside turned up, good plaster and whitewash always appeared. Not content with throwing down the roofs and walls, the very foundations have been turned up; and here I must explain what, a moment ago, I stated, namely, that only a portion of the walls were pulled down in the first instance. That is fine; but, on the night of Friday, the wretched creatures pitched a few poles slantwise against the walls, covering them with the thatch, in order to procure shelter for the night; but when this was perceived next day, the bailiffs were despatched with orders to pull down all the walls, and root up the foundations, in order to prevent the 'wretches' (this, it appears, is a favourite term applied to these poor people) from daring to take shelter amid the ruins.

"When this last act had been perpetrated, the 'wretches' took to the ditches on the high road, where they slept in parties of from 10 to 15 each, huddled together before a fire, for the two succeeding nights. I saw the marks of the fires in the ditches; everybody can see them, and the temporary shelter which the 'wretches' endeavoured to raise around them. These, with the sticks rescued from their recent dwellings, the thatch and the dung, remain there as evidence of the truth of my statement. The whole extent of ground connected with the village is over 400 acres. It may be some acres more or less, but I believe, from the best information, that this will be found about the number of acres which Mrs. Gerrard has recovered, and over which her fat bullocks may now roam, without a solitary hut to intercept them."

The writer concludes his statement with a list of the families, and their names, ejected on the 13th of March, from which it appears that 270 persons have been sent on the world without a home or even a shelter.

Nation, 7 **November 1846**

PENALTY ON FAMINE

Sentence of doom has gone forth against the barony of Tulla, in the county of Clare…

Several months ago it began to be given out that public works were to be provided to secure wages to all who could work, that so the poor people, their potatoes being utterly lost, might have wherewithal to get provisions to keep them alive. Men's minds were kept on the stretch by this expectation of Government relief—they were led to rely upon it; tenants began to neglect their own private work; landlords to cast about for the best method of preserving themselves from spoliation; those who had many labourers employed began to dismiss them, and to save money for the expected taxation; mutual hatred and distrust came between even good landlords and their dependants.

Punch, **vol 13., 1847: 22**

HEROISM OF AN IRISH LANDLORD.

THE IRISH TAX-GATHERER.

Nation, 29 September 1849

No later than Monday the 17th inst. a great part of the village of Clare was razed to the ground, and no less than Twenty-Seven families sent adrift on the world by the lord of the soil, Marcus Paterson, Esq., of Killaloe.

The facts of this case are peculiarly distressing, for the evictions could by no means improve the property, as the place where the miserable hovels (of the worst possible class) stood is a commonage, called "the Commons of Clare."

The drama of Monday last was cause of the saddest and most revolting that even this far-famed county ever produced. The shrieking of miserable women and their famine-stricken children, with the mournful wailing of old grey-haired men, is beyond all description. So horrible was the scene that even Mr. Tidd, the sheriff, though accustomed to see misery in its worst shape, could not endure it, and generously endeavoured to alleviate it, by giving money to some of the greatest objects. I cannot proceed with these disgusting details. Suffice it to say that the whole mass of the evicted creatures are now to be seen in groups by the roadside, or stowed away in unoccupied pigsties of their neighbours, with scarcely a rag of covering, and literally without one morsel of food.

London Illustrated News, 20 October 1849

IRISH EVICTIONS

The state of Ireland has again become the one topic of paramount interest. All other subjects of foreign or domestic politics yield to its urgency. Nothing like the misery of the Irish people exists under the sun. Even the gleam of hope that appeared to brighten their prospects a few weeks ago, when a harvest more than usually abundant was ripe for the sickle, has disappeared. The very abundance of the crop has proved a new source of disquietude, of heart-burnings, of agrarian conflict, and of national misery. The transient hope has yielded to a more permanent despair. The landlords evict their miserable tenants by hundreds and by thousands; the miserable tenants go to the Union, or receive out-door relief at the rate of seven-eighths of a penny per day, till the munificent allowance lapses in the grave;—while the small farmers, still in possession of a portion of the soil, struggle with the landlords, and with the constabulary, for the crop. The Irish papers teem with accounts of outrages. Each day's struggle of the farmer with his landlord becomes more fierce than the struggle of yesterday. The landlords are at their wits' end, for to them, also, it is a question of ownership or confiscation—life or death. Their tenants cling with dishonest, but scarcely unnatural, tenacity to a crop, the whole of which is not sufficient to pay rent, poor's-rates, county cess, and arrears, but some portion of which is fairly due to the absolute necessities of the men who ploughed or dug the soil, and sowed the seed. The great bulk of the people either take the part of the farmers against the lords of the soil, or, to use the words of Mr. Poulett Scrope, bear the barbarities they suffer "with a patience and resignation which it is heart-breaking to witness, and which one scarcely knows whether to praise or to blame."

London Illustrated News, 6 April 1850

EVICTIONS OF TENANTRY

Evictions are as numerous as ever throughout the country. It is stated that two-thirds of the land in the North Riding of Tipperary, held by tenant farmers, will change occupiers this year; and the Tipperary Vindicator adds, "never were such shoals of ejectment notices levelled against the unfortunate tenants as the landlords are issuing for the coming Quarter Sessions in Thurles and Nenagh." The Newry Examiner says: We have received a letter from a Drogheda correspondent, stating that between twenty and thirty families (numbering about one hundred individuals) were recently ejected from their holding on the Mornington property, situate on the seashore, three miles from Drogheda, in Meath.

Extracts from Robert Whyte, *The Ocean Plague: Or, a Voyage to Quebec in an Irish Emigrant Vessel* (Boston, 1848), 25, 28, 29, 32, 37, 38, 42–43, 51, 58, 60, 77, 78–79, 80, 88–90, 100

> This book appeared in 1848, one year after the journey the author portrays. On the title page he describes himself as "a cabin passenger." The book portrays a famine-era journey from Ireland to Canada. Later the author made his way to the United States. Aside from this book nothing else is known about Robert Whyte.

ev

Tuesday, June 1st

In consequence of this discovery, there was a general muster in the afternoon, affording me an opportunity of seeing all the emigrants; and a more motley crowd I never beheld;—of all ages, from the infant to the feeble grandsire and withered crone.

While they were on deck, the hold was searched, but without any further discovery, no one having been found below but a boy, who was unable to leave his berth, from debility. Many of them appeared to me to be quite unfit to undergo the hardship of a long voyage; but they were inspected and passed by a doctor, although the captain, as he informed me, protested against taking some of them. One old man was so infirm, that he seemed to me to be in the last stage of consumption.

The next matter to be accomplished was to regulate the allowance of provisions to which each family was entitled. One pound of meal or of bread being allowed for each adult,—half a pound for each individual under fourteen years of age,—and one third of a pound for each child under seven years. Thus, although there were 110 souls, great and small, they counted as 84 adults. That was, therefore, the number of pounds to be issued daily.

June 3rd

The meal with which they were provided was of very bad quality;—this they had five days; and biscuit, which was good, two days in the week.

June 4th

I learned that many of these emigrants had never seen the sea nor a ship, until they were on board. They were chiefly from the county Meath, and sent out at the expense of their landlord, without any knowledge of the country to which they were going, or means of livelihood, except the labor of the father of each family. All they know concerning Canada was, that they were to land in Quebec, and to go up the country; moreover they had a settled conviction that the voyage was to last exactly three weeks.

Tuesday, June 8th

The head committee reported that two women were ill; they were therefore dosed according to the best skill of the mistress.

June 12th

The two women who first became ill, were said to show symptoms of bad fever; and additional cases of illness were reported by the Head committee. The patients begged for an increased allowance of water; which could not be granted, as the supply was very scanty; two casks having leaked.

June 15th

He [the captain] felt much alarmed; nor was it to be wondered at that contagious fever,—which under the most advantageous circumstances, and under the watchful eyes of the most skilful physicians, baffles the highest ability,— should terrify one having the charge of so many human beings, likely to fall prey to the unchecked progress of the dreadful disease for once having shown itself in the unventilated hold of a small brig, containing one hundred and ten living creatures, how could it possibly be stayed,—without suitable medicines, medical skill, or even pure water to slake the patient's burning thirst?

The prospect before us was an awful one; and there was no hope for us but in the mercy of God.

Tuesday, June 22nd

One of the sailors was unable for duty, and the mate feared he had the fever.

The reports from the hold were growing even more alarming, and some of the patients who were mending, had relapsed. One of the women were every moment expected to breathe her last, and her friends—an aunt and cousins—were inconsolable about her; as they persuaded her to leave her father and mother, and come with them. The mate said that her feet were swollen to double their natural size, and covered with black putrid spots. I spent a considerable part of the day watching a shark that followed in our wake with great constancy.

July 9th

We now had fifty sick, being nearly one half the whole number of passengers.

July 17th

The poor passengers were greatly terrified by the storm, and suffered exceed-ingly. They were so buffeted about that the sick could not be tended; and after calm was restored a woman was found dead in her berth.

July 19th

The first thing he did was to open his huge trunk, and take from it a pam-phlet, which proved to be the quarantine regulations; he handed it to the captain, who spent a long time poring over it. When he had read it I got a look at it—one side was printed in French, the other in English. The rules were very stringent, and the penalties for their infringement exceedingly severe; the sole control being vested in the head physician, the power given to whom was most arbitrary. We feared that we should undergo a long detention in quarantine, and learned that we could hold no communications whatever with the shore until our arrival at **Grosse Isle**.

Grosse Isle: Grosse Île in French, an island in Quebec, Canada, which served as an immigration depot during the famine era.

July 28th

I could not believe it possible that here within reach of help we should be left as neglected as when upon the ocean;—that after a voyage of two months' duration, we were to be left still enveloped by reeking pestilence, the sick without medicine, medical skill, nourishment, or so much as a drop of pure water; for the river although not saline here, was polluted by the most disgusting objects, thrown overboard from the several vessels.

July 29th

They remained in the hold for about an hour, and when they returned com-plimented the captain on the cleanliness of the vessel. They staid a short time talking to us upon the deck, and the account they gave of the horrid conditions of many of the ships in quarantine was frightful. In the holds of some of them they said, that they were up to their ankles in filth. The wretched emigrants crowded together like cattle, and corpses remaining long unburied, the sailors being ill, and the passengers unwilling to touch them. They also told us of the vast numbers of sick in the hospitals, and in tents, upon the island, and that many nuns, clergymen and doctors, were lying in typhus fever, taken from the patients. [...]

We lay at some distance from the island [Grosse Île], the distant view of which was exceedingly beautiful. At the far end were rows of white tents and marquees, resembling the encampment of an army; somewhat nearer was the little fort, and residence of the superintended physicians, and nearer still the chapel, seaman's hospital, and little village, with its wharf and a few sail boats; the most adjacent extremity being rugged rocks, among which grew beautiful fir trees. At high water this portion was detached from the main island, and formed a most picturesque islet. But this scene of natural beauty was sadly deformed by the dismal display of human suffering that it presented;—helpless creatures being carried by sailors over the rocks, on their way to the hospital,—boats arriving with patients, some of whom died in their transmission from their ships. Another and still more awful sight, was a continuous line of boats, each carrying its freight of dead to the burial-ground, and forming an endless funeral procession. Some had several corpses, so tied up in canvass that the stiff, sharp outline of death was easily traceable; others had rude coffins, constructed by the sailors, from the boards of their berths, or I should say, cribs.

August 1st

They had on their best clothes, and were all clean, with the exception of one incorrigible family. The doctor came on board in the forenoon, to inspect the passengers, who were all called on the deck, but those who were unable. Placing himself at a barrier, he allowed each to pass, one by one; making those he suspected of being feverish show their tongues. This processing lasted about a quarter of an hour; when the doctor went into the hold to examine those below, and to see if it were clean; he then wrote out the order to admit the six patients to hospital, and promised to send the steamer to take the remainder; and which we should have clean bills. When he had gone, the patients were lowered into the boat amid a renewal of the indescribable woe that followed the previous separations. Two of them were orphan sisters, who were sent for by a brother in Upper Canada. Another was a mother, who had tended all her family through illness,—now careworn, and heartbroken, she became herself a prey....

While the captain was away with the boat the steamer came alongside us to take our passengers. It did not take very long to transship them, as few of them had any luggage. Many of them were sadly disappointed when they learned that they were to be carried on to Montreal, as those who had left their relatives upon Grosse Isle, hoped, that as Quebec was not far distant, they would be enabled by some means to hear of them, by staying there.[...]

Of the passengers I never afterwards saw but two, both of them young men, who got employment upon the **Lachine canal**. The rest wandered over the country, carrying nothing with them but disease; and that but few of them survived the severity of the succeeding winter (ruined as their constitutions were) I am quite confident.

Lachine canal: A canal in southwestern Montreal that was undergoing major extension in the 1840s.

DOCUMENT 40:

Extracts from *Papers Relative to Emigration to the British Provinces in North America and to the Australian Colonies* (London, 1847), 1, 70

The scale and condition of Irish-famine emigrants presented significant issues for the places that received them. Below is some Canadian correspondence dealing with the issues presented by Irish-famine migration.

e

A Letter from the Medical Superintendent at Grosse Isle, 24 May 1847

Sir,

In submitting for the information of his Excellency the Governor-general the report of sick for the week ending Saturday the 22nd instant, I regret to have to call attention to a state of illness and distress among the newly arrived emigrants, unprecedented in this country even during the prevalence of cholera in 1832 and 1834. Every vessel bringing Irish passengers (but more especially those from Liverpool and Cork), has lost many by fever and dysentery on the voyage, and has arrived here with numbers of sick. Since I last had the honour of addressing you, 17 vessels have arrived with Irish passengers; five from Cork, four from Liverpool, and the others from Sligo, Belfast, Londonderry, and New Ross. The number of passengers with which these vessels left port was 5,607; out of these the large number of 260 have died on the passage, and upwards of 700 have been admitted to hospital, or are being treated on board their vessels, waiting vacancies to be landed.

The number now under treatment, as exhibited by the weekly report, is 695, and there remain on board the ships "Aberdeen" and "Achilles" from Liverpool, and ships "Bee" from Cork, and "Wolfville" from Sligo, 164 sick, who receive medical assistance on board, and will be landed as soon as accommodation can be made by turning the passengers' sheds in to hospitals.

I have taken upon me to engage the services of Drs. Jacques and McGrath, while waiting his Excellency's authority for that purpose, but shall require at least two more medical assistants, as these gentlemen have already charge of upwards of 300 sick, and will be unable to give attendance to the large number still to land, without taking into account the number who may arrive among the many thousands now due. May I beg to be furnished with the necessary authority for this purpose; my own time is wholly taken up on inspecting the vessels that arrive, in selecting the sick from them, and in prescribing for those on board who cannot be landed.

I have, in conformity with the authority given me by your letter of the 29th instant, made arrangements for the erection of an addition hospital ward and shed.

G.M. Douglas, Medical Superintendent

Dispatch from Earl Grey to Lieutenant-Governor Sir W.M.G. Colebrooke, 3 September 1847

I have to acknowledge the receipt of your despatches Nos. 60 and 64, of the 6th and 13th July accompanied by returns of vessels which have arrived with emigrants at St. John's, New Brunswick, down to the 7th of that month.

I lament the disastrous consequences which appear from these papers to have resulted from the introduction of whole families of poor persons into New Brunswick, including the aged and infirm, before any provision had been made for the reception and care of them on their arrival. I entirely concur in the opinion that the most healthy system of emigration is that in which the able-bodied members of families proceed first to the colony, and delay sending for their relatives until they can provide for their maintenance; but under the peculiar circumstances of the emigration of this year, conducted as it has been under the pressure of distress and at the expense of individuals, I do not see how Her Majesty's Government could have taken any steps to secure so desirable a mode of proceeding.

I am gratified to observe that the local authorities at St. John's are making every effort to mitigate the sufferings and provide proper accommodation for the sick emigrants in that city and at Partridge Island.

DOCUMENT 41:

Excerpts from the *Annals of the Grey Nuns*[1]

The Sisters of Charity, or the Grey Nuns, at Grosse Île were the first to come to the aid of the Irish emigrants arriving in Canada in 1847. In their annals they describe the conditions of the migrants and the dangers they themselves faced in tending to them.

e

News of my arrival spread, and I was soon surrounded by two hundred (200) ghosts, several of which were delirious. I still hear their savage cries, I still see their haggard eyes, their appearance bleak and wild. When I wanted to leave, I experienced such pain in ridding myself of the hold of a woman who was breastfeeding a newborn. The unfortunate woman and her children were in a state of almost complete nudity. The police opened a house that had been closed for several days; we found on the floor two frozen cadavers, half devoured by rats! A mother in delirium had wanted, for the sake of modesty, to bury and hide her daughter's completely naked cadaver under the rocks, she was twelve years old. The doctor at the clinic found seven people in a house sheltered under the same blanket. One of the members of this group of people had been dead for several hours. The survivors did not have the strength to remove the corpse nor move themselves.

The bishops responded to the Pope's request, from all parts of the world, for abundant donations were sent to the Church's veritable children in green Erin. We estimate $100,000.00 was the total of a collection made in New York for Ireland; an anonymous woman sent $1,000.00; some said that New York contributed $300,000.00, Philadelphia $250,000.00, Washington $500,000.00, Charlestown $100,000.00, New-Orleans $250,000.00. A great quantity of clothing and many provisions were also part of this contribution....

It was written in Dublin on March 6th, in the *Morning Chronicle* "Newspapers from the province still contain the most distressing details about the famine. We are importing food and the government and others make an effort of generosity; but how can we save an entire population succumbing to hunger? In the town of Derrymacash, county Antrim, from January 1st to February 26th, we counted 400 deaths. The county of Armagh has suffered much; in the occidental division of West Carbery, the local

---

1 Reprinted with permission from *The Irish Famine Archive* (http://faminearchive.nuigalway.ie), Project Leader Dr. Jason King.

authority was forced to order the digging of new graves, the land no longer sufficient. In a Mission for the Poor in Kilkenny, 520 with fever succumbed. What renders the fever deadly is that typhus often complicates it...."

Quebec and overseas [international] newspapers did not cease talking of Irish emigration. Some statistics from the time are as follows: "From January 1st to May 17th inclusive, 4,627 passengers arrived at the quarantine stations. 537 died at sea. 1,115 were received by the Hospital of the Marine. 795 of these were ill with typhus. The number of emigrants arriving in Quebec on May 27th was 5,546, and on June 1st, 25 ships were expected to arrive at Grosse-Isle." [...]

We do not neglect the devotion with which QUEBEC attempted to prevent the spread of the scourge and the care with which they tried to wrestle so many victims from death. Despite the diligent services of the Faculty of Medicine and the precautions implemented, a great number of emigrants died at Grosse-Isle and at the Hospital of the Marine.

6,000 Irish disembarked on our shores, 3,500 of which stopped at the sheds or ambulances. 2,000 disappeared in search of more favorable pastures; many died. There nevertheless still remains 250 in the shelters. On June 25th of this same year, the sick numbered 850 in the shelters; around twenty were dying each day. July 2nd, the sick numbered 1,300, the number of those who died went from THIRTY to FORTY a day. Death did not only prey on the ambulances, it also victimized those in the city, as the contagion began to spread, and spiritual relief was becoming more and more urgent in several neighborhoods.

Let us continue.... The first shelters that the fellowship built to receive the emigrants stretched along the canal, this territory belonging to the General Hospital. Point-Saint-Charles, where it was situated, was once a rural valley, and very swampy, as this year saw torrential rains. Despite the mud and other inconveniences, the sisters made their journey within twenty minutes, already hearing the groans of the ill and the wails of the dying.... We disperse ourselves in this unfamiliar maze.... Could we imagine for a moment the spectacle this multitude of men and women piled pell-mell offered, up to three or four in the same bed, indifferent to everything, groaning, however, heartbreakingly?

These sheds are usually 100 to 200 feet long and 25 by 30 in size, separated by walls and contiguous from one another. Some, however, are separated by a distance of 30 feet; this proximity renders service easier. They are furnished but with poor beds made from simple planks, attached to the walls and more or less inclined in the same way seen in barracks or in police stations. We will substitute them soon with bunks; these are poles with crude planks around the circumference of which a layer of straw makes a soft bed....

[A]n Irishwoman recovering from typhus arrived [at the makeshift hospital] searching for her husband and children. After many questions, the sister recognized the unfortunate mother of the little orphans she was caring for. With haste she gave her all the details to satisfy her. This poor woman put her hands together and raised her gaze towards the heavens: Ah! My sister, said she, with the deepest of pain; I am consoled to learn that my children are still alive and that they have been returned to me! Blessed be the Lord! This family's name was McKay.

Now, a glance on the general sanitary state of **Bytown**. Since last June 15th, there were illnesses, as many in the General Hospital of the Grey Nuns, as in the shelters and in the town, regularly, an average of 200 sick. At the hospital, the number of sick always ranged from fifty-five to sixty. Since the said date, there entered in the hospital: in the month of June, one-hundred and eleven (111) sick; in the month of July, one hundred and eighty-two (182) in the month of August, and to now, one hundred and sixty-seven (167) which totaled four hundred and sixty (460). One hundred and forty (140) people died in the hospital; one hundred and sixty (160) in the shelters and one hundred (100) in the city; a grand total of: four hundred (400).

Bytown: Modern-day Ottawa, the capital of Canada; the name was changed from Bytown in 1855.

PART 6

Aftermath

DOCUMENT 42:

Report on the Famine by Sir William Wilde, *Census of Ireland for the Year 1851*, V(I) (Dublin, 1856), 242–44, 246–47

Sir William Wilde was an Irish surgeon and author, and father of the famed Irish author Oscar Wilde. In addition to his writing and medical practice, Wilde also worked with census commissioners to analyse data relating to deaths for the pre-famine census in 1841. For the 1851 census Wilde was appointed Assistant Census Commissioner and wrote a detailed analysis on the mortality of the famine.

e

We have seen, that during the hundred years previous to this date, repeated failures in the potato crop of Ireland were noted. Public aid was afforded, and private benevolence largely contributed, to save, year by year, from absolute starvation, those who were reduced to want by the failure of their favourite and most prolific **esculent**; but which, for upwards of a century, in all weathers, during the extremes of heat and cold, in dryness and moisture, whether planted early or late, was destined to fail, either in whole or in part, leaving those who trusted to its support for food and maintenance nearly destitute for months together previous to the ensuing crop arriving at maturity; so that a state of chronic famine had existed in many districts on the west coast of Ireland for several years antecedent to the late great potato failure....

The potato, as a vegetable support of animal life, possesses in its chemical constituents a remarkable supply of those materials most necessary to the healthy preservation of life, along with other qualities superior to most other known esculents; and as it requires little culinary preparation, either to heighten its flavour or extract its nutrition, can it be wondered at if the Irish peasant, who is most inexperienced in cookery, should prefer this simple article of food, and turn with dislike and distrust from nutriment of a different character offered in an unusual and, to him, a less palatable

esculent: Suitable for food.

form? The potato, by its occasional abundant produce and easy cultivation, tended to promote early marriages and consequent increase of population, and afforded, likewise, a means of rent-paying which largely contributed to the minute subdivision of land in Ireland. It is not surprising, therefore, that when this product of the soil failed, not only did famine and disease accrue to the immediate cultivation, but that the misery consequent thereon should be felt by many of those who derived their chief means of support from it.

No vegetable, perhaps, ever effected the same amount of influence upon the physical, moral, social, and political condition of country, as the potato exercised over Ireland, when cultivated to the extent it was, immediately preceding the famine of 1845. With its failure, these valuable animals, the pigs, were almost extinguished in many districts; which was also, to a great extent, the case with the poultry.

During the prevalence of the famine, food rose to an excessively high price; and some idea may be formed of the loss sustained by the country from the fact that sixteen millions' worth of produce is supposed to have been destroyed up to the autumn of 1846; while the general state of destruction may be calculated by the measures of relief afforded during the crisis of that fearful period; relief, far surpassing in amount, derived from more distant sources, and springing from the excited sympathies of a greater range of society, than any precedent can be found for in our social history upon similar occasions of national distress. Agriculture was neglected, and the land in many places remained untilled. Thousands were supported from day to day upon the bounty of out-door relief; the closest ties of kindred were dissolved; the most ancient and long-cherished usages of the people were disregarded; food the most revolting to human palates was eagerly devoured; the once proverbial gaiety and light-heartedness of the peasant people seemed to have vanished completely, and village merriment or marriage festival was no longer heard or seen throughout the regions desolated by the intensity and extent of the famine; finally, the disorganization of society became marked and memorable by the exodus of above one million of people, who deserted their homes and hearths to seek for food and shelter in foreign lands, of whom thousands perished from pestilence and the hardships endured on shipboard.

It is scarcely possible to exaggerate in imagination what people will do, and are forced to do, before they die from absolute want of food, for not only does the body become blackened and wasted by chronic starvation, but the mind likewise becomes darkened, the feelings callous, blunted, and apathetic; and a peculiar fever is generated, which became but too well known to the medical profession in Ireland at that time, and to all those engaged in administering relief.

In this state, of what may be called mania, before the final collapse takes place, when the victim sinks into utter prostration from inanition, some instances may have occurred at which human nature, in its ordinary healthy condition, revolts. Thus a stipendiary magistrate stated, in the court-house of Galway, in extenuation of the crime of a poor prisoner, brought up for stealing food, that to his own knowledge, before he was driven to the theft, he and his family had actually consumed part of a human body lying dead in the cabin with them.

Generally speaking, the actually starving people lived upon the carcasses of diseased cattle, upon dogs, and dead horses, but principally on the **herbs of the field, nettle tops, wild mustard, and water cresses,** and even in some places dead bodies were found with grass in their mouth. The shamrock, or wood-sorrel (*oxalis acetosella)*, mentioned by **Spenser** as forming part of the food of the famished people in his time, does not now, owing to the extirpation of woods, exist in sufficient quantity to afford any nutriment; but along the coast every description of sea-weed was greedily devoured, often with fatal consequences; even the dillisk, or "salt-leaf," though a safe occasional condiment, became the cause of disease when used as the sole support of life.

Some approximation to the amount of the immense mortality that prevailed may be gleaned from the published tables, which show that within that calamitous period between the end of 1845 and the conclusion of the first quarter of 1851, as many as 61,260 persons died in the hospitals and sanitary institutions, exclusive of those who died in the workhouses and auxiliary workhouses. Taking the recorded deaths from fever alone, between the beginning of 1846 and the end of 1849, and assuming the mortality at 1 in 10, which is the very lowest calculation, and far below what we believe really did occur, above a million and a-half, or 1,595,040 persons, being 1 in 4.11 of the population in 1851, must have suffered from fever during that period. But no pen has recorded the numbers of the forlorn and starving who perished by the wayside or in the ditches, or of the mournful groups, sometimes of whole families, who lay down and died, one after another, upon the floor of their miserable cabin, and so remained uncoffined and unburied, till chance unveiled the appalling scene. No such amount of suffering and misery has been chronicled in Irish history since the days of Edward Bruce; and yet, through all, the forbearance of the Irish peasantry, and the calm submission with which they bore the deadliest ills that can fall on man, can scarcely be paralleled in the annals of any people. Numbers, indeed, were sent to prison for petty crimes, often committed to save themselves or children from starvation, and there met their death from pestilential diseases arising from the overcrowding and contagion in those institutions; yet the slight amount of crime of a serious nature which prevailed throughout Ireland

herbs of the field ... : It was common for these to be eaten during times of famine, but they do not provide enough nourishment to live on.

Spenser: Edmund Spenser (1553–99), an English poet who wrote extensive descriptions of Ireland during the Tudor reconquest.

during the years of extreme destitutions was remarkable; and instances occurred in which the judges, feeling that want alone drove the prisoners to its commission, directed their discharge without further punishment.

According to the Report of the Census Commissioners for 1841, the annual average emigration between 1831 and 1841 was 40,346, and from the 30th June in the latter year to the end of 1845 it was averaged 61,242 per annum. Such, however, was the effect of the potato blight and the warning voice of the pestilence, that the number rose to 105,955 in 1846, after which the emigration seemed to partake of the nature of an epidemic, and in 1847 the numbers who left the country more than doubled those who departed in the previous year. Owing to a slight mitigation of the potato blight, and a consequent improvement in the harvest of 1847, there was an arrest of the exodus in the beginning of 1848, when the numbers who emigrated only amounted to 178,159; but in the following year they again rose to 214,425. In 1850 the amount of emigration was 209,054. The emigration reached its highest point in 1851, when the numbers amount to 249,721, after which they gradually decreased to 150,222 in 1854; yet, even in 1855, long after the extreme poor, the panic-stricken, and the destitute, had passed to other countries, or had found a refuge in the workhouses, or rest in the grace, the remarkable spectacle of whole families—usually well-dressed, intelligent-looking people—of all ages and sexes, the mere infant as well as the extremely aged—might be observed passing through the metropolis on the way to the emigrant vessel....

Concurrent with the foregoing state of famine, and the disruption of the social condition of the people, pestilence came upon the nation in the following order: Fever, Scurvy, Diarrhoea and Dysentery, Cholera, Influenza, and **Ophthalmia**. Respecting the mooted question of famine and fever being cause and effect, we have evidence from the foregoing examination of the social and medical history of Ireland, that while fever may spread epidemically, without being either preceded or accompanied by famine, but as simply the result of a peculiar epidemic constitution, of which the memorable period dating from 1814 is an example—yet it is scarcely possible to lessen the physical strength of a people by withholding their customary amount of food, or to alter suddenly the chemical constituents of that people's usual source of sustenance, without rendering them liable to epidemic disease; while it is without the range of all probability that depression of mind, amounting to the despair, consequent upon parents witnessing the lingering starvation of their offspring, or children observing the haggard looks and wasted forms of their parents and near relatives, could occur without fatal effects on the human frame. Furthermore, it is an established fact, that we cannot congregate together human beings, in crowded masses, whether in camp or in huts, in barracks or workhouses, in overcrowded cities, or even

Ophthalmia: Inflammation of the eye; Wilde was primarily an eye surgeon.

upon the public works, without pestilence of one kind or another being generated. And when once epidemic disease has sprung up under any of the foregoing circumstances, experience proves that it will spread rapidly and extensively unless checked by moral combined with physical treatment, such as the substitution of hope and happiness for misery and despondency—of nutritious, and what is of paramount consequence, accustomed dietary, for the unusual, insufficient, innutritive, and often unpalatable food which want and necessity may have forced upon the people. Lastly, there must be immediate and total separation of the sick from the healthy, the living from the dead. Epidemics may be said to prevail, when the mortality from the class of epidemic diseases is in the proportion of more than one-third of the total deaths from all specified causes. In the returns for 1841, this class of disease was to the general mortality from all causes, as 1 in 3.11 for the entire kingdom; but in the present decade, the returns give a proportion of deaths from this class, to the total deaths from all other diseases as 1 in 2.5....

The rise and progress of this epidemic disease is, however, equally remarkable with the amount of persons who fell victims to it. Up to the end of the year 1845, the annual average mortality from fever in Ireland was but 7,249, although it must be borne in mind that the means of arriving at an approximation to the truth increases as we get back to the early period of the inquiry. According to the information with which we have been supplied, the disease increased gradually from 1840 to 1846, when the deaths reached 17,145 in the latter year. In 1847 there were 57,095 death from fever; in 1848 there were 45,948; in 1849, as many as 39,316; and in 1850 23,545.

Extracts from Mary Anne Sadlier, *Bessy Conway; Or, the Irish Girl in America* (New York, 1861)

Born Mary Anne Madden in Co. Cavan, Ireland, Sadlier emigrated for Canada in 1844 and married the publisher James Sadlier. Sadlier primarily wrote didactic novels about the Irish-American experience, influenced by her fervent Catholicism. *Bessy Conway* tells the story of the trials of a young Irish woman who works as a domestic servant in New York. She is tempted by a secular life in the United States but remains a devout Catholic and is eventually able to return to Ireland and rescue her family from destitution.

Preface

It seems to me that there is little need of a Preface for *Bessy Conway*. The object of the book is plain enough; so plain, indeed, that there is no possibility of any one's mistaking it for a better or a worse. It is simply an attempt to point out to Irish Girls in America—especially that numerous class whose lot it is to hire themselves out for work, the true and never-failing path to success in this world, and happiness in the next. Perhaps in the vast extent of the civilized world, there is no class more exposed to evil influences than the Irish Catholic girls who earn a precarious living at service in America. To those who are even superficially acquainted with the workings of that chaotic mass which forms the population of our cities, of the awful depth of corruption weltering below the surface, and the utter forgetfulness of things spiritual, it is a matter of surprise that so many of the simple-hearted peasant girls of Ireland retain their home-virtues and follow the teachings of religion in these great **Babylons** of the west.

The subject looms up before us in tremendous proportions as we come to consider it, and the mind shrinks appalled from the consequences and probabilities presenting themselves on every side. The vast number of these girls, their unprotected state, generally speaking; the dangers of every kind awaiting them after they have slipped the moorings which bound them in safety to the old Christian land, where virtue and religion are the basis of society; and, unfortunately, the mischief is not confined to themselves. Every woman has a mission, either for good or evil; and, unhappily for society, the lax, and the foolish, and the unprincipled will find husbands as well as the good and virtuous. The sphere of influence thus extended, who can calculate the results, whether good or ill?

Babylons: Originally an Ancient Mesopotamian city, in this case Sadlier is referencing a great but sinful city called Babylon in the Book of Revelations.

Some may say that I have drawn too gloomy a picture. Such persons know little about it. The reality exceeds my powers of description, and I have only to say in conclusion, that the fathers and mothers who suffer their young daughters to come out unprotected to America in search of imaginary goods, would rather see them laid in their graves than lose sight of them, did they know the dangers which beset their path in the New World.

I have written this book from a sincere and heartfelt desire to benefit these young country-women of mine, by showing them how to win respect and inspire confidence on the part of their employers, and at the same time, to avoid the snares and pitfalls which have been the ruin of so many of their own class. Let them be assured that it rests with themselves whether they do well or ill in America—whether they do honor to their country and their faith, or bring shame and reproach to both.

————

We will now leave Bessy Conway for awhile, and return to the old homestead she left behind,

"On that bright spring morning long ago,"

When she went to seek her fortune in America. Full seven years had passed away since Bessy left her father's cottage, and eventful as those years had been to her they were not less so to "the old folks at home."

"The summer sun was sinking
 With a mild light calm and mellow,"

And its slanting rays rested on the straw-thatched roof of Denis Conway, but there was no beauty in the picture, for the look of comfort and neatness that belonged to the place in former days was gone, and had left scarce a trace behind. The thatch so trim and smooth in those by-gone days was broken in many places, and covered with patches of moss, whilst chicken weed and darnel flaunted their unwelcome verdure on the gable-tops. The white walls beneath were discolored and stripped here and there of the "pebble-dash" that had covered them all so neatly. The small windows, too, were disfigured with sundry pieces of board nailed on as substitutes for broken panes, and altogether the house had a desolate, neglected look in painful contrast with its former appearance. The haggard was empty, and so was the byer [byre]—the horse was gone from the stable, and even the sty had lost its tenants—the overgrown sow was no longer there with her squeaking brood, nor the well-cared bacon pigs, which, in other days, furnished so important a share of the winter's store for the family. The fowl were gone from the barn-door, for no grain was there to gather them round it. The discordant chorus of the farm-yard was no longer heard; the very hum of the bees in the adjacent garden had ceased, and silence sat brooding over

Denis Conway's cottage. Decay, too, was there, and, beneath its withering touch, all things were hastening to ruin.

This was the aspect of affairs without, and within it was nothing better. The same look of desolation was everywhere visible, but its saddest imprint was on the people. Famine and disease had found their way into that happy household, and misery sat on the threshold. The aged father and mother sat opposite each other in their old straw chairs, by the dull, flickering fire, watching with distended eyes the unsavory mess which Nancy was making for the family supper, consisting of water and nettles, with a handful or so of oatmeal. Nancy herself as she bent over the pot was a living picture of hunger, and the low, suppressed moans which came at irregular intervals from a straw "shake-down" in the corner indicated the presence of one who suffered bodily pain. It was Ellen, the bright-eyed, dark-haired fairy, whose laugh used to ring the loudest, whose foot sprang the lightest in days not long gone by. But the terrible fangs of hunger had fastened on her vitals, and disease was wearing her young life away....

Truly that was a dismal time in Denis Conway's cottage, and in many a cottage through the length and breadth of Ireland. It was the terrible year of the Famine, as the reader will have guessed, and the ruin which had been progressing rapidly during the previous years of dearth and commercial depression, and the failure of crops, had at length reduced the small farmers of the country, and amongst the rest Denis Conway and his family, to the pitiful state in which we have seen them. What money Denis had had was long since gone, no corn or wheat was ripening in his fields, for in the spring-time he had not the means to purchase seed, the stock could not live without eating, and one after another every hoof was taken to the fair and sold. Milk and butter, of course, went with them, and what was worse than all, the money which they brought—it was little compared with what it would have been at another time—had most of it to go to satisfy the clamorous demands of Mrs. Herbert's bailiffs. So from bad to worse things went on, till everything was wanting in the once-plentiful household, everything except the grace of God and His holy peace. That was still there in as great abundance as ever, and faith and hope, though at times, perhaps, dimmed by the heavy clouds of suffering and privation, were never wholly obscured. The old man himself never allowed distrust or fear to enter his mind: no patriarch of old ever trusted more firmly in the Lord Almighty, and the darker the clouds that gathered around him the more steadily he fixed his eyes on the light that glimmered afar in the firmament. It was sad to see the failing old man wandering in the morning or evening twilight around his fallow fields where in other years the golden grain would, at that season, wave luxuriant, ready for the sickle, and the rugged leaves of the potato stalk covering whole acres with their dark green hue of promise. Now the tall rag-weed nodded in the summer breeze, the dock-weed spread its broad leaves on the arid soil, and the fiery nettle grew and flourished where a weed dared not rear its head before, to dispute possession with the carefully-tended grain-stalk. As Denis noted all this, and thought how many other farms in that fertile district were like unto his own, he would sit down on a broken stile, or one of those huge boulders—geological puzzles—so common in the inland as well as the maritime counties of Ireland, and burying his face in his hands, give free vent to that natural sorrow which he could not but feel at sight of so much desolation. At home, the old man tried to conceal his feelings, for he knew that the wife of his youth and the children of his love were pining and wasting day by day under the blighting hand of misery, and he felt it incumbent on himself to set them an example of fortitude and resignation. One of the hardest of his trials was the apparent neglect of Bessy, for, although he tried to excuse her to the rest of the family, he was far from being satisfied himself, and feared either that something must have happened to her, or that her heart had grown hard and cold, as hearts often do in the lapse of years, especially away from home and home-ties....

"Well! have you the rent for us, Conway?" said the insolent bailiff who was Mrs. Herbert's factotum—the other was merely an assistant.

"'Deed I haven't, Alick!" said poor Denis Conway trembling all over; "I told the mistress I couldn't raise a penny till I'd get it from America—I'm expectin' a letter every day from my daughter Bessy that's in New York **beyant**."

beyant: Irish variant of beyond.

"Fudge!" was Alick Bowman's emphatic reply. "You might as well give us a draft on the man in the moon. As you haven't the money, Conway! we have a duty to perform—you must march!"

"Why, sure, Mister Bowman! it isn't turn us out you'd be doin'?—sure Mrs. Herbert wouldn't do that on an old tenant like me that's on the estate since—since the old master's time—that's Mr. Mullady, the heavens be his bed, this day!"

"Can't help it," was the man of law's curt reply. "Come, Charlie!" to his companion, "lend a hand, will you? We've got plenty of work to do before night!—it's like there's not much here to detain us."

In the bailiffs went, but Denis was in before them, trying to soothe as well as he could his wife and their daughter Nancy who were sobbing and crying and wringing their hands in a paroxysm of grief. Ellen was just sitting up for the first time, propped up in her mother's old arm-chair, and on hearing the direful news she fell back fainting, though not insensible. She had not strength enough to make any demonstration of her feelings.

The poor father had only time to say, "don't despair, for your lives don't! the darkest hour, you know, is the hour before day, and I tell you God won't desert us though the world may!"

The words were still on his lips when the two officials were hard at work turning the poor ménage inside out. The beds—such as the hard times had left—chairs, tables, pots, pans, and so forth, were flying through the door-way with little regard to "loss or damage" on the part of those who trundled them out. The family within sat looking on in hopeless anguish waiting for the moment when they, in turn, were to be sent after their goods and chattels.

"Well! God sees all this," said the afflicted father of the family as he saw his wife wrapping a thin shawl round Ellen—the blankets were gone with the rest. "God sees all this!"

"What are you about, young woman?" cried Alick suddenly. A little hand had been laid on his arm, and a soft feminine voice bade him stop. "Who the d—l are you?"

The Conways answered the question. Father, mother, sisters—even Ellen—rushed forward with hands outstretched and the one word "Bessy!" escaped the lips of each with a thrilling cry of joy.

Bessy put them all gently aside with her hand. "Let us get the bailiff out first," said she; "oh! father, father! how did it ever come to this with you? —Ellen, darling, sit down—you're not able to stand—oh! you haven't a seat, I see—hand in a chair!" said she to the astonished bailiff.

"Can't do it," said he scratching his head, "the things are all under seizure, and they're a-going to be sold by and by."

"They're not going to be sold," said Bessy with quite an air of authority; "give in the chair, I say!" Mechanically the man obeyed.

"Now all the other things—put them in, I tell you?"

"I tell you I won't," said Bowman doggedly, "unless the old man is ready to hand out the cash." This by way of a taunt.

"How much is it, father?" demanded Bessy.

"Oh! indeed, it's little use to tell you, astore!"

"Well! well! let us hear it, anyhow."

"Why I'll soon tell you, if you want so bad to hear it," said Bowman impudently, "it's twenty-three pounds, ten shillings, and seven pence halfpenny." He and his colleague looked as though they expected the young woman to be quite confounded by so startling an announcement. She was not, though, but appeared rather to enjoy it as something particularly amusing.

"Go up now to Mrs. Herbert," said she with a quiet smile, "and tell her she will oblige us by sending a receipt in full—in full, mind you!—for all rent and arrears of rent due on Denis Conway's farm."

"But what'll I say to her in regard of the money?" demanded Alick. "Of course, she's not such a fool as to give a receipt without knowin' for what?"

"I'll tell you what you'll do, father," said Bessy after a moment's thought, "I'll give you the money, and you can go up yourself with this man and pay Mrs. Herbert and get your receipt."

"An' have you that much money, Bessy?" said the father with tears in his eyes—tears of joy.

"Yes, and a trifle more to the back of it," said Bessy in her gayest tone.

Extracts from Anthony Trollope, *Castle Richmond* (London, 1860), 121–25

Anthony Trollope (1815–82) was an English novelist. He moved to Ireland in 1841 to work as a postal clerk, and he lived there until 1859. Trollope set five of his novels in Ireland; *Castle Richmond* was the third of them. The plot, which is set in southwestern Ireland, revolves around two Protestant cousins competing for the hand of a noble but impoverished young woman. Trollope took the opportunity of the novel to comment extensively on the famine, and to reject the idea that the famine was somehow a punishment visited upon Ireland by God.

⁊

They who were in the south of Ireland during the winter of 1846–47 will not readily forget the agony of that period. For many, many years preceding and up to that time, the increasing swarms of the country had been fed upon the potato, and upon the potato only; and now all at once the potato failed them, and the greater part of eight million human beings were left without food.

The destruction of the potato was the work of God; and it was natural to attribute the sufferings which at once overwhelmed the unfortunate country to God's anger—to his wrath for the misdeeds of which that country had been guilty. For myself, I do not believe in such exhibitions of God's anger. When wars come, and pestilences, and famine; when the people of a land are worse than decimated, and the living hardly able to bury the dead, I cannot coincide with those who would deprecate God's wrath by prayers. I do not believe that our God stalks darkly along the clouds, laying thousands low with the arrows of death....

The idolatry of popery, to my way of thinking, is bad; though not so bad in Ireland as in most other Papist countries that I have visited. Sedition also is bad; but in Ireland, in late years, it has not been deep-seated—as may have been noted at Ballingarry and other places, where endeavour was made to bring sedition to its proof. As for the idleness of Ireland's people, I am inclined to think they will work under the same compulsion and same persuasion which produce work in other countries.

The fault had been the lowness of education and consequent want of principle among the middle classes; and this fault had been found as strongly marked among the Protestants as it had been among the Roman Catholics. Young men were brought up to do nothing. Property was regarded as having no duties attached to it. Men became rapacious, and determined to extract the uttermost farthing out of the land within their power, let the consequences to the people of that land be what they might.

We used to hear much of absentees. It was not the absence of the absentees that did the damage, but the presence of those they left behind them on the soil. The scourge of Ireland was the existence of a class who looked to be gentlemen living on their property, but who should have earned their bread by the work of their brain, or, failing that, by the sweat of their brow. There were men to be found in shoals through the country speaking of their properties and boasting of their places, but who owned no properties and had no places when the matter came to be properly sifted....

And thus a state of things was engendered in Ireland which discouraged labour, which discouraged improvements in farming, which discouraged any produce from the land except the potato crop; which maintained one class of men in what they considered to be gentility of idleness, and another class, the people of the country, in the abjectness of poverty.

It is with thorough rejoicing, almost with triumph, that I declare that the idle, genteel class had been cut up root and branch, has been driven forth out of its holding into the wide world, and has been punished with the penalty of extermination. The poor cotter suffered sorely under the famine, and under the pestilence which followed the famine; but he, as a class, has risen from his bed of suffering a better man. He is thriving as a labourer either in his own country or in some newer—for him better—land to which he has emigrated.

Extracts from John Mitchel, *The Last Conquest of Ireland (Perhaps)* (Dublin, 1861), 131, 158–59, 323–35

John Mitchel (1815–75) was an Irish nationalist and writer. He was an active member of the Young Ireland movement, and worked on its newspaper, the *Nation*. Mitchel was convicted of treason against the United Kingdom in 1848 and was transported to jail in Bermuda, from where he escaped from in 1853. While living in the American South he became a pro-slavery advocate, and in 1861 wrote *The Last Conquest of Ireland (Perhaps)* in which he lays out his views on British culpability for the famine.

Irish landlords are not all monsters of cruelty. Thousands of them, indeed, kept far away from the scene, collected their rents through agents and bailiffs, and spent them in England or in Paris. But the resident landlords and their families did, in many cases, devote themselves to the task of saving their poor people alive. Many remitted their rents, or half their rents; and ladies kept their servants busy and their kitchens smoking with continual preparation of food for the poor. Local Committees soon purchased all the corn in the government depots (at market price, however) and distributed it gratuitously. Clergymen, both Protestant and Catholic, I am glad to testify, generally did their duty; except those absentee clergymen, bishops, and wealthy rectors, who usually reside in England, their services being not needed in the places from whence they draw their wealth. But many a poor rector and his curate shared their crust with their suffering neighbours; and priests, after going round all day administering Extreme Unction to whole villages at once, all dying of mere starvation, often themselves went supperless to bed. [...]

The Code of Cheap Ejectment was therefore improved for the use of Irish landlords. As the laws of England and of Ireland are extremely different in regards to franchise and to land-tenure; and as the Ejectment laws were invented exclusively for Ireland, to clear off the "surplus population,".... In many parts of the island, extermination of the people had been sweeping. At every quarter sessions, in every county, there were always many ejectments; and I have seen them signed by Assistant-Barristers by hundreds in one sheaf. They were then placed in the hands of bailiffs and police, and came down upon some devoted townland with more terrible destruction than an enemy's sword and torch. Whole neighbourhoods were often thrown out upon the highways, in Winter, and the homeless creatures lived for awhile upon the charity of neighbours; but this was dangerous; the neighbours were often themselves ejected for harbouring them. Some landlords contracted with Emigration companies to carry them to America "for a lump sum," according to the advertisements I cited before. Others did not care what became of them; and hundreds and thousands perished every year, of mere hardship....

The Census of Ireland, in 1841, gave a population of 8,175,125. At the usual rate of increase, there must have been, in 1846, when the Famine commenced, at least eight and a half millions; at the same rate of increase, there ought to have been, in 1851 (according to the estimate of the Census Commissioners), 9,018,799. But in the last year, after five seasons of artificial famine, there were found alive only 6,552,386—a deficit of two millions and a half. Now what became of those two millions and a half?

The "government" Census Commissioners, and compilers of returns of all sorts, whose principal duty it has been, since that fatal time, to conceal the amount of the havoc, attempt to account for nearly the whole deficiency by emigration. In Thom's Official Almanac, I find set down on one side, the actual decrease from 1841 to 1851 (that is, without taking into account the increase by births in that period, 1,623,154. Against this, they place their own estimate of the emigration during those same ten years, which they put down at 1,589,133. But, in the first place, the decrease did not begin till 1846—there had been till then a rapid increase in the population: the government returns, then, not only ignore the increase, but set the emigration of ten years against the depopulation of five. This will not do: we must reduce their emigrants by one-half, say to six hundred thousand—and add to the depopulation the estimated increase up to 1846, say half a million. This will give upwards of two millions whose disappearance is to be accounted for—and six hundred thousand emigrants in the other column. Balance unaccounted for, a million and a half.

Now, that million and a half of men, women, and children, were carefully, prudently, and peacefully slain by the English Government. They died of hunger in the midst of abundance, which their own hands created; and it is quite immaterial to distinguish those who perished in the agonies of famine itself from those who died of typhus fever, which in Ireland is always caused by famine.

Further, I have called it an artificial famine: that is to say, it was a famine which desolated a rich and fertile island, that produced every year abundance and superabundance to sustain all her people and many more. The English, indeed, call that famine a "dispensation of Providence;" and ascribe it entirely to the blight of the potatoes. But potatoes failed in like manner all over Europe; yet there was no famine save in Ireland. The British account of the matter, then, is first, a fraud—second, a blasphemy.

The Almighty, indeed, sent the potato blight, but the English created the famine.

And lastly, I have shown, in the course of this narrative, that the depopulation of the country was not only encouraged by artificial means, namely, the Out-door Relief Act, the Labour-rate Act, and the emigration schemes, but that extreme care and diligence were used to prevent relief coming to the doomed Island from abroad; and that the benevolent contributions of Americans and other foreigners were turned aside from their destined objects—not, let us say, in order that none should be saved alive, but that no interference should be made with the principles of political economy....

The subjection of Ireland is now probably assured until some external shock shall break up that monstrous commercial firm, the British Empire; which indeed, is a bankrupt firm, and trading on false credit, and embezzling the goods of others, or robbing on the highway from Pole to Pole; but its doors are not yet shut; its cup of abomination is not yet running over. If any American has read this narrative, however, he will never wonder hereafter when he hears an Irishman in America fervently curse the British Empire. So long as this hatred and horror shall last—so long as our island refuses to become, like Scotland, a contented province of her enemy, Ireland is not fully subdued. The passionate aspiration for Irish nationhood will outlive the British Empire.

Maud Gonne, "The Famine Queen," *United Irishman*, 7 April 1900

Maud Gonne (1866–1953) was an English-born Irish revolutionary and actress. She famously played the lead role in **William Butler Yeats**'s play *Cathleen Ní Houlihan* and was the muse for many of his famous poems. In 1897 she, along with Yeats and **Arthur Griffith**, was active in organizing protests against Queen Victoria's Diamond Jubilee. In 1900, when Queen Victoria was planning a visit to Ireland, her first since 1861, Gonne published this piece in Arthur Griffith's *United Irishman* newspaper.

William Butler Yeats: (1865–1939) Irish poet and playwright, Yeats was a leading force in the Irish Literary Revival.

Arthur Griffith: (1871–1922) Irish nationalist and political leader, Griffith founded the political party Sinn Fein and was President of Dáil Éireann, the revolutionary Irish republic in 1922.

ϵℓ

"The Queen's visit to Ireland is in no way political," proclaims the Lord Lieutenant, and the English ministers. "The Queen's visit has no political signification, and the Irish nation must receive her Majesty with the generous hospitality for which it is celebrated," hastens to repeat Mr. **John Redmond**, and our servile Irish members whose nationality has been corrupted by a too lengthy sojourn in the enemy's country.

"The Queen's visit to Ireland has nothing at all to do with politics," cries the fishmonger, **Pile**, whose ambitious soul is not satisfied by the position of Lord Mayor and who hankers after an English title.

"Let us to our knees, and present the keys of the city to her Most Gracious Majesty, and compose an address in her honour."

"Nothing political! Nothing political! Let us present an address to this virtuous lady," echo 30 town councillors, who when they sought the votes of the Dublin people called themselves Irishmen and Nationalists, but who are overcome by royal glamour. Poor citizens of Dublin! Your thoughtlessness in giving your votes to these miserable creatures will cost you dear. It has already cost the arrests of sixteen good and true men, and many broken heads and bruised limbs from police batons, for you have realized—if somewhat late—the responsibility of Ireland's capital, and, aghast at the sight of the men elected by you betraying and dishonouring Ireland, you have, with a courage which makes us all proud of you, raised a protest, and cried aloud, "The visit of the Queen of England is a political action, and if we accord her a welcome we shall stand shamed before the nations. The world will no longer believe in the sincerity of our demand for National Freedom!"

And in truth, for Victoria, in the decrepitude of her eighty-one years, to have decided after an absence of half-a-century to revisit the country she

John Redmond: (1856–1918) An Irish politician and member of Parliament, Redmond was leader of the Irish Parliamentary Party, a moderate nationalist party that sought Home Rule.

Pile: Sir Thomas Devereux Pile was Lord Mayor of Dublin from 1900 to 1901.

hates and whose inhabitants are the victims of the criminal policy of her reign, the survivors of sixty years of organized famine, the political necessity must have been terribly strong; for after all she is a woman, and however vile and selfish and pitiless her soul may be, she must sometimes tremble as death approaches when she thinks of the countless Irish mothers who, shelterless under the cloudy Irish sky, watching their starving little ones, have cursed her before they died.

Every eviction during sixty-three years has been carried out in Victoria's name, and if there is a Justice in Heaven the shame of those poor Irish emigrant girls whose very innocence renders them an easy prey and who have been overcome in the terrible struggle for existence on a foreign shore, will fall on this woman, whose bourgeoisie virtue is so boasted and in whose name their homes were destroyed. If she comes to Ireland again before her death to contemplate the ruin she has made it is surely because her ministers and advisors think that England's situation is dangerous and that her journey will have a deep political importance. England has lived for years on a prestige which has had no solid foundation. She has hypnotized the world with the falsehood of her greatness; she has made great nations and small nations alike, believe in her power. It required the dauntless courage and energy of the Boers to destroy forever this illusion and rescue Europe from the fatal enchantment. Today no one fears the British Empire, her prestige has gone down before the rifles of a few thousand heroic peasants.

If the British Empire means to exist she will have to rely on real strength, and real strength she has not got. England is in decadence. She has sacrificed all to getting money, and money cannot create men, nor give courage to her weakly soldiers. The men who formerly made her greatness, the men from the country districts have disappeared; they have been swallowed up by the great black manufacturing cities; they have been flung into the crucible where gold is made. Today the giants of England are the giants of finance and of the Stock Exchange, who have risen to power on the backs of a struggling mass of pale, exhausted slaves. The storm approaches; the gold which the English have made out of the blood and tears of millions of human beings attracts the covetousness of the world. Who will aid the pirates to keep their spoils? In their terror they turn to Victoria, their Queen. She has succeeded in amassing more gold than any of her subjects; she has always been ready to cover with her royal mantle the crimes and turpitude of her Empire, and now, trembling on the brink of the grave, she rises once more at their call. Soldiers are needed to protect the vampires. The Queen issues an appeal in England, the struggling mass of slaves cry "Hurrah"; but there is no blood in their veins, no strength in their arms. Soldiers must be found, so Victoria will go herself to fetch them; she will go over to Ireland—to this people who have despised gold, and who, in spite of persecutions and threats, have persisted in their dream of Freedom and idealism, and who, though reduced in numbers, have maintained all the beauty and strength and vitality of their race.

Taking the Shamrock in her withered hand she dares to ask Ireland for soldiers—for soldiers to protect the exterminators of their race! And the reply of Ireland comes sadly but proudly, not through the lips of the miserable little politicians who are touched by the English canker but through the lips of the Irish people:

> "Queen, return to your own land; you will find no more Irishmen ready to wear the red shame of your livery. In the past they have done so from ignorance, and because it is hard to die of hunger when one is young and strong and the sun shines, but they shall do so no longer; see! Your recruiting agents return unsuccessful and alone from my green hills and plains, because once more hope has been revived, and it will be in the ranks of your enemies that my children will find employment and honour! As to those who today enter your service to help in your criminal wars, I deny them! If they die, if they live, it matters not to me, they are no longer Irishmen."

GLOSSARY OF KEY FIGURES AND TERMS

Absentee: Absentee landlords were those who owned Irish land but did not live in Ireland and rarely visited, preferring to live in England.

Acts of Union 1800: Formally united the Kingdom of Great Britain and the Kingdom of Ireland to create the United Kingdom of Great Britain and Ireland. This went into effect in 1801; as a result Ireland lost its independent Parliament.

British Relief Association: A private charity formed by prominent members of the British aristocratic and financial elite to provide relief to victims of the famine. The organization was active from 1847 to 1848.

Conacre: A speculative system of leasing small patches of land, for short periods of time, with rent paid in cash or in labor and with few legal rights granted to the tenants. Only desperate landless laborers leased land on these terms.

Corn Laws: Trade legislation in the United Kingdom between 1815 and 1846 that imposed tariffs on imported grain. The intent was to keep grain prices high in order to favor domestic producers. During the famine these laws made it expensive to import food and were repealed at the urging of Prime Minister Sir Robert Peel in 1846.

Cottiers: Laborers who held a cabin with a small amount of land (0.25–3 acres) from an occupier whom they were bound to work for at a certain fixed price whenever called upon.

Encumbered Estates Acts: Series of acts passed in 1848 and 1849 which allowed the sale of mortgaged Irish estates whose owners were unable to meet their obligations. The hope was that this would encourage English investors to buy these estates and transform Irish agriculture. No protection was provided for the existing tenants of these estates.

Gregory Clause: An amendment to the Poor Law Amendment Act of 1847, this required that relief applicants surrender all but a quarter acre of their land in order to qualify for assistance.

Guardians: Boards of Guardians were committees elected by rate-payers in the Poor Law Unions tasked with administering the Poor Law.

Indian corn: Maize, Indian corn, or meal ground from Indian corn was imported to Ireland during the famine by the Peel administration to offset the skyrocketing cost of food. Indian corn was sold to the Irish at cost.

Land agent: Employee hired by absentee landlords to handle their Irish landholdings.

O'Connell, Daniel: Irish politician, popularly referred to as "the Liberator." O'Connell campaigned for Catholic emancipation and the right of Catholics to sit in Westminster Parliament. This was achieved in 1829. O'Connell spent the rest of his political career working for the repeal of the Acts of Union. He died in 1847 while on a pilgrimage to Rome.

Outdoor relief: Assistance to the poor that did not require the recipient to enter the workhouse.

Peel, Sir Robert: British politician and member of the Conservative (Tory) Party. Served as prime minister 1834–35 and 1841–46. In 1846, Peel repealed the Corn Laws in response to the famine. The move was unpopular enough within his Conservative party that he resigned as prime minister in June of 1846.

Poor Law of 1838: Modeled on the English Poor Law of 1834, this created the first national poor relief system in Ireland.

Quakers: Members of the Religious Society of Friends, there had been a small community of Quakers in Ireland since the seventeenth century. Notable for their charity work, the Quaker community organized a relief association in 1846 and raised funds from Great Britain and the United States. The Central Relief Committee of the Society of Friends was active throughout the famine.

Rates: Poor rates were a tax on property levied in each Poor Law Union used to pay for poor relief. During the famine the government preferred to have local poor rates pay for local relief.

Repeal Movement: Political campaign organized by O'Connell designed to repeal the Acts of Union.

Russell, Lord John: British politician and member of the Whig (Liberal) Party. Served as prime minister 1846–52 and again 1865–66. An adherent of laissez-faire economics, Russell refused to intervene against Irish food exports to England during the famine, and halted the government's relief works.

Three Fs: Fair rents, fixity of tenure, and free sale. Beginning with the Tenant Right League founded in 1850, these became the primary goals of Irish land reformers through the rest of the nineteenth century.

Workhouse: A common form of poor relief in the nineteenth-century. These institutions were designed to house, feed, and put the poor to work.

Young Ireland: Nationalist movement begun in the mid-nineteenth century associated with the newspaper the *Nation*. Members founded the Irish Confederation, and some went on to found the Irish Republican Brotherhood. In 1848 some members of the movement attempted to provoke a nationalist uprising by besieging a police unit in South Tipperary.

SELECT BIBLIOGRAPHY

Bourke, Austin. *"The Visitation of God"?: The Potato and the Great Irish Famine*. Dublin: Lilliput Press, 1993.

Boyle, Phelim P. and Cormac Ó Gráda. "Fertility Trends, Excess Mortality, and the Great Irish Famine." *Demography* 23, no. 4 (1986): 543–62.

Crawford, Margaret E., ed. *Famine, The Irish Experience 900–1900: Subsistence Crises and Famines in Ireland*. Edinburgh: John Donald, 1989.

Cullen, L.M. "Irish History without the Potato." *Past and Present* vol. 40 (1968): 72–83.

Daly, Mary. *The Famine in Ireland*. Dundalk: Dundalgan Press, 1986.

De Nie, Michael. "Curing 'The Irish Moral Plague.'" *Eire-Ireland* 32, no. 1 (1997): 63–85.

Desmond, Norton. "On Lord Palmerston's Irish Estates in the 1840s." *The English Historical Review* 119, no. 484 (2004): 1254–74.

Donnelly, James S. *The Great Irish Potato Famine*. Sutton: Stroud, 2001.

Edwards, R. Dudley and T. Desmond Williams, eds. *The Great Famine: Studies in Irish History, 1845–1852*. Dublin: The Lilliput Press, 1994 (1957).

Fitzpatrick, David. *Irish Emigration 1801–1921*. Dundalk, Dundalgan Press, 1984.

Geber, Jonny. "Mortality among Institutionalised Children during the Great Famine in Ireland: Bioarchaeological Contextualization of Non-adult Mortality Rates in the Kilkenny Union Workhouse, 1846–1851." *Continuity and Change* 31, no. 1 (2016): 101–26.

Goodbody, Rob. "Quakers and the Famine." *History Ireland* 6, no. 1 (1998): 27–32.

Gray, Peter. *Famine, Land and Politics: British Government and Irish Society 1843–50*. Dublin: Irish Academic Press, 1999.

Grossman, Virginia and Donnacha Sean Lucey. "'One Huge Abuse': The Cork Board of Guardians and the Expansion of Outdoor Relief in Post-Famine Ireland." *English Historical Review* 126, no. 523 (2011): 1408–29.

Haines, Robin. *Charles Trevelyan and the Great Irish Famine*. Dublin: Four Courts, 2004.

Harling, Philip. "Assisted Emigration and the Moral Dilemmas of the Mid-Victorian Imperial State." *The Historical Journal* 59, no. 4 (2016): 1027–49.

Harzallah, Mohamed Salah. "Food Supply and Economic Ideology: Indian Corn Relief during the Second Year of the Great Irish Famine (1847)." *Historian* 68, no. 2 (2006): 305–23.

Hoppen, K. Theodore. *Elections, Politics and Society in Ireland 1832–1885*. Oxford: Oxford UP, 1984.

Kennedy, Liam, Paul S. Ell, E.M. Crawford, and L.A. Clarkson. *Mapping the Great Irish Famine: A Survey of the Famine Decade*. Dublin: Four Courts, 1999.

Kerr, Donal A. *A Nation of Beggars: Priests, People and Politics in Famine Ireland 1846–1852*. Oxford: Clarendon, 1994.

Kinealy, Christine. *This Great Calamity: The Irish Famine, 1845–52*. Dublin: Gill & Macmillan, 1994.

Kinealy, Christine. *Charity and the Great Hunger in Ireland: The Kindness of Strangers.* London: Bloomsbury, 2013.

Miller, Kerby A. *Emigrants and Exiles: Ireland and the Irish Exodus to North America.* Oxford: Oxford UP, 1985.

Mokyr, Joel. *Why Ireland Starved: A Quantitative and Analytical History of the Irish Economy, 1800–1850.* London: George Allen & Unwin, 1983.

Mokyr, Joel and Cormac Ó Gráda. "What Do People Die of During Famines: The Great Irish Famine in Comparative Perspective." *European Review of Economic History.* 6, no. 3 (2002): 339–63.

Nusteling, Hubert P.H. "How Many Irish Potato Famine Deaths? Toward Coherence of the Evidence." *Historical Methods* 42, no. 2 (2009): 57–80.

Ó Ciosain, Niall. "Approaching a Folklore Archive: The Irish Folklore Commission and the Memory of the Great Famine." *Folklore* 115, no. 2 (2004): 222–32.

Ó Gráda, Cormac. *Black '47 and Beyond: The Great Irish Famine in History, Economy, and Memory.* Princeton, NJ: Princeton UP, 1999.

O'Neill, T.P. "The Scientific Investigation of the Failure of the Potato Crop in Ireland, 1845–6." *Irish Historical Studies* 5, no. 18 (1946): 123–38.

O'Neill, T.P. "The Society of Friends and the Great Famine." *Studies: An Irish Quarterly Review* 39, no. 154 (1950): 203–13.

O'Rourke, Kevin. "Did the Great Irish Famine Matter?" *Journal of Economic History* 51 (1991): 1–22.

Poirteir, Cathal, ed. *The Great Irish Famine.* Dublin: Mercier Press, 1995.

Reilly, Ciaran. *The Irish Land Agent, 1830–1860: The Case of King's County.* Dublin: Four Courts, 2014.

Reilly, Ciaran. *Strokestown and the Great Irish Famine.* Dublin: Four Courts, 2014.

Shrout, Anelise Hanson, "'Distressing News from Ireland': The Famine, the News and International Philanthropy." PhD Dissertation, New York University, 2013.

Solow, Barbara L. *The Land Question and the Irish Economy.* Cambridge, MA: Harvard UP, 1971.

Scally, Robert James. *The End of Hidden Ireland: Rebellion, Famine and Emigration.* Oxford: Oxford UP, 1996.

Woodham-Smith, Cecil. *The Great Hunger: Ireland 1845–1849,* New York: Penguin, 1992 (1962).

Woodward, Nicholas. "Transportation Convictions during the Great Irish Famine." *Journal of Interdisciplinary History* 37, no. 1 (2006): 59–87.

From the Publisher

A name never says it all, but the word "Broadview" expresses a good deal of the philosophy behind our company. We are open to a broad range of academic approaches and political viewpoints. We pay attention to the broad impact book publishing and book printing has in the wider world; for some years now we have used 100% recycled paper for most titles. Our publishing program is internationally oriented and broad-ranging. Our individual titles often appeal to a broad readership too; many are of interest as much to general readers as to academics and students.

Founded in 1985, Broadview remains a fully independent company owned by its shareholders—not an imprint or subsidiary of a larger multinational.

For the most accurate information on our books (including information on pricing, editions, and formats) please visit our website at www.broadviewpress.com. Our print books and ebooks are available for sale on our site.

broadview press
www.broadviewpress.com